Market Whys and
Human Wherefores

MARKET WHYS AND HUMAN WHEREFORES

Thinking Again About Markets, Politics and People

DAVID JENKINS

CASSELL

Cassell

Wellington House, 125 Strand, London WC2R 0BB

370 Lexington Avenue, New York, NY 10017-6550

First published 2000

British Library Cataloguing-in-Publication Data

A catalogue record for this book is available from the British Library.

ISBN 0-304-70608-6

Typeset by Paston PrePress Ltd, Beccles, Suffolk

Printed and Bound in Great Britain by Redwood Books, Trowbridge, Wilts.

Contents

Acknowledgements

This book would never have been completed and made presentable for publication if my various scribbles and drafts had not been transcribed and re-transcribed, edited and re-edited, by my daughter Rebecca in the midst of her own writing activities. But this is a family matter – as is my immense debt to my wife, Mollie, for her support in all I do. Acknowledgement there simply must be, but evaluation is beyond me.

At a more formal level I am glad to acknowledge the stimulus to the shaping of the argument of this book which I received through my invitation to be the Samuel Ferguson Lecturer at the University of Manchester in the academic year 1995/6.

As a result of this invitation I gave four lectures at the end of February 1996. The theme of the lectures was *Ideology, Exploitation or Inevitability? – Theological Reflections on the Market and Providence.* The sympathetic but penetrating questions which I received from members of the audience, and in the accompanying seminars, sharpened many issues for me.

The publication of this book, therefore, is offered to the Department of Religions and Theology at Manchester University as an addition to their series of Samuel Ferguson Lectures. With it I offer also my gratitude for the discussions and intellectual stimulus which I received at the University. In particular I wish to thank Professor David Pailin for all the care he took over my arrangements and hospitality.

David Jenkins

Further Acknowledgements

The author and publishers gratefully acknowledge the permission of various parties to quote extracts from their publications, as follows:

The Economist (all articles © *The Economist* London)

'The disappearing tax payer' (Leader article – 31.5.97); 'The myth of the powerless state' (7.10.95); 'Power politics' (7.10.95); 'Who's in the driving seat?' (7.10.95); 'Back to the future' (7.10.95); 'Judge and jury' (7.10.95); 'A walk on the wild side' (7.10.95); 'Not so divine intervention' (7.10.95); 'Governments that live in glasshouses' (7.10.95); 'Ten lessons to learn: Summers on Mexico' (23.12.95); 'Growth in Africa: it can be done' (29.6.96).

The Financial Times (all articles © *The Financial Times*)

Brian Riley: 'The birth of enclave man' (20.9.97)
Brian Riley: 'Statistics can prove a real minefield for the unwary' (8.2.97)

The Guardian (all articles © *The Guardian*)

Victor Keegan: 'Missing out on the share boom' (20.1.97)
John Gray: 'Culture of containment' (20.11.95)
Andrew Rutherford: 'Enemy behind bars' (13.3.96)
Paul Johnson: 'Reporting on a book entitled "*Inequality in the UK*"' (28.7.97)

The Times

Anatole Kaletsky: 'Explain(ing) the American miracle' (9.7.96); article on Bank of England Inflation Report (8.8.96); 'Economic view' (8.8.97); 'Economic view' (12.9.97); 'Why I am a prophet of boom' (23.9.97); 'Wall Street: cheap at the price' (17.9.96); 'Why Mexico has done the market a good turn' (2.2.95); 'Economic view' (17.8.95); 'Economic view' (13.12.96); 'Article of Davos' (7.2.97). © Times Newspapers Limited.

Lord Rees-Mogg: 'Society's dicey prospects' (10.2.95); 'The end of nations' (31.8.95); 'Decline of the past' (31.1.97); 'When tax revenues slip through the net' (2.12.96). © Lord Rees-Mogg/Times Newspapers Limited.

George Riddell: 'Blair's big idea' (10.1.96); 'Over the horizon' (leader – 13.2.86). © George Riddell/Times Newspapers Limited.

Philip Bassett: 'CBI limbers up for election, intent on running in neutral' (19.7.96). © Times Newspapers Limited.

Janet Bush: 'Keeping up the UK allure' (11.2.97); 'US and Europe play power games' (19.11.97); 'How the West cages Asian tigers in IMF TRAP' (24.12.97). © Times Newspapers Limited.

Business Commentaries (12.12.97; 6.1.98; 9.1.98). © Times Newspapers Limited.

Bernard Connolly: 'No such thing as the "right exchange rate"' (27.5.97). © The author.

'Gilt edged' (regular Monday article – 10.1.96). © The author.

Anthony Harris: 'Exploring the high demand for nonsense' (20.11.96); 'Sterling at 100' (22.4.97). © The author.

Lord Alexander of Weedon: 'Executive voice' (11.5.96). © The author.

The Observer

J. K. Galbraith: 'The war against the poor' (26.9.96). © J. K. Galbraith.

The Atlantic Monthly

George Soros: 'Capital crimes' (January 1997).

1 Initial Scientific Protest – Are We Living the Latest Fatal Conceit?

Everyone knows that since the nineteenth century the capitalist inspired Free Market has delivered amazing growth and hitherto undreamed of prosperity across the world. Everyone hopes that this (so far very unevenly distributed) prosperity will continue to expand and the wealth will trickle down to improve the material lot of increasing numbers of the world's population. And – an even greater blessing – this promising expansiveness promotes and extends freedom as well. At last we have discovered a way for the world which promises well for everyone into the indefinite future. There are failures in the system which require modification. There are troubling problems associated with finding individual, governmental and social responses to the casualties of the Market processes; costs which so far the Market has failed to produce sufficient spare resources to deal with. But there is clearly no other way available and we do well, if we want to do well for both ourselves and our neighbours across this earth, to follow and develop the way of the Free Market.

The Free Market enthusiasm sounds simplistic and oddly naive. Logically, politically and practically are we being led towards a promised land? Or are we being enticed (possibly in fairly good faith) to pursue a random walk along which some people are enabled to grow very rich indeed but many people do very badly, sustained by the promise of jam tomorrow, although never jam today? In search of illumination, I decided to examine step by step the typical language and claims of the regular Market commentators and commenders. I started out uneasy about our current enthusiasm for the Free Market, suspecting that radical questions had to be raised. I did not realize how radical these questions would prove to be.

It may be practically, politically and obviously true that seeking some *total replacement* for the Market way would be to look for a different physical, historical world than the one we have arrived at. However it is equally true that current economic theories relating market practices to this world are not supported by coherent theoretical arguments. What is more, these arguments are shored up by data insufficient to bear the weight put upon them. This is not to claim that the operations of the Market do not deliver immense amounts of goods and services which are as real as anything else in the world in the sense of 'being there' and 'making a difference'. The data collected with reference to the activities and products of the Market have as good a claim to be real as any other set of accurately observed and reliably organized data. The problem lies in the relation of this data to the world as we commonly experience it. The theories we are sold about the Market, and the promises we are told we may or must invest in it, are much more like stories or myths than convincingly articulated scientific theories. Consequently these Market predictions and promises have insufficient substance to guarantee our several and collective futures.

This sounds like a remotely theoretical argument about logic and language. But it is the concrete and remarkably productive practices of the Market – practices on which practically all our livelihoods depend – which are being questioned. What my investigation has shown me about these 'remarkably productive practices' is that, whatever they may have produced *so far*, there are no sound reasons for believing that they will continue to be 'remarkably productive' indefinitely. Further, this remarkable productivity has produced, and is increasingly producing, many negative effects alongside the good. Perhaps most decisively – there are insufficient grounds for the claim that Market processes have a built-in *self-correcting* mechanism which in the longer run will enlarge prosperity and promise while diminishing deprivations and threats.

The material for my investigation is drawn from the arguments of proponents of the optimistic Market way and not from its critics. Readers must judge for themselves whether my conclusions are justified. This initial scientific protest is written by way of introduction to stake the claim that even if my conclusions are not as conclusive as I believe them to be, the questions I raise are unavoidable. Whatever may be their current prestige, the proponents of the Free Market maintain their claims about, and prescriptions for, the actual world only by plainly misdescribing it and ignoring literally vital features in it. My basic challenge to market rhetoric arises from an extended critical analysis of the nature of the data on which Free Market promoters rely for the strength of their case and the way they use those data.

The fundamental trouble with the nature of economic and financial data – and one which has discomfited me by implying a far deeper scepticism and doubt than I had anticipated – is that the data selected for use are highly partial and limited while the *application* of theories related to this data is total. Thus the Market dominates our expectations of prosperity while the data on which it operates, by which its success is measured, and from which its future promises are derived, have no direct relation to *people, the future,* or the *use* to which market products are put.

In currently applied economics the Market is presented as an essential information system for the optimum allocation by the price mechanism of economic resources via economic production to chosen human ends. Yet the workings of the markets as described have no direct relationship to actual persons in the realities of their particular lives. This is a statement of fact, for the Market works by price signals. The whole point about these signals as they are defined in Free Market theory is that they *abstract* from the transactions involved and from their effects everything but the money value of the exchange. That is the definition of a price, and that is how it works. All the complications of real markets and the real desires, intentions, and resources of real people are abstracted into, and focused by, the price of any or all transactions. Thus the workings of the Market through the price system have no direct relation to people in their particular reality.

The implications of the Market (and economic theories) having no interest in, or place for, registering anything to do with the future, first dawned on me as I began to pick up hints that the rules formulated about the operations of the Market in classical economic theory are timeless. They are statements, hypotheses or stories about how the economy works as if it were a *machine* (which, being a machine, always works in the same way and therefore timelessly). They are not statements about how the economy works as an organic – or organic-like – process which is affected by its own serial progression, and therefore is related to time and to what happens in the future.

The practical effects of this on how one should evaluate the products and possibilities of the Market was clarified for me by a discussion of the Market's ability to solve the problem of the dwindling of scarce resources in the chapter on 'Professional Reservations' in Paul Ormerod's *The Death of Economics.* Ormerod refers to

> a number of important papers which address the question of whether the price mechanism could always be relied upon to save the world from running out of exhaustible resources. In a word, the answer was no.

He cites *Economic Theory and Exhaustible Resources* by Das Gupta and Heal (1979), commenting:

> The key reason why Das Gupta and Heal, among others, arrived at this conclusion [that is about the price mechanism being unable to cope with the problem of disappearing resources] *was that in their theoretical models they allowed the future to exist* [my emphasis]. This may seem a bizarre statement to make, but it is not. The model of competitive equilibrium which has been discussed so far is set in a timeless environment. People and companies all operate in a world in which there is no future and hence no uncertainty.[1]

At first sight this seems amazing but it fits in with the frequently made point that economic models do not pretend to be maps of the real world but are abstracted models which are supposed to be helpful in getting to grips with economics in the real world.

My basic question is this. If the models are *theoretical abstractions* from the real world, and if the Market system works by prices which are *actual* (money-expressed) abstractions from the real world, then how can it be claimed that the Market as described is an inevitable ruler of our behaviour and that the Market as experienced is bound to produce beneficent and prosperous results for the greatest good of the greatest number as time goes on?

This – as it would appear – unlikely and certainly unscientific act of faith in the Free Market is made all the more questionable by at least three other considerations. The first, as I have already mentioned, is that the abstracting nature of market operations means that the Market pays no attention to 'use'. If the whole mechanism works as an information system informed by prices, all that the Market responds to is *money* 'valuations'. There is nothing meritorious or valuable (in any humane sense) or useful (in any sense of contributing to beneficence, human support or celebration) in this money 'valuation'. In the Market economy there is no such thing as worthwhile use – all is reduced to exchange value. Even worse from the point of view of any long-term beneficent effect of the Market, the 'value' of money in exchange use is increasingly determined by the value of money and financial transactions whereby money is made out of money.[2] Oft-repeated statistics show that the financial markets are dominated by transactions which are conducted 'for no other reason than for pecuniary gain'.[3] In other words, the Market is increasingly run by money for money. The *power* of the Market in the real world is increasingly obvious. But the *beneficence* of the Market for the uses of real people in the real world is, correspondingly, increasingly questionable.

In this first introductory chapter I am simply outlining the conclusions to which the investigations described in the rest of the book have led me. As the account which follows shows, I am well aware that the proponents of this faith in the Free Market have theories about how individual choices, issues about use, worth and future prospects for the individuals in their diversely particular situations, are aggregated into results which, under the balancing effects of the Market, will ultimately be beneficial for the increasing majority of us all. These theories, however, do not stand up to detailed investigation, particularly when considered critically as an allegedly coherent and logically compelling whole.

The case for doubting the theory of the Free Market is a strong one.[4] But practical men and women of business and commerce may well reply that theory is all very well, but they have to deal with the way things work in practice – and that means business as usual. And yet business as commended in the Free Market is conducted on partial and often misleading data. The way operators in the Free Market do their *accounts* regularly distorts the world. Their accounting takes no account of people as persons, nor of our common future, nor of the effects of both production and consumption on communities and the earth. The account is of profits and losses solely in money terms. Hence my prefacing my investigations into the validity of the Free Market faith with an initial scientific protest about data. The data that count in market accounting cannot properly be assumed to take sufficiently realistic account of what men and women need to live decently and properly, nor of what has to be taken into account if our earth is to be sustained and maintained in its supportive capacities for life.

This central worry about the scientific status of market data in their relationship to the whole field of the realities of human living, human environment and human productive and trading activities, is reinforced by the economic notion of 'externalities'. 'Externalities' are real effects in the real world which interact with market behaviour, and indeed, often arise out of market behaviour. Because, however, they are not paid for (i.e. not specifically taken account of in market and money transactions) they are 'external' to the Market and to market calculations.

This very concept is itself something of a diagnostic give-away. It highlights the presence of a vast range of independent promising things, threatening things and uncertain things which are not taken into account by the Market, despite the claim that the Market is determinative for prosperity overall. Take, for example, market data calculations about gross domestic product. How would the world survive, for instance, without the *unpaid* activities of women? But as there is no money price assigned to their work, there is no money 'value' placed on it. One wonders how economists and economic commentators dare to make decisive claims about the limits of ways to manage the world when such basic realities are ignored. There ought, surely, to be more humility and much more openness to radical criticism of the way in which the whole system works and what it actually delivers.

The increasing presence of 'externalities' is, indeed, becoming one of the main challenges to the hegemony and optimism of the current market way. From the environmental damage caused by the motor car to the limitations of natural resources, the real world is forcing its way back into the abstractions and limited accounting of economic theories. One of the hopeful signs developing in public opinion, in some reactions in the world of industry and in some economic thinking is that there is a growing recognition of the importance of externalities given the major pressures on environment and communities of economic processes. But so far these partial recognitions do not add up to general awareness leading to action within the Market activities and propaganda which I am investigating. I do not see how such challenges can be coped with within current free market capitalist assumptions which enable things to be done only if they generate sufficient profit to provide a high rate of return on capital. It is still the case that the generation of this profit is worked out by a method which takes no signals into account other than those of prices.

We are confronted with two sets of data with at least equal claim to reflect the real world which are increasingly in conflict with one another on many vital matters including realistic assessments of prospects for the future. The 'alternative' sets of data about such things as pollution, poverty indices and the pressure of migrants, demonstrate both the limits to the effectiveness of market growth overall and the increasing inadequacy of market operations to cope with particular human problems of great urgency. The 'escape' of treating these sets of data as 'externalities' may well prove to be the Achilles' heel for the lingering idea that the Market is, in the longer run, persistently promising because it is self-correcting. It is becoming increasingly obvious that the 'externalities' are *internal* to the real world in which the Market operates and *internal* to the very operations of the Market itself. Market theorizing is thus exposed as a vast and indeed, impressive, attempt to adapt the real world to an optimistic faith in the Market. It is obvious that for any sane or hopeful future the Market has to be adapted to the real world. This is the point of this initial scientific protest. My case is that the market theorizers and enthusiasts are partial and hence in grave danger of being wrong about the effects of indisputably observable data which arises concerning the real world and the effects of the Market therein. The market data are 'partial' in the two-fold sense that they only cover a part of the activities and survival possibilities of the real world as a whole, and that they are selected for recording and response by partial (that is highly selective and somewhat doubtfully coherent) theories of 'economics'.

A reasonable tradition of arguing about economic theories and economic data in relation to the Market has taken a wrong turn into an applied ideology which has descended into an idolatry. The vast network of market activities which have been a vitally important and largely positively productive good (full, of course, of limitations and difficulties) have been transformed into a dominating and defining god on which we are all obliged to be helplessly dependent. Yet this system, allegedly, is the best guarantor of our freedom. This is an example of the way the paradoxes of economic idolatry override the restraints of reason, of scientific observation and of prudently organized political activity. These paradoxes also, as I shall argue, divert and distort the potential prosperity which markets could and should continue to deliver for us.

Once the view that the Market 'knows best' and will 'do the best that can be managed' for us all indefinitely is clearly laid out, it hardly seems a likely one. Why should the world of human environment and interaction work as the Market faith says it does? The answer of our contemporary apologists for the Free Market appears to be – because it has turned out so in the past, and continues to do so in the present. Look as we tell you to look and you will see that this way of looking at our world is the proper and hopeful way.

I have looked at how we are told to look at the world and I have found the arguments and descriptions insufficiently coherent in their own terms, and unconvincing on wider grounds of practicality, morality or any claims to scientific demonstrability. I have gone on to examine the way in which enthusiasts for the Free Market describe the prospects and effects of its current operations, particularly in the area of the financial markets.[5] After such an inspection (and note that this inspection is of what is said and described by enthusiasts for the Free Market) I do not see how anyone who is not determined to go on seeing the world in terms of the Free Market Myth can assume that the case for trusting the promises of the Free Market is vindicated or even rendered reasonably plausible. Why, then, do all our politicians persist in taking it for granted that we can and must all trust in this Free Market and regard financiers, entrepreneurs and capitalists as the source and guarantee of our future prosperity and freedom? It seems we have been co-opted into a bastardized version of the nineteenth-century Marxist theory of the material dialectic based on a faith in the endless possibilities of modern enterprise, technology and productivity.

Once upon a time it was believed in some quarters that the Party (the Communist Party, with the guidance of Marx) knew the practical truth and direction of this progressive dialectic. Now it is believed that the business community, together with its acolytes and guardians, the central bankers (with the help of selected economic gurus such as Hayek, Friedman and possibly, Keynes – descendants of a line stretching back to Adam Smith), know the practical truth and direction of this progressive dialectic through the Market. But the whole idea of this progressive dialectic is highly suspect. It assumes that the world, history and human interactions are such that the processes we are involved in proceed in regular and observable ways. If we discern and collaborate with these ways then the processes develop into progress for us as human beings.[6] Both sets of ideas reflect nearly identical superstitions about the role of economic production as the basic dynamic of human life and hope; both are allied to forms of economic determinism. But what of our freedom? Progress of any viable, promising, shareable and sustainable sort, surely, depends on us. To imagine that an alleged evolutionary force has miraculously or fortuitously emerged to smooth out our abuses of self-interest into steadily beneficial outcomes for everybody is to take refuge in a delusion.

In 1988 the leading philosophical guru of liberal Free Market individualism, F.A. Hayek, published *The Fatal Conceit: The Errors of Socialism*, an extended summary of his case for the Free Market, setting out his argument against the rival contentions of communism and socialism. In 1989 the Berlin Wall and the socialist system collapsed. To the proponents of the Free Market this was decisive proof of the necessity and promise of liberal capitalism. The falsity and illusion of socialism and communism had been overthrown by the truth and promise of the capitalist Free Market, now established as the one, only and assured way to human prosperity and freedom.

Reviewing Hayek's *The Fatal Conceit* in November 1988 in *The Times* (25.11.88) Professor (now Lord) Dahrendorf referred to '*the fatal conceit that we can impose one comprehensive view on a recalcitrant world*'. To put our faith in some force of nature guaranteeing the evolutionary system named 'the Free Market' would appear to be quite as much a fatal conceit as the now discredited fatal conceit of socialism ever was. To be truly realistic and down-to-earth about our possibilities and our future, including our future expectations from and uses of markets, we need something much more open, experimental and democratic than passing from the strait-jacket of one fatal conceit to another. Any hopeful future depends, as it has always done throughout history, on ourselves and on the ways we combine to pursue freedom and handle the issues of power through the development of pragmatic politics (issues which occur in and through markets as much as elsewhere).

Economic theories do not break down into the sort of practical common sense which any sensible person can and should simply take for granted. During my investigation I have found myself describing a formulation which operates as a comprehensive worldview while claiming dogmatic authority and demanding economic obedience. The message is: There Is No Alternative but we may cheerfully follow TINA, for obedience to her rules promises all of us – at least eventually – enough prosperity to be sufficiently content. We shall be sufficiently free in the nearest thing to an earthly utopia – a globalized earth living off the cornucopia of the Free Market's productivity. Trust us, say the practitioners of the Free Market and the gurus of liberal economics, that is where we are going.

Where did this hope come from and how did it get such a grip on us all? I believe this enquiry to be a hopeful one for if we can but clear away this absolutizing of hope in the Free Market, then we have every chance of being liberated to collaborate in finding more hopeful ways forward at every level from the local, through the regional and national to the global. Worldwide we need to revive a democratic and pragmatic politics; a politics rescued from our present mind-numbing subservience to the mantras of the Market so that the Market itself can be rescued for what it is undoubtedly worth. If we can only organize ourselves effectively to that end, we might be able to recapture profit for people at large and develop trading and exchange operations which take seriously both the sustaining and the sharing of the earth.

There are troubling grounds for being concerned about where the untrammelled operations of the Free Market are taking us, our communities and our world. Is it not worth exploring one's anxiety in a systematic way, even if one risks, as I consider in the next chapter, being taken for an idiot? Everyone who is anybody across the world – and certainly anybody who holds political power – seems to be convinced that the way of the Free Market is the only way forward. Even the Chinese are falling into line. When the governments of the world together with their voters are all putting their hopes in one direction and moving towards one economic system, how can the agreed way of hope be called into question? That is the multi-billion dollar question. But what is the practical worth of nominal billions of any currency when the nominal values need to be 'cashed' to help all people to live decently on a sustainable earth into the indefinite future? I hope to show that in this present 'case of the anxious idiot', it is my anxiety which proves creative and hopeful. I am well aware that there will be many who will start with and maintain the view that it is the idiocy which is definitive. That issue is what the whole argument of this book is about.

Notes

1   Paul Ormerod, *The Death of Economics* (Faber & Faber, 1994), p. 75.
2   See Chapter 12 for a discussion of this.
3   As for example a Chancellor's Bank of England 'wise man', Charles Goodhart, points out in his standard work on *Money, Information and Uncertainty* (Macmillan, 1975; second edition, 1989) (cf, for example, pp. 21 and 445).
4   See Chapters 3–11.
5   See Chapters 12–14.
6   For an extended treatment of this issue, consider the discussion of the Market as an evolved information system and Hayek's theory of this in Chapters 4 and 8.

2 The Apology of an Anxious Idiot

The basic logic of the theory of the Free Market is simple. Markets make money and money makes human prosperity. So as long as the Free Market is left untrammelled by appropriately restrained government, it sets us free as if by an Invisible Hand to pursue our human quest for what the Founding Fathers of the USA described as: Life, Liberty and the Pursuit of Happiness. It is no mere historical accident that the American Declaration of Independence and the first publication of Adam Smith's *Wealth of Nations* both took place in 1776. History was preparing for both the freedom and the prosperity of the Market.

It is not only right and proper, therefore, but also profitable and promising that our political, social, and personal lives, should be dominated by the Market litany – or rather the Market mantra. This mantra, to put it crudely, is:

> The Market works, OK
> The Market rules, OK
> and (even more OK) the way the Market works and rules is the only way to freedom and prosperity.

Therefore, go with the Market and profit, prosperity and freedom shall be added unto you.

This book is written because I have become convinced that this 'Market mantra' is neither a gross oversimplification nor a gross caricature. It is a simple statement of faith held to be an obvious statement of fact. It is the creed of our Free Market faith and the hymn of our salvation. As human beings on the verge of the twenty-first century we no longer share any common good nor any convictions or visions about common goods. Our common good, the investment which unites us all, is in the Market.

When I started writing this book the Conservatives were still in power. Now we have New Labour. It seems that New Labour led by Mr Blair as Prime Minister and Mr Brown as Chancellor are as clear as anyone that we have to take the Free Market for granted. I invest a great deal of hope in Messrs Blair, Brown and their colleagues. At least some of the right questions are being restored to the political agenda. But I find that I remain a frequently angry and often deeply frustrated citizen.

In the March 1998 Budget New Labour began to develop measures directed to help people into work but it is yet to be proved whether they have grasped what they are up against. By the 1999 Budget, we see Mr Brown proceeding on his determined way to at least the modified plaudits of the sober and sound commentators of *The Times*, *The Financial Times* and, to some extent, *The Economist*. He seems, if growth is restored, to have some chance of both satisfying financial orthodoxy and of finding some sums to expend on health, education and training people to get back into work. But what if growth does not recover? And even if it does, a substantial minority of people seem to be guaranteed great uncertainty and 'rewards' which are not only uncomfortably smaller than those of the select successful, but are distressingly near or below any civilized subsistence level. And how long will the promised improvement take to develop? The prospects look uncertain and the prospectus doubtful.

Meanwhile, Mr Brown is seen requesting corporate management to show restraint in their remuneration policies. At the same time he presses workers to shoulder their responsibilities and accept the flexible arrangements about pay and security which the Free Market requires. Yet corporate industry continues to hand out rewards and bonuses to chief executives (even those forced to relinquish their posts because of association with corporate failures or inadequacies). Economic orthodoxy demands that the unemployed be targeted and labour be flexible while executives are to be lavishly rewarded. The Free Market both requires and justifies this.

Is New Labour sufficiently aware of the difficult issues once the Free Market is accepted as the basic way forward for the provision of prosperity for all? Can the individualistic model of human trading and choice which lies at the heart of Free Market theory be reconciled with the desire, shared by so many who voted for Labour on 1 May 1997, that the Government and the State should exercise a more direct concern on behalf of all of us *for* all of us? Or has such a desire been dispelled by the brute fact of market necessity?

I am not only a frustrated and often angry citizen, I am an increasingly troubled human being. I cannot but question the present emphasis on growth in productivity, profit and consumption. I suspect not only a false promise but also a threatening prospect. How realistic is it to believe that we can go on developing our present patterns of production, resource use and consumption, and then multiply it by the ten-fold increase (or is it the twenty-fold or even forty-fold increase?) which current projections suggest would be required if there were to be enough 'trickle down' to spread market prosperity effectively around the majority of the population of this globe? I fear for my grandchildren and I fear for our still lovely and lively world.

Perhaps I underestimate the adjustments entrepreneurial ingenuity can achieve and the power of sheer human inventiveness. Perhaps it is true that all limits exist to be surpassed – as they have been repeatedly transcended in the last two hundred years or so. Am I simply a misinformed pessimist? As yet I am not persuaded. I remain a disturbed human being – unsettled not simply by questions about long-term prospects but over the particular prospects of my grandchildren, well-loved human persons of direct concern to me.

I am not just an angry and frustrated citizen and a frequently troubled human being, I am also a disturbed Christian. That is to say, I seek to relate what goes on around me to values which I believe to be given me from a shared and corporate faith in the God who is particularly (although not exclusively) known in and through Jesus of Nazareth, believed to be the Christ. As a Christian I am clear (and I share this clarity with many other people who look at the world from different perspectives) that it is offensive, unworthy and dangerous to treat the materials and living systems of the world as if they exist simply for our individual exploitation rather than as resources to be husbanded for neighbourly use and the future sustenance of the community.

I am prepared to take it for granted that the mechanism of market trading is important for a whole series of interactions which supply both necessities for the survival of life and many embellishments for its enjoyment. However I cannot believe that the whole dynamic of societal interchange and personal relationships depends upon the magnification of self-interest to and beyond the threshold of greed. As a citizen, a human being and a Christian, I cannot justify investing so much in the putative growth of the Market. Consumption cannot do away with the need and duty to promote community. Profit-making and taking cannot replace the necessities and opportunities for mutual sacrifice and sharing, for the maintenance and enhancement of human living together.

This is not to claim that there is a simple way forward. I recognize the concerns of those who fear the moralistic tyranny of the Grand

Inquisitor (whether imposed from political ideologies or religious moralisms) more than the allegedly amoral operations of the Market. But I cannot see that shunning communal responsibility, or taking refuge in the near-absoluteness of individual freedom, are anything but an irresponsible escape, a political sham which fails to face up to issues of power. (Power that may be exercised in the Market as well as through pressure groups in politics.) To locate all human reality, potential and value in 'the individual' (treated apparently as an isolated and isolatable unit) is oddly simple-minded and contrary to observable basic facts. I cannot be an individual in my person and personality without relationships – however stifling or corrupting some relationships may be. To set up an acute and necessarily negative polarity between the individual as the focus of human being and the relational (and, up to a point, collective) exercise of being human flies in the face of simple facts, and is dangerously impractical.

As a citizen, and as a human being who also finds himself a Christian I am deeply worried about the morality of the overweening dominance of 'the Market' in public affairs. I doubt its present operations and fear its future effects. Are our prospects and significance as human beings to be determined primarily by the extent to which we have access, via the possession of cash or credit, to those economic transactions which are commonly held to determine life according to the laws of the overriding Market?

I am well aware that this conviction of mine flies directly in the face of current political orthodoxy in developed and democratic countries. Every election for a parliament, a president or congress, is now evaluated as an exercise in marketing. What political prospectus will the majority of electors buy as being most likely to increase that 'feel good' factor which is assumed to flow from voters having more money in their pockets with which to exercise freedom of choice in that ever-growing cornucopia of possibilities which the Free Market promises to spread before us.

What are the practical chances of challenging what is so widely taken for granted as *common* sense – the only common sense on matters political and economic available to persons of reasonable goodwill? I am haunted by a feeling that to write this book is to make an attempt which verges on the *idiotic*, but I am forced to this idiocy by my concerns as an angry citizen, a disturbed human being and a troubled Christian. 'Idiotic' is a powerful adjective built up from the ancient Greek word 'idios', meaning 'one's own' and so 'private', 'personal'. From this adjective comes the noun 'idiotes' (or, as we might say, 'idiot'). The idea or conception of an 'idiotes' develops in classical Greek times along a fascinating rake's progress which has resonances for our own personal capacities for effective contemporary reflection.

According to my copy of the standard Greek–English lexicon, Liddell and Scott, the meaning of 'idiotes' starts as a 'private person, an individual': 'One in a private station – as opposed to one holding public office.' Then the decline in the meaning of the word appears – on the way to the disenfranchising of the ordinary person by 'the experts'. 'Idiotes' comes to encompass: 'One who has no professional knowledge – whether of politics or any other subject, as we say, "a layman".' That trend in usage leads on to: 'Generally, a raw hand, an ignorant, ill-informed man.' And so we are practically ready for the corresponding adjective 'idiotikos' to become our 'idiotic'.

These days we have so many self-contained disciplines, not least that of economics itself, alongside the many professional and practical expertises in banking, finance, management and communication. It seems clear that it is 'idiotic' of an ordinary citizen to attempt to explore in any global way across the complex economic field of markets, finance, money, production, distribution and consumption. My undertaking to write this book, therefore, risks being taken as the wonderings and wanderings of 'an ignorant, ill-informed man'. One glance at the sets of statistical tables and diagrams assembled in any copy of *The Economist* ought to be enough to warn off all 'idiots and lay-persons'. All the more so if the rash enquirer is a bishop who has been publicly chastised a number of times for interventions which have led him, so it is alleged, to the betrayal of his spiritual calling and the exposure of his practical inexperience and ignorance.

It occurs to me, however, that a bishop might be just the person to take up the idiotic and questioning stance of a lay-person *vis-à-vis* the dominant orthodoxy of the Market age. For a bishop is by professional training well-initiated into the high priestly traditions of professional and sacred secrets – revelations which the ordinary faithful cannot be expected to understand, and wherein their meddling would be counter-productive to both their current spiritual welfare and their future prospects of salvation. Once upon a time the church was confident that it knew better and knew for the best, and was generally so accepted. It is ironic, although not altogether surprising, that eighteenth-century enlightenment and nineteenth-century liberal rationalism and utilitarianism should have spawned a new high priesthood of the Market and the money men whose mysteries are not to be questioned by the common folk but simply obeyed.

It could be that it is only professional envy arising from the displacement of bishops and other religious authorities by the current authority figures of economists, financiers, industrialists and business-men that motivates me to embark on an idiotic-seeming attempt to call into question the whole Market myth and mantra. But I think not. That we are faced with far-reaching questions is made clear enough by the statements of the apologists of the Market. Their texts are not just concerned with technical details about trade and finance. They present practices which are defended and developed in relation to views about how the world is, and who we are as human beings. The proponents of the fundamentalism of the Market put forward urgent moral, philoso-phical and political arguments for the Free Market. Arguments revol-ving around freedom, the central status and value of the individual, and the evident undesirability and inefficiency of attempts to guide or regulate the Market.

I increasingly doubt the validity of the arguments for the Free Market as at present operating and am increasingly anxious about the results that this Free Market is producing. So it is necessary first to make a case for breaking through the ring-fence with which market proponents and fundamentalists surround their theories. This ring-fence is both sus-tained, and declared to be unbreachable, by the power of TINA. There simply Is No Alternative so no further questions can be asked. It is necessary therefore to demonstrate that even if there is no alternative in sight which offers sufficient signs of being practicable and applicable, nonetheless the *questions* about both the basis of, and expectations from, market operations clearly exist and must be raised. The first step is to establish that the assumed and alleged fundamentals of the Market, when examined, are not as fundamental as all that.

The idiot who persists in pressing this case is undoubtedly raising the question as to whether the idiocy is all on one side. One of the purposes of this book is to explore the possibility that the ultimate idiocy is to polarize everything into arguments and aspirations cleanly divided between the practical realism of market proponents and the idiotic idealism of market opponents. But there is no way open to any more hopeful and common facing of shared idiocies, realisms and aspirations, while an unacknowledged market fundamentalism blocks any serious thinking *beyond* the Market. This is why the limitations and myths of market fundamentalism have to be presented as starkly as possible.

The second reason for challenging the 'fundamentals' of market orthodoxy arises from a consideration of practical politics. At present politics across the world appear to be based on an acceptance of market fundamentalism. The political debates and divisions, such as they are, are about how to adjust within the system. It is not considered practical even to contemplate developing policies of living with the system and mitigating its negative effects, while seeking for serious and far-reaching changes in the system or, indeed, evolving it into something else. The collapse of communism is taken as absolutely decisive evidence that there is no alternative and that is that.

The sheer prudence and practicality of this standpoint deserves to be questioned. Throughout human history politics and power systems have repeatedly been challenged and have evolved. Why should our present systems of politics and power be expected to persist without major change? Does the ideal of democracy inevitably dissolve before the power of the Market, leaving no hint or expectation of anything different? It may be alleged that 'history' enforces the abandonment of attempts at political optimism and insists on the acceptance of market determinism. But on whose authority does this claim rest? What are their reasons for making it? (And how are their interests served by maintaining it?) Does the Market really sanitize all those issues of power, aspirations to freedom and conflicts of interest which have alternately baffled and inspired men and women of vision?

Market realism seems, from some perspectives, to be remarkably naive. It appears to claim that power needs no other legitimation than money, and wealth no other justification than that it has been acquired, and once acquired carries no further responsibilities. How prudent is it to assume that 'the masses', conscious of past political struggles and ideals, and daily informed by the media of the juxtaposition of immense wealth and frequent squalor, will acquiesce in this modern version of feudal distribution of power based on the control of money rather than the control of land?

A precondition of any realistic and hopeful revival of a politics must be a readiness to reconsider fundamentals, and that must include challenging the fundamentalism of the Market. The evident impact of market operations demands a reassessment of the basic theories (and consequently justified practices of) the operation of the Market according to received market fundamentalism. Which problems in the world are to be subordinated to which? By what inevitable law, for example, should Mexican banks be rescued while Mexican peasants are further impoverished? Must we accept that there are no other conceivable ways of co-ordinating locally experienced, but globally spread, problems other than by money handed on and made viable by the global financial markets and servant agencies such as IMF and World Bank? Is ever freer capital and trade bound to be advantageous to every person and area of the world – and, if that premise is accepted, how long must the poor survive before they experience any benefit? And what can be done about the victims en route? Can it be true that the Market is the only source of information and resource management we have for dealing with questions like this?

The examination of market fundamentalism is therefore necessary both politically and economically. Many of its taken-for-granted axioms are more like shibboleths or traditions which, having once been true, have now to be maintained as true in order to keep the system intact and justify the worship of TINA as the guaranteeing and protective deity. But acquiescing in market fundamentalism does not obliterate the questions that are as old as reflective humanity. Those questions to do with morality, citizenship, visions and faith still persist. Indeed market fundamentalism, with its consequent operations and expectations, is itself based on assumptions about how the world works, what motivates people and what is worth promoting.

These wonderings and wanderings of an idiot threaten to raise every question there is about everything there is or might be – which is even more idiotic. Surely such a pretentious investigation can become only a random walk? Not inevitably – although this is clearly a risk. The challenge lies in whether the motivation of faith can be controlled and directed by the discipline of fact and the logic of arguments in pursuit of a specified objective. My objective is, in the first place, to gain a hearing from other frustrated citizens and anxious human beings who, from whatever perspective, are troubled about the hegemony of market fundamentalism. Anxiety, disturbance and discontent need to be focused and rallied if there are to be any effective movements to challenge and change the Market's stranglehold over practical economics and politics.

There is a great and growing volume of work which criticizes the Market from many perspectives, ranging from that of radical opt-out to critical reordering, with the help of a whole variety of experiments in localized but multipliable alternatives. This book does not draw directly on this material, although the knowledge of its existence and its expanding scope has been a major factor in encouraging me to risk following my own particular idiotic way. The particular concern of this book is focused on the imperviousness of the Market fundamentalism to this growing mound of evidence and detailed criticism. The Market establishment is insulated by its combination of ideological conviction and actual control of the resources of market and money power. This insulation is reinforced by the degree to which political conviction, the media and public opinion have been captured by the Market apologists so that criticisms of the Market are dismissed either with the assertion that the system will sufficiently deal with the criticisms as time goes on, or by stating that there are no practical alternatives. The whole argument is reinforced by the claim that this is the practical, proven and theoretically established way to prosperity for ever greater numbers – sooner or later. People are advised, therefore, not to lend credence to those who would derail the beneficent juggernaut of the Market, which is our only hope (however postponed) of prosperity.

This book is not so much aimed at those who are already working in the field of collecting critical data or providing possible alternatives. It is addressed rather to those who are baffled by the strength of the Market mantra, troubled by what they see around them, but unsure of the existence of any alternative way ahead. Previous General Elections have shown that voters, uncertain in a vision-less time, tend to 'stick close to nurse for fear of worse'. Many people hoped that the election result of May 1997 demonstrated the existence of a sufficiently widespread feeling that something more than the Market was required to build a healthy society with a sustainable future. But New Labour thought it prudent to emphasize strict monetarist and fiscal restraint. It has been widely agreed that no set of politicians, whatever their perspective, can ask people with money to allow more of it to go in taxation for social investment in improving long-term social cohesion. The 'common sense' of the Free Market requires that people who make money keep it and people who cannot make money be pushed as quickly as possible into work so they at least make some even if the wage of an insecure and often part-time job is below subsistence. It is not yet clear that New Labour sees how to serve both the Free Market and everybody. But then the Free Market faith is that by serving the Free Market we do – sooner or later – serve everybody and there is no alternative. There are strong logical and practical grounds for worrying about sticking to the nurture of the nurse embodied in the Free Market. There are strong grounds for arguing that 'nurse'and her Market enthusiasts are not aligned on multiplying general prosperity. The probable truth about the powers-that-be who support and put their faith in the Market establishment and market fundamentalism, is that they are out to milk most of us for the increasing benefits of some of us, themselves in particular.

This is not to claim that all market enthusiasts are hardened cynics who know this very well but are simply selling us the prospectus so that they can profit by it. True fundamentalists actually believe in their fundamentals. The connection between the moral commitments and hopes of individuals, and the moral effects of what they commit themselves to, is not simple. In view of the terrible crimes committed historically by religious enthusiasts, it is not proper for a bishop to condemn all market enthusiasts. But it is right and proper for a frustrated citizen and an anxious human being, who is also a troubled Christian, to challenge the basis, assumptions and practical effects of market enthusiasms, upheld by market fundamentalism, and speak out against either the dismissal of basic questioning as based on ignorance or the silencing of criticism because at present there is no alternative.

The first task, therefore, for the anxious idiot is to establish, by examination of what the Market enthusiasts actually say, the existence of the Market faith and the Market fundamentalism summed up in the Market mantra.

3   The Market as Providence

God may not be in his heaven but all is still well with the world. The Market has taken over and will provide increasing prosperity for rising numbers of the world's inhabitants. We should not fret too much about poverty or pollution. We certainly should not attempt to regulate financial markets. Indeed, we should rejoice at the increasing globalization and sophistication of markets in trade and finance, for this enhances their capacity to enforce the necessary restraints and disciplines of the Market on all and sundry in the 'real economy' – governments, the governed, the managers of savings and capital, let alone the users of that capital in industry, commerce and services. This system ensures the greatest possible smoothing out of market volatilities and inefficiencies so maximizing the possibilities of production and consumption. The Market's discipline is often tough but always basically benign. Such is the Gospel According to Economics.

As I am a layman on the subject of economic theories and activities, I shall no doubt be told that to attempt to start a serious discussion about the grip economics has on our lives from such a statement is a gross over simplification, even a parody. Economics, we are told, is the discipline which grapples with the real world of human interaction through production, trading and consumption. Practitioners in the real world of industry, trade and finance are well-known to be the most hard-headed and realistic of men and women. They would be the last people to follow a simple gospel or get caught up in a naive faith. But is that so? Let us consider some of the evidence as reflected in a typical collection of economic and financial commentators.

In October 1995 *The Economist* published, as a forty-four page insert, 'A Survey of the World Economy'.[1] Its cover bears the title, 'Who's in the driving seat?'. The accompanying cartoon depicts a powerful lorry belonging to 'Global Money Inc.' and labelled 'Financial Markets', travelling at speed, and a small car with the number-plate 'GOVT1' perched on its roof. The driver and passenger of this car are having their documents entitled 'Policy' blown away by the momentum of the lorry.

Turning the page on this graphic representation of government at the mercy of global financial markets the reader finds the first leader in the survey ('The Myth of the Powerless State') setting out to refute the claim that global integration of the world economy is emasculating the modern state. The author warns against siren voices calling for the regulation of markets and a return to protectionism. Such an attempt to reverse the trend towards freer trade would be potentially disastrous. This commentator is clear that things are going in the direction of the best of all possible worlds. Indeed there is no alternative, but we can be of good cheer for in submitting to the mechanisms and disciplines of the Market there is the promise of (near) perfect freedom and developing the greatest happiness of the greatest number. This world is not thereby claimed to be ideal, but it is feasible and it is promising – more promising than any other attainable world.

The Economist survey is symptomatic of the basic faith in the Market. It is clearly not intended as an apologia for the Market but simply as an extended exposition of the way it works. The object is to show that the global development of the Market is not a threat to the power of states and governments. The global market should not be feared; all it does is draw attention to limitations which have always existed on the powers of states and governments to influence economic affairs.

In case *The Economist* alone may be thought a biased witness, another example of the prevalence of this absolutist set of assumptions about the Market is to be found in the pamphlet *Coming to Terms: Corporations and the Left* by Roger Warren Evans, published in 1992 by the Institute of Public Policy Research. The IPPR 'was established in 1988 by leading figures in the academic, business and trade union community to provide an alternative to the free market think tanks'. Evans' pamphlet is thus a contribution to 'coming to terms' with the currently established market economy in ways which will enable the pursuit of the basic aims of socialism concerning the liberation of men and women for personal freedom and fulfilment. His description, therefore, of the conditions under which these socialist aims must be pursued is all the more significant in the way it takes the prestige and momentum of the Market idea for granted. He writes:

> The need is to recognise that a new relationship is already emerging, between governments on the one hand, and the corporate sector on the other. Governments have already undergone a metamorphosis; they have become, first and foremost, guarantors of their citizens' supply of consumer goods and services. That is more important to

their political survival than the ability to wage war or promote peace, to conduct diplomatic relationships with skill, or to uphold the traditional political freedoms. And the corporations, operating internationally behind the obscuring screens of company law, have become the most effective suppliers of those consumer goods and services, supplementing their traditional roles as bankers and suppliers of governmental goods. With the collapse of state socialism in Eastern Europe, it is no longer arguable that state agencies are capable of meeting consumer demand. Governments have become wholly dependent upon the corporate sector to meet the imperious demands of their consumer-voters. The advent of the consumer society has shifted power decisively towards the corporate sector, and it is now impossible to imagine any other outcome.[2]

Is it true that 'it is now impossible to imagine any other outcome'? Is the global market economy the final, inevitable and inescapable state, structure and dynamism of the world we inhabit?

It is reported that after one of his powerful ethical and evolutionary lectures, T.H. Huxley was approached by a member of his audience who said, 'Professor, after your lecture I have decided to accept the universe.' The reply is said to have been: 'Madam, you'd better.' We can wonder whether this was received by the lady as good news or bad. If you 'accept the universe' do you *do* better? Or is such an acceptance simply surrendering to fate? It depends, of course, on how we perceive and experience the universe and what resources are discovered in it through our perceptions of, and responses to, this universe. The writers of *The Economist*'s 1995 survey clearly assume both that we 'had better' accept the global market and that by doing so we shall 'do better' – indeed, I think, they assume that we shall do the best we can and that this best is desirable and very much to be welcomed. This, surely, is to believe in the Market as Providence. The grounds for this belief must be considered at the next stage of our investigation. First I must establish that (whether acknowledged or not) this belief exists and informs, if it does not determine, what a representative selection of commentators, such as that brought together in *The Economist* survey describe and prescribe.

We can start where the survey starts, in the words and sentiments expressed in its first leader, 'The Myth of the Powerless State'. The basic thesis is: 'The world has changed, the global economy has indeed arrived; none the less the emasculated state is a myth.' I shall take up the issue of whether or not the state is 'emasculated' later, but what I am concerned with at this point is what this collection of commentators assume to be the *powers* of the Market and the *effects* of these powers.

We start therefore from the presumably indisputably true position that 'the world has changed' and 'the global economy has arrived'. This global economy makes its power felt.

> For Europeans, the wreckage of the Exchange Rate Mechanism (ERM) cruelly symbolises the power of markets and the apparent impotence of governments. First in 1992 and again in 1993, the foreign-currency markets bet heavily that governments would devalue their currencies – and thereby made the prediction come true.

Drawing on evidence from the USA the leader continues: 'So you might think that when it comes to currencies and deficits, markets are indeed in command. They are, in a sense – and so they have always been.' The markets are in command when it comes to currencies and deficits and not directly over anything else. So their power may be considered to be merely consequential and instrumental. But it is very far reaching and active in its effects. For example: 'The collapse of the Bretton Woods system of fixed exchange rates starting in 1971 was . . . a case of "market discipline" applied to inconsistent policies.' The inverted commas are to be noted. Their use presumably indicates that the writer has some sense that the language employed is operating metaphorically rather than literally. What is being referred to are structuring operations rather than disciplining actions. It is 'as if' someone was exercising discipline, just as in another and more famous formulation it was 'as if' someone was exercizing an Invisible Hand.

It is to be observed, however, that the machine – or whatever it is – does seem to operate purposively. In the final paragraph the leader says:

> The myth of the powerless state has also prospered for another reason: politically, it is extremely convenient. Towards the end of the 1970s, governments began lowering their barriers to trade and international finance because of mounting evidence that the barriers were doing more harm than good. In selling this change of policy to their voters, governments chose not to emphasise that the benefits of liberalisation (higher living standards in the aggregate) greatly outweigh the costs (lower wages and higher unemployment in some of the industries facing new competition). To argue that way would only have drawn attention to the costs. Better to say that changes in the world economy left them no choice but to liberalise.

Reluctant governments are being forced ('disciplined') into doing good things. The results are good, for the benefits outweigh the costs. We may wonder incidentally how the commentator knows that there are 'higher living standards *in the aggregate*'. Is this derived from a utilitarian calculus and, if so, based on what set of statistics? Also, for that matter, is it clear that these (calculated?) advantages 'outweigh the costs'? By what system of evaluation can we demonstrate that, for example, the costs borne by displaced miners and their dependent communities in County Durham, Yorkshire and elsewhere, are outweighed by raised living standards? One is reminded of Norman Lamont's celebrated (or infamous) remark when Chancellor that unemployment was 'a price worth paying for low inflation and economic recovery'.

Such questions, however, fall below the horizon of assumption of this leader writer. He or she is secure in the assurance of the superior workings (if not the superior wisdom) of the markets.

> It seems churlish to complain that politicians are using a bad argument ('our hands are tied') in a good cause (lowering the barriers to international trade and finance). On balance, however, it is best to bear in mind that this is so. The barriers politicians have lowered can be raised again.

Clearly the price of economic liberty is eternal vigilance. The discipline of the markets is not only inescapable, it is far wiser than governments, politicians and electorates. It is therefore appropriate to use a patronizing and condescending tone.

> For a good deal of the past fifty years . . . governments aimed to keep deficits small. Whenever that approach was abandoned, the results were bad – and it was the financial markets that delivered the news.

Or, again,

> In fiscal policy the timing has been relaxed – the global Market often lets countries borrow more, more cheaply, than they otherwise could. However, since this can allow deficits to run further out of control, the eventual punishment may often be worse.

The global markets deliver bad news, exercise discipline and exact punishment and all the while 'the benefits . . . greatly outweigh the costs'.

The assumptions of this leader are prevalent throughout the survey. Thus, the opening article in the review contains observations such as:

> The increasing clout of the global Market is said to be eroding governments' ability to steer their economies. This may be no bad thing if it prevents them from acting unwisely.... The past two decades have seen a revolution as domestic financial markets have been opened up to create a massive global capital market, beyond any government's control... [As a result the] policy tool-kits with which [governments used] to steer their economies ... have been plundered by the de-regulation of domestic financial flows, the liberalisation of international capital flows, the arrival of powerful computers and telecommunication, and rapid financial innovation.

Despite the 'plundering' language, I want to underline the market optimism general among *The Economist*'s commentators. This first article has a subsection entitled 'Three Cheers for the Market': 'Financial liberation has developed huge benefits. The free capital market ensures that savings are directed to the most productive investments without regard for national boundaries.' I waive for later discussion the issue of 'productive of what for whom?', and note simply the assertion of the maximizing and optimizing effects of the globalized and liberalized markets. The three full cheers are justified because: 'The global capital Market is simply a mechanism for pricing capital and allocating it to its most productive uses.' (Same caveat as before about 'most productive'.)

> In this increasingly uncertain environment one thing is sure; plenty more clashes between global markets and national governments lie ahead. The danger is that some governments will be tempted to respond to market excesses by trying to force the global capital market back into a strait-jacket. But they would be bound to fail. Governments would do better to rethink the way they conduct policy to avoid destabilising market expectations, and ensure that markets are better informed so that they can become stricter disciplinarians.
>
> The challenge is to help the global capital market to become more effective in encouraging good behaviour. To increasingly frustrated politicians, it will appear that governments have been defeated. Their scope for promising voters heaven (and delivering hell) is shrinking. But in the long-term the real victors are not just the

financial markets but also companies, workers, savers and pensioners.

In an uncertain world one thing is sure. The global markets are in charge. The important thing is to help them to become stricter disciplinarians. This does not defeat governments, it corrects them so that the real victors will be 'not just the financial markets' (who will, presumably, continue to earn huge sums for their practitioners out of the profits and fees arising from the manipulations conducted on them) 'but also companies, workers, savers and pensioners'. It may be worrying that it looks as if poor-ish pensioners are having a bad time and are threatened with worse. It may be disquieting that in this country over half the population has less than £475 in savings so that interest rates cannot affect them greatly. It is bothersome that unemployment remains so stubborn while job security ebbs away. But we may, presumably, trust that the Market will 'in the long-term' deal with all this. For not a few of us 'in the long-term' means we shall be dead. It is however no doubt comforting to know that our children and grandchildren will have these prospects.

This is indeed a 'gospel' – the Good News of the Market. It is taken for granted that any reasonable set of human beings, taking a balanced or objective view of this articulation of how things work will agree that this is how things indeed are, and that this is indeed good news.

Is then the 'gospel' not a faith but a science? I suspect that such commentators as I am considering in this *Economist* survey would be inclined to reply – 'neither a faith nor a science but common sense derived from practical observations and experience'. 'Pragmatism' and 'pragmatists' seem to be generally approved of in the circles of economic analysis. But whether they believe themselves to be writing from faith, science or pragmatic common sense, all these writers are resolutely optimistic. So resolute is their optimism that it is *as if* they believed in the Market as Providence – a truly benign Providence which guarantees their conviction about the goodness of the Market. This conviction is demonstrated incidentally but all the more effectively by the way in which this collection of commentators in later articles in the survey handle the deficiencies and inefficiencies which they discern in the operations of the Market.

The argument is that the Market deals with its own faults and, eventually, delivers – whatever the odds. This it does because it is the mechanism or communications system by which 'economic forces' eventually assert themselves. The short article entitled 'Back to the

Future', whose theme is 'Fears that financial markets have too much power go back a long way', ends with a reference to the collapse of the Bretton Woods System for managing international currency arrangements and the scrapping of all controls on all international capital movements in the 1970s. It concludes: 'The pressure to lift controls rose not just from free-market ideology, but from economic forces which undermined the effectiveness of the rules and caused business to move away.' There is something deeper and more powerful than ideas, organized into an ideology, about the Capital Free Market which undermines attempts at regulation and impels the movement of business. The underlying, and where necessary undermining, power of these economic forces always prevails. But we need not fear for 'the Force' is not only with us, it is for us.

A long article entitled 'Judge and Jury' is devoted to the subject 'as economic watchdogs go, financial markets have their faults'. The issue of the value of market power is the starting point:

> The debate on whether financial markets are too powerful really turns on the issue of whether market power is a good thing. If the markets judge economies correctly, then the answer must be yes. If they get it wrong, the answer is no.

The panel illustrating the economic data which supply the author's way into considering his posed problem is taken from an OECD study on the relationship between real long-term interest rates and the economic indicators provided by budget deficits, inflation and current account balances. This panel is given the label 'Judgement Day'. Is it just because I am, both by conviction and by profession, theologically inclined that I perceive in this labelling one more indication that there are latent assumptions of a quasi-providential or pseudo-theological nature floating around in the whole universe of discourse in which these commentators are operating?

Elsewhere in the survey another panel on the foreign exchange market ('Not So Divine Intervention') compares the quantity of reserves held by 'industrial countries' to the size of *daily* foreign exchange trading. In 1983 the reserves are shown as more than twice the size of the daily foreign exchange trading. By 1995 the volume of both reserves and daily trading has grown greatly, but the growth in daily foreign exchange trading has far exceeded the growth in reserves. In 1983 the reserves dwarfed daily foreign exchange trading. By 1995 the value of daily exchange trading towers over the value of the reserves. This dominating position is reflected in the title given to the panel – 'Masters of the Universe'. The powers of the Market do indeed dominate – which could easily be translated, via the Latin 'dominus' into 'have the mastery over', or 'lord it over', all of us.

The point, is that the writers in *The Economist* survey share the faith, hope or whatever it is, that we can, on balance and in the long run, be cheerful about this. For, as the marginal note of the article which uses the 'Master of the Universe' panel says 'Markets are not perfect, but the alternative is worse'. So the markets deliver the best of all possible worlds. No doubt we should not worship them but we should certainly welcome and cherish them. In any case we have to give into them sooner or later.

The 'Judge and Jury' article lists a series of inefficiencies in the markets. An IMF study is cited as concluding that

> the discipline organised by Markets on policy is neither infallible nor is it applied smoothly and consistently... Discipline is often doled out erratically, with waves of excessive optimism being followed by excessive pessimism.

Three 'striking examples' of this are cited, including the mid-1990s Mexico crisis in which 'the markets simply lost their heads', and the boom and bust in the world bond markets in 1993 and 1994 when

> the Bond Market collapse was a rebound from an over-shoot in 1993 when banks, Hedge Funds and other institutional investors built up large positions, based on over-optimistic expectations about inflation and budget deficits.

These references to 'losing their heads' and building up 'long positions based on over-optimistic expectations' conjure up pictures on television of frenetic young people jumping up and down before their computer screens in international financial exchanges. They may look like highly paid gamblers but we can rest assured. Whatever intermittent vagaries may occur, we are really witnessing what is, overall, a rational communications system related to, and giving discipline to, economic realities. As the writer who is discussing 'whether market power is a good thing' puts it:

> Plenty of horrendous economic errors have been caused by governments rather than financial markets. And although discipline has

been erratic, most of the policy changes forced by capital markets
have been in right direction.

This is good to know, even if one has a lurking worry about how 'the
right direction' is understood, and for whom and for what it is the right
direction.

The writer finally discusses the stubborn resistance of the US dollar
to market rationality: 'One snag with capital markets, however, is that
they impose less discipline on giants than on dwarfs.' One wonders
whether this is why banks, trusts and currency dealers seem to be
merging together into ever bigger units. Is it to protect market discipline
or to escape it? That is for further investigation but for the moment we
return to the basic and simple optimism of the article. For the time being
the almighty dollar has enough momentum left to get away with it. But
this is about to change and the real question is whether this can be
handled well or suffered badly.

The world has been there before. The mismanagement of the shift
in currency pre-eminence from Sterling to the Dollar earlier this
century caused financial havoc that made governments strap their
financial markets into strait-jackets. The global capital market has
only just recovered from that.

This reminds one of a comment in the article 'Back to the Future' to
which I have already referred. This has the further observation: 'the
collapse of the Bretton-Woods System in the earlier 1970s *signalled the
rebirth of the global capital markets*' [my emphasis]. Attempts are
repeatedly made to suppress or strait-jacket the global capital markets
but these attempts cannot be sustained in the longer run and the return
to the inevitable can only be good, despite deep-seated and repeated
inefficiencies of particular market operations. As the survey's next article
('A Walk on the Wild Side') underlines: 'If derivatives amplify price
movements in time of stress, the lesson for policy makers is obvious; they
must ensure that their policies do not cause stress and uncertainty.' The
increasing sophistication, complication and therefore uncertainty in
assessing risks of derivatives is merely a subordinate problem – if it
exists at all. What all the sophisticated innovations do over all is to
enable the Market to improve its discipline, punishment, and delivery of
realistic news, thereby constraining governments into those ways of
fiscal and monetary rectitude which are the proper and guaranteed path
for increasing overall prosperity and welfare.

After all, as the article on 'Not So Divine Intervention' remarks:

> There is no reason why governments should be better judges than the markets . . . Capital flows are an economic barometer, conveying useful information based on the opinion of large numbers of investors who scrutinise economic indicators. Those who favour capital controls are making the dangerous assumption that policy makers know better than all these players in the market.

This leads on to the argument and advice put forward in the next article in the survey ('Governments that Live in Glass Houses . . .') which begins:

> If financial markets, imperfect though they are, cannot and should not be curbed by means of capital control – as this Survey argues so far – then where does that leave Governments? Are they now completely at the mercy of the changing whims of investors? Only up to a point. For although they can no longer affect capital flows directly, they can influence markets indirectly by conveying information. Information is the missing link between financial markets and governments. Markets cannot be expected to be wise disciplinarians unless they have good information on economic goals, policy instruments and performance. If governments try to hold back information, markets are more likely to panic and over-react to rumours and leaks.

If 'all the players in the Market' are given all available information, then their responses will promote economic health and prosperity as widely as possible. New Zealand is held up as an example of good behaviour in this respect.

> New Zealand now has probably the best fiscal and monetary framework anywhere in the world. By itself that does not guarantee good policy; but by making policy more transparent, it will improve the capital markets' ability to impose discipline and reduce the risk of market over-action caused by uncertainty about policy intentions.

With this symbiotic picture of the relationship between governments and markets we are ready for the concluding article entitled 'Power Politics'. This has a motto attached, 'The market – whether stock, bond or super – is a barometer of civilisation' attributed to Jason Alexander in his 'Philosophy of Investors'. The article's opening paragraph reads:

The appropriate attitude to the global capital market is neither blind devotion nor white-knuckle fear, but healthy respect. Inevitably, finance ministers whose policies have been overwhelmed by international capital flows will feel that markets are too powerful; yet most, if not all, of the changes which financial markets have forced on governments in recent years have been in the right direction. This Survey has argued that fears about governments being left powerless to defend their countries' interests have been overdone. On the whole, the market takes power away from governments that do the wrong things; borrow recklessly, run inflationary policies or try to defend unsustainable exchange rates. They thereby encourage governments to adopt policies that will benefit their economies and their citizens.

A little later in the same article a powerful, and in some ways remarkable, claim is put forward:

Still, nobody disagrees that elected governments now have less control over their economies than they used to. Does that mean that non-elected, and ever-more-powerful financial markets pose a threat to democracy? There is no evidence that they do; indeed in some ways capital markets, driven by the decisions of millions of investors and borrowers, are highly 'democratic'. They act like a rolling twenty-four hour opinion poll. Moreover they increase politicians' accountability by making voters more aware of governments' economic performance. Financial markets have much sharper eyes than voters.

At least 'democratic' is put in inverted commas. We may begin to wonder what real world the writer is describing. The author himself (or herself) realizes that some defence is required:

This still leaves the widespread worry that the markets give a vote only to those with money. But financial markets do not just represent the rich; most people have some savings, whether in a small savings account, a mutual fund, or their future pension. The battle between financial markets and governments really comes down to a power struggle over savings. Governments will find it much harder in future to nibble away surreptitiously at the value of people's nest eggs.

It would seem to be very doubtful indeed that 'most people' have some savings even in developed countries, let alone in the world at large. (Unfortunately, for example, in this country the Government has not funded old age pensions.) The statement about most people having some savings, is on the face of it, simply not statistically true. Maybe, however, it is the considered conviction of those who promote this gospel of the Market that if we let the Market have its head then the trickle-down effect will be such that, fairly soon, the statement about savings will be true. Meanwhile therefore we should perhaps give the enthusiasts for the Market the benefit of the doubt. In statements such as those I have just cited it may be that the descriptions are simply extrapolating trends which those who make them have already discerned and which they are convinced will go on into a fuller future. But this would require also settling any doubts we may have over the 'democracy' of 'the decisions of millions of investors and borrowers' which 'drive' the capital markets. How many of the smaller investors that already exist have any but the most remote and diffused control over the actual operations of investment, dis-investment, and speculation, which make up the vast transactions of the global markets?

Clearly there is much to be investigated about the relationship between the rhetoric of arguments like these and the part financial markets play in the ways the real economy in the real world affect the majority of real and ordinary people in that world. These big questions clearly remain as one reads the conclusion to the survey's concluding article:

> If markets send early warnings, and if governments respond, then future economic crises will be less severe than if everyone had carried on as before. As long as these ifs can be met, the world economy can look forward to a more prosperous future – though still a bumpy one.

The unshakeable optimism is clear. Keep the economy on track by removing impediments to the natural disciplines of the Market unimpeded and the world economy will continue on its ride to prosperity, albeit the ride will be a bumpy one. Does this conviction really stand up to serious investigation? While the benign juggernaut of the Market pursues its bumpy way there are casualties. There are not a few persons, communities and overexploited areas of the world, who are bruised, knocked out or even wiped out as the Market propels the governments and peoples of the world on its way to this more prosperous future.

Why are people so sure that whatever the temporary or local evidence of effects and results, the main thrust of the Market to prosperity is guaranteed and, further, that no other way can be found or imagined? Until this issue is faced, detailed discussion of cases, causes or symptoms is useless. What is the real source of, and basis for, the note of almost bland assurance and superiority which seems to be sounded again and again in a set of discussions like those laid out in the October 1995 *Economist* survey on the world economy. Is it a blandness which is soundly based in unshakeably reasonable assurances, or is it blindness, perhaps encouraged and maintained by the blinkered self-interest of those who so obviously profit from the way the Market operates?

Notes

1   *The Economist*, 7.10.95.
2   Roger Warren Evans, *Coming to Terms: Corporations and the Left* (Institute of Public Policy Research, 1992), p. 3.

4 Not Really Providence – So What?

Market enthusiasts seem sure that their descriptions are more or less a matter of fact. Therefore their prescriptions have the force of necessity. To attempt to interfere with the workings of the Free Market is worse than useless for to do so is to put oneself up against – what?

We need to be clear about who or what this 'What?' is, for it is the arbitrator of innumerable and important decisions. It is consulted about taxation policies, about what can (or, more often nowadays, cannot) be afforded for welfare payments. It is the crystal ball to be consulted about such things as Maastricht criteria, and in its name Central Bankers must be heeded as some sort of oracle. Presidents and lesser politicians expect to win or lose elections according to its behaviour. After all, 'it is the economy, stupid'. Under the influence of their reading of this 'What?' international organizations such as the World Bank and the International Monetary Fund set terms of financing, trading and even internal fiscal policies for needy developing countries, and under its shadow the World Trade Organization resolutely pursues ever freer trade so that the blessings of this 'What?' shall become irresistible worldwide.

Perhaps there is no mysterious 'What?' but only simply and obviously the Market. Perhaps the Market is a development (possibly a 'natural' development?) rooted in time immemorial, its growth vastly enlarged through the great take-off of mechanization, capital investment and production from the late eighteenth century onwards. The significance for human prosperity of this development was most notably reported on by Adam Smith in the second half of the eighteenth century. His analysis of, and observations on, what was then happening have been studied (possibly 'scientifically' studied) ever since. Consequently, now we understand the Market and can have confidence both in our knowledge of it, and in the predictions which we may draw from that knowledge. One might as well query the truth of evolution as call in question the truth of the Market. Here it is and it provides the context and dynamism within which we all live.

With the advent of New Labour the UK political establishment universally adopted this market truth and market mantra. At the opening of 1996, as he began the campaign which was to bring Labour back into power after eighteen years of Tory rule, Mr Blair – as leader of New Labour – made a series of carefully worked out speeches in the Far East on his way home from a Christmas holiday in Australia. He assured his listeners in Japan and in Singapore (the then much-praised leader of the then much-admired Asian Tiger economies) that Britain under Labour would be just the place for market leaders to invest in. He accompanied this with a message to the electorate back home that he was out to develop a stake-holders' market economy in which everybody (and not just stock-holders) had a stake in both the activities and the prosperity which the Market would produce. He subsequently paid a visit to Washington where he pressed home the Market orthodoxy of the Labour government-in-waiting to the US political and financial powers-that-be.

As reports of Mr Blair's eastern speeches were arriving in Britain, Peter Riddle wrote in *The Times* – 'In concrete terms, it can be argued that Labour is arguing that social cohesion promotes economic growth, while the Tories maintain that economic growth leads to social cohesion.'[1] The subsequent General Election campaign of 1997 was fought on whether the Market mantra should be performed in a major or minor key. All political and social possibilities depended on the Market making more money. The question at issue was simply whether this basic momentum could be steered rather more sharply to the libertarian Right or rather more slightly to the communitarian Left. This was thankfully recorded in a regular Monday article on 'Gilt-Edged' in the financial section of *The Times* of the same date.[2]

> the scale of the threat to the Market from a Labour Government has been much exaggerated. Firstly, macro policy under Labour is likely to be little different from that under the Tories. The Labour leadership has undergone a philosophical revolution. They no longer believe in massive state spending and borrowing. Moreover, whatever they might think, their scope for action is tightly circum-scribed by the power of financial markets.

So that was all right. The gilt markets could dismiss worries that a change in government might interrupt their task of making profits out of dealings in bonds and gilts in a way which would decisively influence the dealings in currencies, stocks and shares. These, in turn, could continue to take profits in such a way that enterprise in 'the real economy' (where goods are manufactured and services delivered) would make and take profits in such a way that all these transactions would work 'efficiently', granting us all the best chance of being better off.

Can any reasonably reflective person believe such a thing? Obviously they can, and many of them write not only articles but books about it. This book is written precisely to engage with such works. But is there not a *prima facie* case for being puzzled about such a view? Can the term 'the Free Market' explain anything unless one has an explanation of the Free Market? What *are* we up against when we try to influence governments to regulate the Market? It looks as if any such attempt is held to go against the grain of the way of the world of human intercourse and history. To introduce what is perhaps an old-fashioned way of putting it, to attempt to 'buck' the Market is held (at least implicitly) to be contrary to Nature. (I give 'Nature' a capital to prepare for my discussion of this old-fashioned way of putting things below.)

Consider a symptomatic passage from what one might suppose to be an unlikely source of evidence for a metaphysical belief in the relationship of the Market to 'the What?' of the natural order of things – an article in the Business Section of *The Times*. 'CBI Limbers up for Election, Intent on Running in Neutral',[3] by Philip Bassett related to the launch of a CBI document entitled 'Prospering in the Global Economy'. Bassett describes the document as 'setting out [the CBI's] priorities for the election' and cites it as saying: 'ultimately the management of macro-economic policy must become politically *uncontroversial* [my emphasis]. In an ideal world, election results would not effect the fundamental economic background against which business plans.' This is a remarkable metaphysical statement in view of what it implies. It appears to assume that 'the management of macro-economic policy' and 'the fundamental economic background' cannot be a matter of controversy or political judgement. They are presumably, in the case of the fundamental economic background, a simple matter of fact, and in the case of the management of macro-economic policy, a matter of generally correct policy decisions to be drawn from non-controversial matters of fact in a manner which all reasonable and informed persons will agree is obvious and appropriate. This would seem to imply a simple belief (a 'metaphysical' one, because it seems likely to go beyond simple physical evidence) that the workings of the Market are part of a natural order of things which can or should be commonly agreed upon, for they can be determined by a scientific-like observation of agreed and accepted matters of fact. On such a basis decisions can be taken which no reasonably informed person of goodwill could find to be inappropriate or undesirable.

I suppose the authors of the document from the CBI could get out of this by making the most of the phrase 'in an ideal world'. Further, it may be that the document is not really a statement of a general position but a highly politicized occasional document designed to keep the CBI's position as open and as 'neutral' as possible in the face of the then anticipated advent of a Labour Government. Nonetheless I would argue that the statement, whether simply *ad hoc* or intended as a more principled expression of belief, is symptomatically significant. Business is what has to be done in relation to the nature of the market world in which business operates, and what is good for Business is good for Britain. For that is the way the world is and in an ideal world this would be uncontroversial.

In the actual world, of course, it is highly controversial both in principal and in relation to details of the operations of business in the Market. One example which is of a fairly high order of both generalization and controversy is identified by J.K. Galbraith in the closing pages of his *A History of Economics*.

> For some, monetary policy had (and has) another, and even greater, appeal which was curiously, even unforgivably, overlooked among economists: it is not socially neutral. It operates against inflation by raising interest rates which, in turn, inhibit bank lending and resulting deposit – that is, money-creation. High interest rates are wholly agreeable to people in institutions that have money to lend, and these normally have more money than those who have no money to lend, or, with many exceptions, those who borrow money ... In so favouring the individually and institutionally affluent, a restrictive monetary policy is in sharp contrast with the restrictive fiscal policy, which, relying as it does on increased personal and corporate income taxes, adversely affects the rich.[4]

Even if this observation is just – as it seems to be – it does not absolutely settle what monetarist policy a government might have to decide to follow in particular circumstances. It might be that at a particular stage of an economic cycle a serious case could conceivably be made for a decision which profitably helped the rich and adversely affected the poor. ('Unemployment is a price worth paying'; 'if it does not hurt, it does not work' – and so on.) But it surely could not be uncontroversial – unless everybody was agreed that the Market was the equivalent of Fate – delivering good luck for some and bad luck for others while working onwards in its inexorable, if observable, way. This, however, is not what market enthusiasts, at least publicly, claim to believe.

The belief and hope that there *is* such a thing as a neutral position in relation to economic matters is widely held – or at least widely aspired to. Another diagnostic utterance occurs in the powerful and often persuasive book by Paul Krugman from the Massachusetts Institute of Technology entitled *Peddling Prosperity: Economic Sense and Nonsense in the Age of Diminished Expectations*. While discussing growth he comes to the role of the Federal Reserve System in the USA with regard to monetary policy and employment.

> The important point is that the institutions whose decisions have the greatest impact on the short-run performance of the economy, a short-run that may easily extend the length of a Presidential Term, is a non-partisan body controlled by more or less apolitical technocrats.[5]

The most important word here is 'technocrats'. The people who are performing the important function of the Federal Reserve System in relation to the American economy can be (by and large) relied upon to perform that function both in a more or less apolitical way and in a fashion that promotes the efficient running of the economy because of their *expertise*. This expertise enables and authorises them to make judgements which are neutral. That is to say there is an independent 'art' (techne) with its appropriate set of 'techniques' for dealing with these economic and monetary matters.

My dictionary associates 'technocrats' with 'technocracy', defined as 'a theory or system of society according to which government is controlled by scientists, engineers and other experts'. Are the implications of Krugman's phrases about apolitical technocrats therefore that 'the economy', for instance, works like a *machine* with various rates in the flow of money producing, so to speak, differing 'hydraulic' pressures for pumping up, say, production and therefore employment? In short, are these experts rather like economic engineers? Alternatively, is the economy like an *organism* with biological-type laws of operation which are to be identified then managed by scientific methods, in which case these experts are better described as economic scientists? (or, even, as economic doctors). Or have economic experts evolved as a unique form of network organization in response to 'the Economy'? We need to be able to make a judgement about the relative authority and neutrality of these and other relevant experts. After all some sort of reliable expertise is supposed to lie behind the decisions which politicians are obliged to take because of economic pressures and realities. Hence my pursuit of this rather uncouth notion of 'the What?' which lies behind, and gives power and shape to, the workings of the Free Market.

As I hunt this 'Snark' (or is it a 'Quark'?) which shapes the economy, it should be noted that the body Krugman judges 'non-partisan', he also describes thus:

> The Federal Reserve System, legally at least, is an association of private member banks, given the privilege of controlling the monetary base by a 1914 law. It's Open Market Committee which decides interest rates, is a hybrid, with some members appointed by the President, while others are chosen by the member banks. Even the presidential appointments are, however, for fourteen-year terms designed to ensure immunity to political pressures. (The Chairman's term, though, is only for four years; it is not a completely insulated institution.)

It rather looks as if the impartial experts are largely recruited from banking and business. Whether, therefore, the expert judges are in fact judges in their own cause must remain an open question. An open question subsumed in the wider investigation into how definitive and determinative the Market is, and who defines and determines the answer to this question.

Consider a further hint about assumed or implicit models of the working of the economy underlying arguments pursued by economic commentators. In *The Times* of 9 July 1996 Anatole Kaletsky's regular column had the subheading: 'Anatole Kaletsky Explains the American Miracle'. He argued that

> The main credit for America's success in the 1990s should not go to Mr Clinton ... but to Alan Greenspan, the chairman of the Federal Reserve Board, who has achieved something that was widely dismissed as impossible a few years ago; he has revived the art of economic fine-tuning.

Here is a testimony, to be joined to that of Krugman, to the work of the Federal Reserve Board of experts. But it was a preceeding passage which drew my particular attention to this article.

Experience shows that governments can do little to accelerate the growth of an economy through so-called 'supply side' measures. Capitalism can adapt to all kinds of different social and regulatory conditions, but such evolution takes decades or even generations. What governments can do is *reduce* a market economy's natural propensity for investment, job-creation and growth.

How can a market economy have a *natural* propensity for anything? The notion seems to be that it evolves – presumably as something like a natural organism. Is this a simple empirical observation? (Compare the opening of the quotation, 'Experience shows ...'.) Does observation show that market economies behave *as if* they were organic entities, operating according to laws and tendencies such as might be observed in the behaviour of a living, natural organism? Or, is there an assumption of something deeper and non-metaphorical? Do market economies, for example, run according to (or are they run and given dynamic and direction by) a *vis naturae*, a force of nature (or, even, The Force of Nature), which keeps them on course and maintains their particular modes of operation?

This is neither an abstract theoretical puzzle nor an irrelevant practical quibble. As has been demonstrated in the previous chapter, there is a class of market proponents who maintain that the Market exercises a discipline on human transactions which sooner or later is inevitable and beneficial in the aggregate. This brings us back to the question of 'the What?'. Where does the persistent, corrective and beneficence-guaranteeing dynamic of the Market come from; and what and how do the experts and initiates of the Market *know* about it? If the whole set of market theories, which some people with very considerable political power turn into the Market mantra, is really an assemblage of metaphors based on interpretations of experiences of the Market so far, then the claim that the Market way of looking at the world is both the correct and the most hopeful perception of the world (so that we may combine believing that there is no alternative with being hopeful about it) rests on very shaky ground.

Metaphors based on experience have to be discarded if the relevant experiences no longer support the metaphors. Thus market metaphors and the Market mantra cannot be defended by expressing the providential-type faith outlined in the last chapter unless that faith is based on some adequately observed and organized facts. If sheer and mere experience is the only ground for the metaphor-system used to explain the Market currently and to claim that, appearances and irregularities to the contrary, the Market will go on working with the hope of benefit for all, then one is simply peddling a false faith. There must be some causative explanatory grounds for maintaining the Market theory against evidence that denies the theory because, in the longer run and in aggregate, the Market is both natural and beneficent.

Is the Market so natural and observable in its regularities and structure that experts can take neutral decisions about how it should be responded to, and advise the rest of us as to how we must bow to its discipline while rejoicing in its hope? It is worth noting here that there are two caveats for further investigation arising out of the Kaletsky article quoted above. The first is that Kaletsky's (and most other economic commentators') enthusiasm about 'the American miracle' is open to debate. As will be discussed in my later chapter, 'Facing the God of Our Production', the American economy may be doing quite, or even miraculously, well but the gap between rich and poor is widening and the wages of very many American citizens are stagnant or declining. In a number of ways the USA provides a model of how at the same time as market capitalism flourishes many people do not. Second, Kaletsky is himself ambivalent about 'experts'. While he consistently approves of Greenspan and the American Federal Reserve Board, he is very suspicious of European Central Banks – and especially the Bundesbank. In an article in *The Times* on 8 August 1996, when discussing a Bank of England quarterly inflation report which forcefully warned the Chancellor of the Exchequer against neglecting inflation risks, Kaletsky makes the tart comment:

> To judge by the relative performance of the British and German economies, our approach to monetary policy also seems preferable to the German (and European) system of giving *dictatorial powers to supposedly infallible bureaucrats* [my emphasis].

Experts, apparently, are not guaranteed to deploy their expertise correctly. It all depends on, again, 'What?'. Perhaps it depends on a judgement of the effects of what the experts propose or impose – a judgement made, presumably, from the perspective of the commentator and his or her own expertise. Expertise, after all, turns out to be as expertise does.

This is not a trivial point to make. I am not merely exploiting a form of nit-picking wherein the writer of a series of short articles by way of commentary on current affairs or current economics can often be convicted of inconsistency because he or she has to expand arguments without safeguards and caveats, while in different articles different points are being made from different perspectives on different issues. My argument is related to a consistent attempt to illustrate that economic comments and advice are insufficiently coherent, when considered as a whole universe of discourse, to give proper support to the presently accepted force of the arguments for observing the rules of the Free Market.

I am concerned with a sceptical investigation of the claim that the operation of the Free Market is something like a force from nature or a consistently operating machine. Investigation of the language commonly used by economic commentators indicates that there is no coherent theory to support such a view. Nor is the actual practice of economic commentary and advice sufficiently consistent to lend practical support to any particular theory. It is in this connection that the *obiter dicta* of economic commentators on policy and the economy, and those of economists commentating on policy and particular issues, are so important. For they betray the fact that in facing up to current economic activities and looking for future economic possibilities as set forth in the common discussion, we are not facing up to what *must* be. That is to say, we are not being confronted by some laws of nature or some inevitable dynamic of evolution. Rather we are engaged in something which human beings have developed for their own ends and which some human beings have from time to time succeeded in dominating for their own purposes. 'The Market' is in all probability, more like a human artefact informed and supported by a built-up momentum and convenient ideology, than a natural organism or evolved machine. It can therefore be changed quite radically if we have the will and the political power to collaborate. Whether or not there is any likelihood of this is the subject of the final chapters of this book. But the possibility is not ruled out by the proven and established givenness of the Market system as at present put forward.

Hence my persistence in searching out what market enthusiasts take for granted as given, and in what way they think it is given. Can the continuing progress of the Market process be taken for granted, except as an act of faith or optimism? A good way to pursue this investigation is to examine what status we can reasonably assign to Adam Smith's famous 'Invisible Hand' to which reference was made at the beginning of this chapter. Whatever Adam Smith himself meant by it, the phrase has become the label attached to that central mystery and power which both describes and guarantees the working of the Free Market. The prestige and influence on economic thought of this almost incidental

phrase of Smith's is remarkable and, almost, uncanny. I propose
therefore to investigate where this uncanny power of the idea, intuition,
theory or myth, of this reliable and promising 'Invisible Hand' comes
from. In investigating how this prestige became established we shall, I
believe, pick up important clues as to what sort of talk about the world
economic talk really is, and therefore about how much inevitable
necessity, or indeed how much guaranteed optimism, is involved in
particular economic descriptions or prescriptions.

Experts in Adam Smith's writings inform us that there is only one use
of the phrase in the whole of the classic *Enquiry Into the Nature and
Causes of the Wealth of Nations*. This occurs in a comment on the way an
individual employs his capital.

> He generally, indeed, neither intends to promote the public interest,
> nor knows how much he is promoting it . . . he intends only his own
> gain and he is in this, as in many other cases, led by an invisible hand
> to promote an end which has no part of his intention.

Smith then dryly comments: 'nor is it always the worse for society
that it has no part of it . . . I have never known much good done by those
who affected to trade for the public good'.[6] The Invisible Hand is much
more clearly related to an overall picture of the world and of human life,
morals and political and economic activity within it, in a philosophical
enquiry of Smith's which is parallel to *The Wealth of Nations*. This is his
The Theory of Moral Sentiment. This work, a treatise on ethics and
morality, I deliberately describe as parallel to *The Wealth of Nations*
(which is clearly a treatise on economics) because, at least until fairly
recently, the trend among economic commentators has been to treat *The
Theory of Moral Sentiments* as an earlier and more generally philosophical and ethical work which has little direct relationship to 'the more
mature' economic work. *The Theory of Moral Sentiments* was first
published in 1759 while *The Wealth of Nations* was published in 1776.
But Smith went on publishing editions of both works – including some
alterations and additions to *The Theory of Moral Sentiments* – up to
1790, the year of his death. It seems likely, therefore, that in Smith's
own understanding and purposes the two works were intimately related,
and that the overtly ethical work is an essential complement to the
overtly economic work.

This is not just a matter of scholarly interpretation of a particular
'classical' author, nor of mere bibliographical detail about his writings.
The decision to keep *The Theory of Moral Sentiments* and *The Wealth of*

Nations apart and to ignore the former in pursuing economic discourse which makes reference, for example, to the influence of the Invisible Hand, is symptomatic. It is directly relevant to the issue of the 'neutrality' allegedly available in making economic judgements. Economics is supposed to have developed as a discipline and tradition of social knowledge which approaches a value-free science. Suggestions that economic understanding, economic theories and the taking of economic decisions always involve both a view about the way the world is, and a perspective which involves a moral stance about what human beings are, are unwelcome. Economic matters are quite complicated enough, while agreement about moral values, or about the nature of the world, or what is involved in being a human being, is quite impossible to attain. Further, as will be considered later, if one raises moral issues it is essential to face the case that agreement about values and morality might lead to the enforcement of the same – and this is a morally bad thing anyway. So far better to keep Adam Smith's 'moral sentiments' as far away as possible from his pursuit of the 'wealth of nations'. Indeed, that is precisely the alleged gift, and one might almost say, the grace of the idea of the Invisible Hand. We can rely on doing well in the matters of the Market, not only for ourselves but for people at large without having to puzzle ourselves about morality or, I suppose about any belief, faith or theory about the way the world is and how it operates or functions. Get on with the Market according to its perceived and perceivable rules, laws or trends, and all will be reasonably well.

It might be convenient if this were so. As a thought experiment it certainly looks as if it would make life simpler. But I do not think we can rely on Adam Smith, or his 'Invisible Hand', to support such a conclusion. Let us take a closer look at the one reference to the Invisible Hand I have already quoted from *The Wealth of Nations*, along with the following reference to it from *The Theory of Moral Sentiments*. This latter is in a passage where Smith is discussing how 'the rich' make a greater contribution to general well-being than one might suppose.

> The capacity of [the rich man's] stomach bears no proportion to the immensity of his desires, and will receive no more than that of the meanest peasant. The rest he is obliged to distribute among those, who prepare, in the nicest manner, that little which he himself makes use of . . . They consume little more than the poor, and in spite of their natural selfishness and rapacity, tho' they mean only their own conveniency, tho' the sole end which they propose from the labour of all the thousands whom they employ, be the gratification

of their own vain and insatiable desires, they divide with the poor
the produce of all their improvements. They are led by an invisible
hand to make nearly the same distribution of the necessaries of life,
which would have been made, had the earth been divided into equal
portions among all its inhabitants, and thus without intending it,
without knowing it, advance the interests of the society, and afford
means to the multiplication of the species.[7]

The almost cynical description of how the rich man's activity benefits
all should be noted in both these descriptions of the operation of the
Invisible Hand. As Professor A.L. Mcfie observes in one of his collected
papers on Adam Smith published as *The Individual and Society*:

> Certainly his invisible hand doctrine helped him to avoid the
> assumption of the Economic Man, rational and clear-sighted,
> which later became basic for the classical economists. For this
> assumption would have been in too stark conflict with his very
> realistic grasp of actual Economic Man, as vain, self-centred, narrow
> and grasping.[8]

If there is no 'economic man' whose rational calculations regularly
inform the price mechanism in such a way that the Invisible Hand is
internally powered by this rationality, how does it work in Adam
Smith's understanding? This is an important question for us for,
surely, Adam Smith's economic man sounds much more like real
people in real markets than does the rationally choosing economic man
of economic theory. Is the Invisible Hand, then, a phenomenon which
exists by lucky chance in the nature of things?
    Although the debate about Smith's religious views continues, it seems
to me that the most reasonable position to take is that for Smith the
Invisible Hand was not a random but fortunate phenomenon or
empirically observable tendency. It was a feature of the harmony of
nature, as arranged and guaranteed by God. Much discussion by
nineteenth- and twentieth-century commentators on Adam Smith and
on the Invisible Hand shows that it is inconceivable to many moderns
that as rational, observant and hard-headed a man as Adam Smith
should have taken the idea of God so seriously that it radically affected
his worldview. But there should be no real doubt that he did. For it is
also clear that this worldview I am attributing to him, involving (and
indeed depending on) God, was a worldview that was widely present in
the early stages of enlightenment thought. Thinkers in the early

Enlightenment held that there was a combination, believed to be a basic convergence, of religion (of a deistic and rationalistic sort), of science (of the Newtonian sort) and of civic and moral sensibility (of the 'moral sentiment' sort).

The God of this pattern of belief, science and society was not the transcendent and active God of biblical tradition and orthodox christianity, but he was held to be a reality who was essential to the holding together of everything in an harmonious, beneficent system. As such, and although a pale shadow of the fully theistic God of biblical revelation and christian faith, he played a key (although scarcely active) role in sustaining and guaranteeing the universe of human life, discourse and history in which the Invisible Hand operates.

Thus the Invisible Hand of Adam Smith is not simply an observational intuition but part of a deistic worldview in which the basic doctrines of a biblical and christian faith survive in the attenuated form of a taken-for-granted belief in the existence of a creator God, his providence and the fact of an after-life with rewards and punishments. The last is necessary to provide ultimate sanctions for enforcing good behaviour, while God's providential creation ensures that nature is a harmonious whole wherein rational and appropriate action by human beings ensures a fruitful functioning of the whole. The goodness of God manifests itself in the beneficence of the regular order of things. What makes entities in the world into an order is that their natures fit together with one another. That is to say that the purposes sought by each entity, according to its nature and function, interlock with the nature and function of other entities so as to come together in a *harmonious whole*. Each in serving itself serves the entire order. This is where the Invisible Hand fits in and why and how – at any rate in its original conception – it operates so effectively and beneficially. Thanks to *Providence* the way of the world is ultimately and in aggregate good, despite the ambiguities, distortions and distresses of particular acts, temperaments or classes of people.

This deistic and providential understanding of things dovetailed with the success, scope and promise of science as focused in the work of Sir Isaac Newton. His theory of gravitation showed that the universe was a great machine, whose workings could be divined by the application of mathematics. Given the prevailing form of deistic religion a machine points to an operator. Science, therefore, was taken to reinforce a deistic philosophy of the universe while deism upheld science in its discoveries of the harmonious operations of the universe. So the logic of the machine combined with the notion of an optimistic God-established harmony, laid down and operating in nature. It is no mere accident, therefore, that the orthodox approach to economics which is at present so widely acquiesced in should show signs of treating the Market as Providence. Adam Smith, whose idea of the Invisible Hand has played so significantly symbolic a part in the development of orthodox economics, saw this Invisible Hand as not metaphorically but actually providential. The harmonious and beneficial results of individual self-interest at work in the Market come about because God either *as* nature or *in* nature had provided this harmony out of his benevolence towards humankind. We can therefore rely on the *beneficence* of the Market for the Market is part of the harmony established by the benevolence, that is the goodwill, of Providence.

Belief in this theory, of course, is an act of faith not a discovery and conclusion of reason. But Adam Smith thought it was a reasonable conclusion because according to a widely held philosophy of his time the essential truths of revelation were held also to be directly accessible to reason. On the same understanding therefore Adam Smith could, and seemingly did, hold that his theory of the operations of the Market, and of relating these to the moral sentiments of human beings, was scientific. But if the idea of a divine being – or even of a Providence immanent in nature – is no longer taken for granted the Invisible Hand surely evaporates. Without any benevolently planned or willed harmony, what possible grounds are there for supposing that any utterly materialistic process should be intrinsically related to the self-correcting production of what we, from our human point of view, regard and welcome as progress. Surely any persistently hopeful universal expectation of doing well must arise out of a reasonable conviction that somebody or something is somehow *willing* well. Beneficence implies, and is underwritten by, benevolence. Adam Smith believed in the benevolence of the providential Creator and that is where the original Invisible Hand comes from.

Although faith in a benevolent Providence as an operational and scientific-like factor in the natural universe has disappeared, optimism in the Market as some sort of organism, machine or sheer economic process, has not. This optimism is repeatedly put forward to manipulate politics and justify policies. The modern election theme is always, 'We are the ones best able to manage the Market and so we shall deliver what you want'. Adam Smith's metaphysical version of the Invisible Hand has thus disappeared but his intuition that in certain important, persistent and beneficial ways the Market operates *as if* there were an Invisible Hand has not. What, then, now justifies and sustains this insight? In our pursuit of 'the What?' it is in the Market that demands our obedience we seem to be back to square one. But are we? There has been a great deal of economic thinking and analysis since Adam Smith. Perhaps, having cleared our minds of any lingering traces of a metaphysical Providence, a sufficiently strong case can be made for something else which is more modern, more believable and equally valuable. I turn next, therefore, to investigate the possibility that the metaphysical Invisible Hand can perform its necessary task as an idea which fits the real world because it encapsulates in a formula what has turned out to be a reasonable observation of the way the world of human interactions actually works.

Notes

1   'Riddle on Politics', *The Times*, 10 January 1996.
2   'Gilt-Edged', *The Times*, 10 January 1996.
3   'CBI Limbers up for Election, Intent on Running in Neutral', *The Times*, 19 July 1996.
4   J.K. Galbraith, *A History of Economics* (London: Penguin, 1989), p. 273.
5   Paul Krugman, *Peddling Prosperity: Economic Sense and Nonsense in the Age of Diminished Expectations* (New York and London: W.W. Norton & Co., 1995), Chapter 4, p. 121.
6   Adam Smith, *Enquiry Into the Nature and Causes of the Wealth of Nations* (*The Works and Correspondence of Adam Smith*, Oxford: Oxford University Press, 1976; Vol. II: Glasgow edition), IV, ii, 9.
7   Adam Smith, *The Theory of Moral Sentiments* (*The Works and Correspondence of Adam Smith*, Oxford: Oxford University Press, 1976; Vol. I: Glasgow edition), IV, i, 10.
8   A.L. Mcfie, *The Individual in Society (Collected Papers on Adam Smith)* (George Allen & Unwin Ltd, 1967), p. 112.

5 The Invisible Hand as a Reasonable Observation

How can what looks like a metaphor have operational force? Clues to this must lie in the history of the development of economic thinking in the two hundred and thirty years since Adam Smith. As my main method for pursuing this investigation of 'the Truth of the Market' lies through examination of the language currently employed by proponents of the Market, I propose to proceed with an analysis of the exposition of the Invisible Hand with reference to a statement of the case for the Market put forward by Sir Samuel Brittan in his *Capitalism with a Human Face*, published in 1995. I find this statement particularly appropriate to this stage of my argument because Brittan makes it clear that he is not all that enamoured of the elaborate theorizing wherein economists from around 1870 onwards attempt to produce scientific-like models and explanations, endeavouring to integrate concepts such as competitive equilibrium, *pareto optima* and other generalizations into a system. One of these attempts at generalization was to turn Adam Smith's observations on the Invisible Hand into an 'Invisible Hand Theorem'. I think it is sufficiently clear that this is precisely what Brittan does *not* do.

Brittan's commendation of the Market with the help of the Invisible Hand is much more pragmatic than theoretical. This is significant for it may well turn out that reasons for expecting growing prosperity from the Market are not providential but simply practical. What counts is what the Market delivers, not what may be theoretically expected from it. But if that is so, it becomes at the least doubtful whether the apparently dogmatic arguments I examined in Chapter 3 have any validity other than the momenta or inertia of their present prestige. This raises sharp questions about which facts, cited as empirical evidence by whom, and with what interpretations, are put forward as the evidence justifying conformity to the Market as it operates at present. This is an important point to keep in mind for the Market is generally commended (and is certainly so commended by Brittan) as a *practical information* system.

Brittan's extended commentary on the Invisible Hand is found in his second chapter entitled 'Two Cheers for Self-Interest'. In the middle of this discussion Brittan dismisses overmuch theorizing and explains why he chooses to concentrate on Adam Smith himself.

> This sort of approach seems to me a blind alley. The true case for the Market mechanism is that it is a de-centralised and non-dictatorial method of conveying information, reacting to change and fostering innovation. That is why I have made Adam Smith rather than more recent formal work my starting point.[1]

Smith gave an immensely influential and creative formulation to an essential understanding of the works of the Market. As Brittan puts it:

> One cannot brush aside two centuries of normative economic teaching – from Adam Smith to economic reformers in post-communist countries – which argues that, *in some areas and under some conditions*, the use of markets avowedly based on self-interest will prove more beneficial than an overt attempt to achieve the public good directly. This normative view was entitled by Adam Smith 'Natural Liberty' as well as the 'Invisible Hand'. It has also been called 'free market competition', the 'profit' or 'gain' motive, and so on. Although these terms are not identical, between them they convey the main idea.[2]

The American economist George Stigler concludes an oft-quoted article entitled 'The Successes and Failures of Professor Smith':

> So Smith was successful where he deserved to be successful – above all in providing a theorem of almost unlimited power on the behaviour of man. His construct of the self-interest seeking individual in a competitive environment is Newtonian in its universality.[3]

In other words, Adam Smith's discovery of the Invisible Hand was something like the discovery of gravity.

I do not think that Brittan has any such scientific-like confidence in what he calls Adam Smith's 'normative view'. It is, rather, just a view which has become common sense ('normative' for the way we now think about economic matters) because of its obvious appositeness and applicability. Moreover it is a view which, if adhered to, discourages attempts to meddle with the Market in ways which interfere with the most efficient delivery of the goods of the Market. Further, and most importantly, this perception discourages attempts to enforce some ideological morality on to human beings in their economic (and therefore other) interactions which are offensive to individual freedom, dangerous to beneficent transactions and all too likely lead to tyranny. Thus Smith's formulation of the Invisible Hand has profound implications, but historically and philosophically speaking it is a matter of serendipity. ('The faculty of making fortunate discoveries by accident', as the dictionary tells us. The word was coined by Horace Walpole in a Persian fairy tale about the three princesses of Serendip, 'whose hero had this fortunate capacity'.) So serendipity replaces Providence, supported by empirical evidence and some important moral considerations and preferences.

Friedrich Hayek, one of the fiercest proponents of the utmost respect for and obedience to the Free Market, indicates that he at least entertains the notion that Adam Smith's *The Wealth of Nations* is the next best thing to – or, more probably, is a replacement for – the Bible. So there is, it seems, serious support for taking *The Wealth of Nations* and the Invisible Hand as some sort of revelation – although, of course, it cannot be revelation as God and Providence have disappeared. Indeed there are grounds in the history of ideas for holding that our present crude and political hope in the Market is very like the rapidly disappearing smile on the face of a cosmic rather than Cheshire Cat, which used to be called 'Providence' and is now rechristened 'TINA'. For as far as human prosperity in the Market goes, there is no alternative. We are, however, to be encouraged to face this lack of alternative with hope in our hearts because at least the aura of the erstwhile providential smile lingers.

Brittan, however, is much more pragmatic than that. In his chapter on 'Two Cheers for Self-Interest' he tries 'to summarise the logical status of the Invisible Hand doctrine':

> It is in my view easiest to explain both the strengths and limitations of the 'Invisible Hand doctrine' in terms of a system of utilitarian morals ... By 'utilitarianism' I mean the view that actions are to be judged by their consequences for the welfare of other people.[4]

He then discusses the need to stick to a fairly simple doctrine of 'utilitarianism', while it does not do away with the need for all sorts of traditional *prima facie* rules of conduct. He comments:

> choices are unavoidable, both about which rules of conduct to follow and whether accepted rules should be overridden in exceptional

circumstances ... The Adam Smith 'Invisible Hand' doctrine is one of the more surprising *prima facie* rules to have been suggested, as it has more of a cynical than a pious flavour. The suggestion is that in matters such as buying and selling, or deciding what and how to produce, we will do others more good if we behave *as if* we are following our self-interest rather than pursuing more altruistic purposes.

The fact that pious people find this rule-of-thumb shocking is not an argument against it. The fact that it sanctions and removes guilt-feelings about what most people do any way is – other things being equal – a positive recommendation.[5]

Brittan is very afraid of 'piety' when organized into a moral ideology allied to forces of public enforcement. But this substantial point can, for the moment, be left to one side. There are three further points to be commented on here with direct reference to the issue of the logical status of the 'Invisible Hand' doctrine.

The first is that Brittan seems to be indicating that the status of the doctrine is that of a pragmatic generalization to be used as guidance to behaviour in the Market with due regard to circumstances, context and the provisions of a wider morality.[6]

The second point to be noted and pursued is that while it may or may not be a good thing to remove guilt feelings about certain common forms of human behaviour, is it transparently desirable simply to sanction 'what most people do any way'? There is forceful evidence that human progress and civilization have developed precisely because what might be called 'moral pioneers', reflective groups of morally concerned human beings, have challenged the decency, and indeed, the welfare-promoting effects of 'what most people do any way'. In any case there is surely a great deal to be said for as many people as possible monitoring what most people do any way in case it is now turning out to be not so good a way of going on. This also raises an important issue about the seemingly innocuous phrase 'two centuries of normative economic teaching'. How can we be sure that by, say, about 1973 the two hundred years in which Adam Smith's insight and the insights developed from his work were suitably normative, were not drawing to their end? The issue of how far it is proper and profitable to rely for the future on something like 'what history has taught us so far' is important and will be pursued in the following chapters.

The third point raises a fundamental matter which is one of the major themes running through the argument of this book. It arises now because, in the second point above, I have already found myself raising a question about morality, even if I am not yet engaged in discussing questions of morality. This is an example of what happens when one investigates the grounds for putting hope in the Market, developing theories about its workings, describing its observable effects, making claims for its benefits or giving warnings about its threats. Such investigations reveal that when the theories, descriptions, claims and warnings are related to advice about decisions, actions or policies then a *moral preference* is disclosed which arises from sources other than straightforward observations of economic processes and events.

Brittan is clearly aware of this, which is a principal reason why his book is both interesting and challenging. Thus he writes:

> What has gone wrong with economics is the over-emphasis on technique as opposed to underlying ideas. Perhaps the time has come for a less strenuous insistence on economics as a science. Most of the hard-core economic doctrines about the gains from international trade, analysis of opportunity costs, and the linking of prices to allocate resources, are neither falsifiable propositions nor just political value judgements. They are ways of looking at the world. Economists do not need to pose as *ersatz* physicists. Philosophers and literary critics know more about their subjects than lay outsiders without their being in a position to supply authoritative answers; and economists may be nearer to them than they are to hard scientists.[7]

This statement invites its own set of questions but at least it allows them to be raised, in contrast to the dogmatic optimists in the Market whose stance and influence it seems so necessary to challenge. This same openness to questions is reflected in Brittan's main discussion of 'Prima Facie Maxims'. At the opening of this section, Brittan writes:

> Too much current discussion is unhelpfully polarised. There are those on whom Adam Smith has made no impact whatever ... For the other side, Market forces are self-evidently the best way of supplying the consumer with 'what he or she wants' and not only promote efficiency, but enlarge choice and freedom. Most people feel one way sometimes on some issues and the other way at other times on some issues, but *without any real reconciliation* [my emphasis].[8]

In the following chapters I shall seek to show that this 'unhelpful polarisation' is symptomatic of far deeper divisions about 'ways of looking at the world' than Brittan seems to recognize in the somewhat unquestioning respect he accords 'two centuries of normative economic teaching'. The issue of how to go beyond the situation of being without any real reconciliation between the two opposing views is clearly of great political and practical importance. I think it will prove to be a good deal more far-reaching than Brittan would be likely to contemplate. Nonetheless we surely have here a much more pragmatic approach to issues about the Market than the dogmatism from which I started my enquiry.

How hard are the 'hard-core economic doctrines' which are 'neither falsifiable propositions nor just political value judgements'? This returns us to the issue of the logical and practical status of the economic doctrines we are pursuing. Can there be any consensus about making 'political value judgements' if economists more closely approximate philosophers and literary critics than hard scientists and thereby are in no position to give 'authoritative answers'. Presumably, on this view, economists should be confined to giving informed advice which has to be blended with other sorts of informed advice about other matters in the world not covered by economic expertise. This is hardly in accordance with the current apparent subordination of politics to economics – but that may be the fault of politicians, or perhaps of the media.

In the investigation of the status of hard-core economic doctrines (including that of the *prima facie* maxim of the Invisible Hand) the disquieting point about the effect of moral preferences will have to play a part. I say 'disquieting point' because the possibility of the pervasive influence of *moral* preferences on economic theorizing and derived advice about decision-taking, suggests that the search for some sort of neutral guidance in matters of economics is a will-o'-the-wisp. Where on earth shall we be if the choices which the proponents of the Market so cheerfully tell us we must make – and which are the essence both of our freedom and of our prosperity – always have to be either *moral* choices or, at least, choices taken within a framework of some sort of shared morality? But I leave this disquieting dilemma until later.

Meanwhile Brittan provides plenty of evidence for a moral stance in his discussion of economic activity and decision-taking. His use of the adjective 'pious' already cited and his anxiety to distance himself from pious sentiments, indicates an embarrassment about handling moral issues which arise. While aware of the moral element involved, he seems anxious to play it down. Thus he continues his evaluation of the status of the Invisible Hand doctrine:

The doctrine of 'natural liberty' is nevertheless more convincing as a permissive one – 'people should be allowed to follow their self-interest in the Market and should not feel guilty in doing so' – than as a positive injunction: 'maximise your own self-interest'. If the maxim is converted into a positive one, it may be misinterpreted as a duty to make more profits when you would rather lie in the sun, or to make your life a misery by grasping at an uncongenial, highly paid job.[9]

This, surely, is going too far in writing down the claims made for the Invisible Hand in the currently orthodox case for the Market. It *is* supposed to justify and require a positive maxim in economic affairs of maximizing your own self-interest. This is both the imperative and the incentive which motivates every human being as they participate in the Market, and thus it drives the Market. There is, for example, a duty on every manager to maximize profits, and if he chooses instead to 'lie in the sun' he will, as orthodox marketeers are always pointing out, be risking losing his enterprise in a take-over bid. This, after all, is the basic justification for the hectic and stressful lifestyle of chief executives and the reason why they are so plainly entitled to six-figure salaries, substantial pension plans, and even more considerable share options. The Invisible Hand is a rewarding hand for its accolytes.

On a rather different issue, the example Brittan gives of the effects of misinterpreting the Invisible Hand (as implying an imperative about duty, rather than permission for a certain form of conduct) provides another instance of the give-away significance of *obiter dicta* from economists and economic commentators. The examples of 'rather lie in the sun' and 'make your life a misery by grasping at an uncongenial, highly paid job', point up the extent to which people who comment authoritatively on financial and market matters live in a world which is simply not the world of most of us. (The world of most of us does not contain easy options of withdrawing to lie in the sun, or of grasping at highly paid jobs.) This world of theirs may indeed determine the real world of all the differing worlds in which various groups of us live. But if so, it would seem to be all the more important to find out what it is that makes this financial and economic world of theirs tick and insists that it should continue ticking in the same way. What is it that holds this dominion over us?

Hence the importance of Samuel Brittan's statement that 'most of the hard core economic doctrines are . . . ways of looking at the world'. What justifies these ways of looking at the world – and how hard and fast are they? Brittan's discussion of the Invisible Hand, as I have argued, would seem to suggest that they are working generalizations which have emerged out of careful and sometimes 'inspired', observations and formulations of competent observers. The inverted commas around 'inspired' are not meant to be ironic. They are intended to preserve a position which does not need to recognize any claim to outside revelation, but does recognize that rare influential thinkers can so 'resonate' with the world around them that they produce formulations which are highly influential in how people in a particular time see that world, and so respond in such a way as, to some extent, to shape their engagement with that world. As Brittan himself says:

> It is only very occasionally that an outside theorist is able to suggest a new maxim, as with Adam Smith's 'natural liberty', and he will usually be most successful if he can encourage some kinds of behaviour that actually exist, and perhaps discover others. In interpreting and applying these suggestions, we still need the help of the traditions and unformulated rules which embody more knowledge than any individual can hope to have.[10]

This last comment raises the question of where do we go from here in following up the pragmatic givens of economic theory and practice clustered around the notion of the Invisible Hand. By 'pragmatic givens' I mean that as a matter of fact Adam Smith hit upon these observations which he himself believed responded to and described observable matters of fact. His account seemed so to fit matters of fact in the estimation and activities of those who followed him that they came to be received as 'normative' and set up a tradition. It should be borne in mind, as already pointed out, that this is almost certainly not what Adam Smith thought he was doing. In his own estimation he was perceiving the harmonious interaction of human faculties and wills with the harmony of the world which had been laid down by God as Providence and nature. This belief, however, played no overt part in the subsequent development of economic thinking (although I suspect it lingered in the optimistic enthusiasms of the nineteenth-century Utilitarians, helping to sustain optimism even while Ricardo and Malthus were earning economics the name of the 'the gloomy science'). However, the take-off of factory production, domestic and foreign trade on the back of technological advance and the investments of early nineteenth-century capitalists provided much more earthly reasons for optimism. We must necessarily return to this impetus to economic optimism.

At this stage it is sufficient to note that this cause for economic optimism is also severely pragmatic. It depends upon the facts and effects of what economic activity produces. At the moment I am investigating whether there is any sustainable theory, as one might say, 'over and above the facts', or perhaps 'beneath and within the facts', to give us reliable guidance about the future of market operations. Are we correct in assuming, as a working hypothesis or a matter of faith (and therefore as a given and necessary basis for political decision-taking), that the Market is self-correcting?

Brittan's account of the logical status of the 'Invisible Hand' doctrine does not seem to provide for such an intrinsic theory of the Market. That is to say that the operations and dynamics do not carry their own inner logic. As he writes: 'In the last resort *an empirical* [my emphasis] comparison of the prosperity and freedom achieved in collective market-orientated and intermediate societies must provide the test.'[11] (How one might carry out such a comparison, and with what reasonable hope of agreement about the results, will be investigated in a subsequent chapter.)

The appeal to 'empirical comparison' is both strengthened and modified in Brittan's chapter entitled 'There is No Such Thing as Society'. This reprints a lecture which Brittan declares to be 'a statement of what I really *do* wholeheartedly believe'. It is, therefore, a *confesso fidei* and as such, contains some moving passages. It goes far to explain why, for Sir Samuel, capitalism has 'a human face'. In my final chapters I shall investigate the inescapable connection between our convictions and our diagnosis of 'markets, politics and people'. At this stage, however, I am concerned with the particular passage which follows as it provides an important indication of Brittan's views on the logical status of the Invisible Hand, natural liberty and so on.

Brittan is examining 'the argument between the real Margaret Thatcher and her more reflective opponents': '[She] implicitly accepted as a positive doctrine the tough-minded version of the economic approach: that people are mostly moved by the gain motive.' This led her to a particular approach to matters of public policy. Brittan then sets out 'the collective reply' and concludes his paragraph:

> As a matter of public policy, collectivists would say that there are so many examples of Market failure and of the short-comings of private good works that the free market doctrines are systematically misleading ... Who is right on the last issue is partly an empirical matter, but not entirely. It is also a matter of where you place the

onus of proof, and also what you fear most: the excesses of authority or the defects of commercialism . . .: Are you more worried about the horrors inflicted in the name of social morality – re-read the Grand Inquisitor scene in *Don Carlos* – or the evils of private greed? From some points of view they have a lot in common. Wagner's *Ring* is intended as a warning against putting both power and money above love. But in many contexts there is some difference between power and money; and the practical individualist would be inclined to agree with Dr Johnson: 'men are seldom so harmlessly employed as in making money'.[12]

The almost dismissive coda to the argument provided in the Dr Johnson quote is characteristic of Brittan's arguing where it touches on morality and values. Whenever he appears to be developing the issue in a major key he quickly signs off with a minor observation. Thus in his last and summary chapter entitled 'Finale' when once again discussing 'the Adam Smith self-interest doctrine' he writes:

> There will be occasions when the normal citizen will suspect that the 'Invisible Hand' is giving the wrong signals, even in spheres where he might expect it to apply. No maxims of political economy can then absolve him from exercising his own moral judgement. The absence of effective legislation should not excuse a chemical company that pollutes the air – although the competitive advantage gained by an unscrupulous firm over others suggests that the law should be put right soon, so that the public-spirited firms are not forced out of business.
>
> But I risk being too pious. I would rather record my conviction, that people in the grip of greed often do much less harm than people in the grip of self-righteousness.[13]

Thus a serious point about personal morality and the responsibilities of citizens, with its political implications, is foreclosed by a Johnsonian quasi-epigram. This may well be excused in a summarizing final chapter for reasons of space, but I suspect it has more significance than that. In his opening chapter on 'Economics and Ethics' Brittan has an important couple of paragraphs entitled 'Immoral Morality'.[14] The issue raised in the paradoxical title is both pungent and important. It will have to be faced in the concluding discussion of this book where the issue of the possibility and practicality of bringing morality to bear on the Market (and if so what morality and whose morality) is a central theme. All that can be registered at this point in the argument is this: The fact is, alas, all too obvious that people are often liable to pursue what to *them* are moral ends in immoral ways. (It is, of course, always 'they' who are immorally immoral while 'we' strive to be morally so.) But this observable fact does not enable us to exorcise morality from important areas of human activity – not least from the economic areas. It simply adds to the complexities we have to face while seeking an appropriate and realistic *modus vivendi* for ourselves and in relation to our neighbours and to humanity in the world at large.

Questions cannot be excised from some particular area of human attention and concern because they are, apparently, unanswerable. If circumstances, realities and human sensibilities perceive and pose questions, they have to be lived with. To live as if the questions were not there is to live unrealistically, inhumanely and so surely without hope. For to ignore a factor which is really present in the context and substance of our lives must be to live in ignorance of something which is, or could (should?) be shaping our responses to what is going on. Thus our responses are likely to be uncreative and, in all probability, distorting.

It may well be some awareness of the unanswerable questions posed in the complexities of modern economic life and the perplexities of modern pluralistic life, that have led to such a widespread acquiescence to the Market. By the Invisible Hand, the Market relieves us of the complications of moral decisions in our business, commercial and purchasing affairs while promising us a growing prosperity and affluence. An affluence we can then use in pursuing whatever moral ends seem individually proper to us in our family and private affairs. This indeed does look like a providential dispensation which has dispensed with Providence.

Yet, if we take Brittan's pragmatic assessment of the normative tradition of the Invisible Hand doctrine as having force and accuracy, it is not as simple as that. I have quoted Brittan as stating that in choosing between a 'Thatcherite' version of tough enthusiasm for the free market and a 'collective' argument that an alternative approach is essential: 'who is right ... is *partly* [my emphasis] an empirical issue but not entirely. It is also a matter of where you place the onus of proof and what you fear most.' Nothing could indicate more clearly that Brittan defends the Invisible Hand doctrine as a brilliant generalization found to illuminate the pragmatic developments of the Market which has hitherto worked so well in the estimation of those who attend to these matters that the 'onus of proof to the contrary' (that is for acting practically and politically in some way contrary to, or different from, the currently assumed implications of the Free Market doctrine) lies with those who contest that doctrine. The normativeness of the tradition, therefore, carries more weight than particular examples where the Market does not work. Moreover there is the issue of moral and personal fears. What does one fear as the greatest threat to humanity and humaneness? Brittan is passionately clear that the greatest threat comes from the self-righteous who are so sure that they are morally correct, or from the committed moralistic politicians who are so certain that they are ideologically correct, that they are prepared to use political power to enforce their views. Brittan would far rather risk the money-makers getting, perhaps quite frequently, over-greedy. In his view that promises less harm.

All sorts of questions arise here. Brittan, perhaps more by implication than by admission, has revealed a crucial problem about investing optimistic expectations in the Market. The Invisible Hand doctrine turns out to be a working hypothesis, invested with greater dignity and weight by two hundred years of normative economic teaching. The validity of a working hypothesis depends on how well it works in practice. This Brittan explicitly admits and he goes on to admit further that one's judgements – that is evaluations – about the working of the Market depend on how one views the world and what moral stance one adopts about what is to be feared most with reference to human life and being. This would seem to imply that the decisive *authority* for making an optimistic investment in the Free Market does not lie in any normative economic teaching but in how one evaluates the way the Market is working according to one's own, in some broad sense, moral stance.

If this is so then 'the Free Market' is not an insulation or a prohibition against having to be concerned with moral evaluations at all sorts of levels. As I have already said, this may be very disquieting – it looks like a complication which cannot easily be dealt with in a highly complex and highly pluralistic world. But it may also be a source of hope – for it indicates that the Free Market, as at present operating and understood according to its propagandists, is not the inevitable machine, network or organism it is commonly alleged to be. Hence there might be greater choice between programmes for new ways of pursuing different ends and aims, than is widely admitted at present.

This is the central possibility which this book is pursuing – a possibility which the fundamentalist proponents of the Market say is so unthinkable that it is not worth investigating. It is necessary, therefore, to proceed step by step, and argument by argument. That is why I move

on to investigate the enthusiastic case for market optimism put forward
by Robert Skidelsky in his *The World After Communism: A Polemic for
Our Times*. The strength and urgency of his optimism is signalled in his
introduction where he states: 'The pessimists are a wearying lot'.[15] Later
he claims that 'economists are a more cheerful breed than historians,
political philosophers, sociologists – and priests'.[16] The challenge is
obvious, strengthening rather than removing the need for careful and
critical argument. But what is the basis for this optimism?

First, however, I must add a final postscript to this chapter about a
central plank in Brittan's argument for, and description of, the Market –
that of his emphasis on the Market as an indispensable information
system. It needs to be recorded here, where I have been chiefly
discussing Brittan's views, for two reasons. First, because it is so central
to his description of the *means* by which the Invisible Hand operates in
the Market. Second, because the part it plays in these operations is
central to the issue of the *power* of the Market to deliver beneficent
results in areas where it is argued that interventions from political bias or
'goodwill' would be worse than useless.

The role of the Market forms part of Brittan's *confesso fidei* in his
'Finale':

> To a liberal the Market is not just a piece of machinery to
> manipulate but a device that has evolved – imperfect and capable
> of much improvement – which reduces the number and range of
> decisions which have to be taken by coercive organs after a struggle
> for votes, power and influence.[17]

What Brittan fears most is the coercive interventions of pressure
groups who interfere with economic processes by political means. The
anonymous and neutral processes of the Market are vastly preferable
and markedly safer. As he writes: 'The true case for the Market
mechanism is that it is a decentralised and non-dictatorial method of
conveying information, reacting to change and fostering innovation.'[17]
This notion is expanded in his last chapter:

> Economic liberals put more emphasis on markets as a discovery
> procedure in a world where tastes and techniques are changing and
> information scarce and expensive ... Markets are means of dis-
> seminating information diffused among millions of human beings
> (who will not be conscious of all the information they possess). This
> information is transmitted in the form of signals – price changes in

flexible markets, but also shortages and surpluses where price changes are delayed by habit or law. These signals provide an incentive to meet unsatisfied needs and to move resources from where they are no longer required. Wants, techniques and resources are not given, but constantly changing, in part due to the activity of entrepreneurs who suggest new possibilities (whether digital records or cheap stand-by transatlantic flights) which people did not previously know existed.

The view of markets as a discovery procedure and coordinating mechanism is now common property to many economists, irrespective of their politics.[18]

Thus the principal manifestation of the Invisible Hand is that through the information system of the Market *prices*. It enables the best possible allocation of the products in goods and services that come on the Market, relative to what people decide they want and where and when they come to want it. This is the most *efficient* way of encouraging the use of economic resources to match changing demand, and distribute the results of economic production to the best possible human use. Such an information system as this, Brittan argues, is essential and inescapable. As he sets out:

Any economic system needs to:

1) coordinate the activities of millions of individuals, households and firms;
2) obtain information about people's desires, tastes and preferences;
3) decide which productive techniques to use; and
4) create incentives for people to act on such information.

It is only the last, incentive, role of the Market, which could be abandoned in a community of saints. Even such a community would need to know how best to serve their fellow men and women. They might proceed best by behaving *as if* they were concerned with their own worldly well-being in order to create the market signals which they could follow in their productive activities.[19]

I shall take up this description of the form and status of the Market as information system, and its bearing on my main enquiry into what it is that 'makes the Market tick' in Chapter 9. There, certain aspects of Skidelsky's case for the Market which I am about to consider lead to the consideration of related aspects in the forceful case for the Market put by the doyen of right-wing liberal economists, Professor Friedrich Hayek. What Hayek has to say is particularly relevant to the evolution of the Market as an information system.

Meanwhile, the idea of the Market as the only possible purveyor of economically essential information serves as an introduction to a consideration of what I have labelled 'the Optimism of the Only Way' as argued by Skidelsky. The connection lies in Brittan's hint about 'evolution'. He refers to markets 'as evolving institutions reacting to unforeseen change'.[20]

That is to say that the Invisible Hand has emerged from evolution, Adam Smith being the observer who spotted its existence and its beneficent effects. Smith was convinced of the beneficence of the effects because he believed that the universe was providentially arranged to work in harmony with rational human purposes and needs. Are we obliged – or even free – to place the same confident trust in the Free Market now that we have experienced a further two hundred years or more of what is, presumably, blind and indifferent evolution? Lord Skidelsky argues that it would be wearisomely pessimistic and politically threatening not to put our trust in the Free Market. What is more, in Skidelsky's view, history joins with evolution in showing how right Adam Smith's observations were.

Notes

1   Samuel Brittan, *Capitalism with a Human Face* (Aldershot, UK: Edward Elgar, 1995), p. 59.
2   Brittan, *Capitalism*, p. 54.
3   George J. Stigler, *The Economist as Preacher and Other Essays* (University of Chicago Press, 1982), p. 158. (Reprinted from *Journal of Political Economy* 84, 1976.)
4   Brittan, *Capitalism*, p. 55.
5   Brittan, *Capitalism*, pp. 55f.
6   Compare also Brittan, *Capitalism*, p. 37: 'The invisible hand makes most sense as a prima facie rule of conduct within a wider morality.'
7   Brittan, *Capitalism*, Introduction, p. 17.
8   Brittan, *Capitalism*, p. 54.
9   Brittan, *Capitalism*, p. 56.
10   Brittan, *Capitalism*, p. 59.
11   Brittan, *Capitalism*, p. 59.
12   Brittan, *Capitalism*, p. 99.
13   Brittan, *Capitalism*, p. 267.
14   Brittan, *Capitalism*, pp. 31ff.
15   Robert Skidelsky, *A Polemic for Our Times* (London: Macmillan, 1995), Introduction, p. xiii.

16   Skidelsky, *Polemic*, p. 162.
17   Brittan, *Capitalism*, p. 268.
18   Brittan, *Capitalism*, pp. 270ff.
19   Brittan, *Capitalism*, p. 59.
20   Brittan, *Capitalism*, p. 268, immediately before extended quotation cited above.

6 The Optimism of the Only Way

I am writing this book because I am increasingly troubled by the uncritical way our political leaders seem to look to the Free Market as the sole sure source of our civic survival and prosperity. Although I have outlined my concerns about the morality of what we were doing, I have not gone on to give details of what angers and disturbs me. Instead I am devoting the first half of this book to an examination of the language in which some current and, I believe typical, proponents of the Free Market give their reasons for advocating policies which conform to the requirements of the Market.

Since the Market language claims indefinite promise, it is the Market language which has to be challenged in as near to its own terms as possible. I believe that the view of the world implied by the language of market proponents is increasingly unrealistic in relation to the real world as experienced by people at large.

We moderns expect evolution. Our experience of rapid and interacting changes leads us to expect that evolving processes in their interactions with one another transform the very nature of both the processes themselves and their effects as they proceed. But Market philosophers are old-fashioned. They believe that the secular revelation that occurred to Adam Smith in the last half of the eighteenth century was a definitive revelation for all times and circumstances. Hayek, for instance, explains:

> Though in Hume ... we can watch the gradual emergence of the twin concepts of the formations of spontaneous orders and of selective evolution ... it was Adam Smith and Adam Ferguson who first made systematic use of this approach. Smith's work marks the break-through of an evolutionary approach which has progressively displaced the stationary Aristotelian view. The nineteenth century enthusiast who claimed that the *Wealth of Nations* was in importance second only to the Bible has often been ridiculed; but he may not have exaggerated so much.[1]

For all his atheism and scientism Hayek displays a propensity to believe there is a definitive truth about the world at large and our place within it which, if perceived, enables us to know assuredly how things are and will be. To Hayek his evolutionary theory of the extended order of the Market (perceived via Adam Smith and Darwin whom Hayek believes picked up a decisive clue to his formulation of his theory of evolution from Adam Smith), is definitive truth. The Bible has a lot to answer for.

It has left us with an ineradicable notion that the world is going somewhere promising for us – or will be if we divine the rules and co-operate. It is to be noted for later reflection that in the case of the Market, the co-operation is with the rules – not between human beings. This, I take it, is to be regarded as a secular miracle and a mercy. For co-operation with one another is notoriously difficult.

Skidelsky's *A Polemic for Our Times* is particularly appropriate for consideration at this stage. His argument appears to be: 'Look at events since the 1939 to 1945 war in the way I suggest and you will see that the interpretation compels us to the promotion of the Free Market and to deny the temptations of collectivism as the only practical *and optimistic* thing to do.' This vigorous appeal to events raises an issue of vital importance. That is, the quite extraordinary history of material progress brought about by the development of the Market economy since the end of the eighteenth century.

The world has literally never seen anything like it before. As Keynes put it in his *Essays in Persuasion* in 1931:

> From the earliest times of which we have record – back, say, to two thousand years before Christ – down to the beginning of the eighteenth century, there was no very great change in the standard of living of the average man living in the civilized centres of the earth. Ups and downs certainly. Visitations of plague, famine and more. Golden intervals. But no progressive violent change.[2]

Wholly unprecedented, progressive and violent change took off in Britain sometime in the eighteenth century and spread across the West in the nineteenth century. As one typical summary puts it:

> The main economic changes were a growing specialisation of labour, a new occupational and industrial structure and the uneven progress towards mechanisation and the factory system. Underlying all was a phenomenal growth in production with its consequent enlargement

of the national wealth. Every production and trade index recorded soaring productivity as machinery came to the aid of human labour. Even allowing for population growth, the gross national product increased four-fold in real terms during the nineteenth century ... through industrialisation increased wealth was generated beyond belief.[3]

Despite two world wars this expansion of wealth continued into the twentieth century. Within a few years of the end of the Second World War the standard of living of Western European countries, even those devastated by the conflict, was higher than ever before. As Paul Ormerod writes in the chapter on 'Measuring Prosperity' in his *The Death of Economics*:

> It is hard to deny that, for example, the average person in Western Europe or North America is much better off now materially than the average person was in the 1930s. There are periods of recession, when growth from one year to the next is close to zero or even slightly negative, but over the course of a decade all Western economies have shown rates of growth which have been consistently positive for the best part of two centuries, and in the case of the early industrializers, such as Britain and the Netherlands, three centuries. [That is to say that the process is very well established in history.] ... Most developed economies achieved average annual growth rates considerably above three percent during the 1950s and 1960s. Of course, Japan and many countries in Europe were starting from a temporarily low base, with poor living standards as a result of the devastation of the War. But growth rates of 5 percent a year were not uncommon, and at such a rate the economy doubles in size over fourteen years.[4]

Professor Krugman in the introduction to his book *Peddling Prosperity* underlines this with respect to the USA.

> For a generation after World War II America had (as Tom Wolfe put it) a 'magic economy'. Some of the magic was measurable: in less than thirty years everything doubled. That is, the real earnings of the typical worker, the real income of the typical family, consumption per capita, all were twice as high by around 1972 as they had been in the late 1940s. But the numbers alone fail to convey the astonishing sense of affluence and economic optimism that pervaded

the country. People worried about many things – social upheaval, nuclear war, the environment – but they took it for granted that the economy would continue to deliver an ever higher material standard of living.[5]

I insert a sample of these well-known statistics at this point in order to strengthen the case for claiming that we can indeed expect great things from the Market. Why should we *question* the process rather than put all our efforts into *promoting* it?

Performance to date is all very well. But does the performance carry within itself a clear guarantee of continuing in the same way as before with increasing benefits? If it is just marvellous luck that the Market processes spontaneously exploded as they did, why should we suppose that our luck will hold? Providence is surely ruled out, however portentously providential commentators such as those previously cited from *The Economist* may sound. Adam Smith's Invisible Hand is reduced from the shadow of Providence to a possible reasonable supposition. Once one gets on to 'reasonable suppositions' then – as is suggested by Brittan – one is into the business of 'partly an empirical issue but not entirely. It is also a matter of where you place the onus of proof and what you fear most.'[6] Is a stable consensus about 'trusting in the Market' possible on that basis or is it a subjective question of how one places one's bets? If it comes down to the placing of bets then it begins to look as if the Market is fine for those with the money to place sufficiently large bets but hopeless for those lacking the money to place any bets at all. Robert Skidelsky in his *Polemic* thinks we can and must be much more decisively optimistic than that. How does he make his case – and what sort of case is it?

Skidelsky locates the dynamic of the Market in history viewed from a particular perspective, combined with a vigorous plea to eschew pessimism and embrace optimism. Let us consider the nature of the faith and realism he displays as he deploys his argument. He begins with a paean of triumph in the opening paragraph of his Introduction:

> The collapse of Communism was greeted with a triumphalism appropriate to a crushing military victory. The failure of Communism and all other forms of collectivism seemed to vindicate Capitalism and political democracy, and to remove any systematic obstacles to their universal adoption. The optimists look forward to the reconstruction of post Communist societies on Western lines and their incorporation into a Western-led international order. A

world integrated by trade and democracy would not only soar to unimagined heights of prosperity but would also realise the nineteenth-century liberal dream of universal peace.[7]

The way in which Skidelsky argues from this optimism with its great expression of hope (which he espouses but does not accept uncritically) reflects the heart of the political faith which inspired Mrs (now Lady) Thatcher and continued (although she might have thought somewhat weakly) to motivate her followers, including her successor Mr Major and his Cabinet. Much of its momentum seems to have been endorsed by Mr Blair and it is certainly, although in a suitably pragmatic and implicit way, the faith of the business and financial communities.

Compare, for example, a piece by Lord Alexander of Weedon, Chairman of the NatWest Group in the series 'Executive Voice' in the Business News of *The Times* of Saturday, 11 May 1996. Entitled 'Two Cheers for Business in Its Search for Legitimacy', the piece includes the following blend of opinion, faith and optimism.

> E.M. Forster once said that he could give only two cheers for democracy. I feel the same about business. But we have come a long way since the Seventies when business attracted more jeers than cheers. What happened? Mrs Thatcher happened. Mrs Thatcher gave management the opportunity to take firm decisions as the power of the Trade Unions waned. As a result our economy is healthier and our firms fitter.

His diagnosis of our present situation is very close to that of Skidelsky.

> Now that socialism and communism are no longer seen as viable alternatives in the West the focus has shifted. No longer do we ask whether business is good or bad. We must move on to ask how business can be better.

The article then discusses in detail what is required to build ethical and customer confidence between firms and those who deal with them and concludes:

> We still have far to go. So we can only give two cheers for business. But *there are no alternatives* [my emphasis] that deserve the full three cheers. Evolution and not revolution is needed. We do have the right political and legal framework. Business has been largely accepted in

the public mind. But business has more to do to win the affection of the public heart.

There is more to be done in detail, but the basic way forward is clear. One can understand why the CBI document referred to in Chapter 4 (see page 37 above) appears to assume, as a realistic possibility, that decisions on macro-economic matters ought to be uncontroversial. The way of business has won through to victory so it must be the realistic way. There can be no argument once this is fully understood. We have been governed by this conviction for years. In *The Times* of 13 February, 1986, there appeared a leader entitled 'Over the Horizon'. It was written by way of comment on the Westland Affair, a dispute over trade and defence policy which led to the resignation of a Cabinet Minister. The leader writer puts the matter clearly and forcefully:

> While the dust and the noise suggest a diversity of future options for Britain, the reality that there are only two fundamental choices remains hidden ... There can either be a strengthening of the opportunities of the individual Mrs Thatcher has pioneered, the further rolling back of the State, the increasing demands on personal responsibilities; or there can be the opposite – more State interven- tion, the sapping of individual will, the easy conditions of corrosive national decline.

The lesson learnt under Mrs Thatcher is that 'the creation of wealth is not an automatic process'. There is a tendency to argue that we should start mixing state power back into our ways of operating, but:

> Mrs Thatcher's model of society, on the other hand, is quite different. It is the one in which a large number of individual decisions are governed by the forces of the market place and set in motion by the free choices of people who have a stake in the wealth of the nation.

The writer is clear about the benefits of this approach.

> While workers' living standards have been rising, inflation is now understood for the cruel and unfair tax on ordinary people's savings that it is ... a massive extension of home and share ownership have been achieved ... every new shareholder has a chance to join the ranks of those in society who earn their living from their capital as

well as from their neighbour ... every new householder gains an asset which could be used to produce wealth as well as shelter ... The prize is an increase in the number of people who are liberated from psychological dependence on the State, who are prepared to consider private provision for education and healthcare, whose new freedoms help the process of defining where the State's responsibilities should end and how they should be paid for. Wealth does not need to be more widely spread, it needs to be seen and felt to be more widely spread. Individuals need to be encouraged to keep the wealth to themselves.

It may be noted that the type of people to benefit from this approach are people with savings, shareholders, householders and those who can consider private provision for education and healthcare. It is doubtful if such people form more than 30 to 40 per cent of our population at the most. In contrast some 30 or more per cent of the population are dependent to some extent on social security payments. But it is clear that the ideal is a property-owning democracy where each citizen enjoys some prosperity. The wider implications of this can be left for later discussion. The present point is the trenchant and optimistic clarity of two fundamental and fundamentally opposed choices presented as the only ones open to us in the running of our political and economic lives. One option is to set the individual as free as possible to operate in and through the Market, the other to be dependent on and constrained by the state. This is the analysis which Skidelsky claims to be optimistic.

It should be noted that an element of morality is held to be involved in choosing and promoting market optimism. Under the headline 'Major Takes Dig at Blair Over Moral High Ground', *The Times* of 19 September 1996 reported a speech given by Prime Minister Major during the 1996 pre-General Election campaign. In it he said,

Morality is a word I usually prefer to leave to the churches but it is apt for what I intend to say ... For example, is it moral to take from individuals the right to make personal decisions? I think not. Is it moral to impose obligations on employers like the Social Chapter and the Minimum Wage that will cost jobs and prevent those without jobs from getting them? Again, I think not ... It is that moral view, just as much as economics, that leads me to the conviction that the State should progressively disengage and do less – but that what it does it should do well.

We are confronted therefore with what is held to be a triumphant and obvious economic faith which supports, or is supported by, a morality of freedom and responsibility invested in the Free Market which requires a certain type of politics. The victory of this faith has already been won for its opposing faith has collapsed. This reflects an essentially dialectical way of looking at things. Two opposing views and moralities (perhaps a thesis and an anti-thesis) were in opposition to one another. One has collapsed. The other is therefore not only the victorious but also the morally correct and the prosperity-promising way. Is this dialectical form a realistic way of looking at our prospects for the future? Is the 'Invisible Hand' reinforced or, perhaps, replaced by locating the process of the Market in a particular process of history?

Skidelsky is conscious of 'violently opposed assessments of the future' but in his estimation ultimately judgements 'depend on our state of mind'. In his brief Introduction he presents a confession of faith:

> Pessimists are a wearying lot. They tend to say that nothing new will work. When never the less it does work somewhere they produce subtle arguments to prove it will not work anywhere else. I am an optimist. I regard the end of Communism, the rolling back of the frontiers of the State, the globalisation of economic intercourse, as the most hopeful turn of the historical screw which has happened since 1914.[8]

He believes that we can have some idea of the purpose for which, or direction in which, 'the historical screw' is turning, for he says: '[The task is] so to manage the transition that *the job can be completed* [my emphasis].' The definition of that job will be discussed shortly, but first let us examine the concept of there being an historical job which can be so specifically perceived and described as to be capable of 'completion'. This appears to be a variant of the dialectical view of history developed by Hegel and, in a different form, by Marx. I shall shortly follow up this suspicion, but first we should consider how Skidelsky himself describes his understanding of the enterprise.

> What follows is an essay in political economy, not international relations . . . I try to explain how we have reached post-communism, not by means of historical narrative but in terms of a single organising idea which I call the rise and fall of collectivism. Collectivism – the belief that the State knows better than the Market, and can improve on the spontaneous tendencies of civil

society, if necessary by suppressing them – has been the most
egregious error of the twentieth century ... My contention is that
this belief in the superior wisdom of the State breeds pathologies
which deform, and at the limit destroy, the political economies
based on it.

This explanatory scheme makes a pattern of twentieth century
history. It is not its only possible pattern, but it is the only one which
can account for the *worldwide* character of the shift in political
economy which took place in the nineteen-eighties.[9]

Thus Skidelsky's polemic for our times is an essay making the case for
giving decisive importance in the running of our political affairs to the
conviction that our best chance of prospering is to rely on 'the Market'
and 'the spontaneous tendencies of civil society'. I take it that this is
more or less the same as relying on what *The Economist*, for example,
calls 'the wisdom of the Market' and on the spontaneous tendencies
displayed by individuals making free choices based on self-interest in the
Market. I find Skidelsky's book particularly central to my enquiry
because its tone resonates more with the supposedly pragmatic attitudes
of the political, commercial and financial proponents of the Market than
with the seemingly academic arguments to do with the Market as
Providence and the logical and material status of the Invisible Hand.
With his appeal to the worldwide pattern of what took place in the 1980s,
Skidelsky's case conforms with the position that the really decisive
argument for being optimistic about the Market is the obvious way in
which it has worked so far.

However, on inspection Skidelsky's argument is by no means as
straightforward and obvious as all that. (The arguments of practical
men are very often not as practical as all that. For the arguments of
practical men tend to be limited by their practices so that their view of
the world is considerably narrower and less complex than the world
within which they have to practice.) In his opening confession of faith
and optimism Skidelsky implies by his definition of 'collectivism' – 'the
belief that the State knows better than the Market' – that he assumes that
the Market 'knows better than' the state. This assumption lands us amid
all the questions about how the Market 'knows'; what guides its knowing;
and whether that guidance includes something which reliably promises
us good guidance leading to prosperity. He also tells us that 'collectivism'
is the belief that '[the state] can improve on the spontaneous tendencies
of civil society'. This raises perennial questions about freedom and,
further, whether Skidelsky's choice of optimism about the Market is not

least because of his moral commitment to, and judgements about, this freedom. Is his optimism chosen because of 'what he fears most'? What grounds does he offer to persuade us to follow him in this moral choice?

Skidelsky's decision to start his polemic from statements about optimism and pessimism itself gives grounds for suspicion about the likely validity of his arguments – especially when he is trying 'to explain how we have reached post-communism ... in terms of a single organising idea'. It might just be that the single organizing idea was a fortuitously perceptive insight which turned out to be of great assistance in guiding politics, business and financial affairs at a particular time. At this stage in my investigation I am still holding open the possibility (although not a very strong one) that Adam Smith's Invisible Hand was a reasonable supposition of this nature. It might also be possible to entertain the notion that a decisive opposition between collectivism and the 'liberal statesmanship' which takes proper account of the Market and 'the spontaneous tendencies of the civil society' is such a reasonable and timely supposition. (That is, obviously, for further investigation – not least with regard to the *sources* of such a supposition.)

But why does Skidelsky propose the acceptance of this 'reasonable supposition' in so forceful a context of optimism and pessimism? Because he believes he has perceived a decisive secular 'revelation' concerning a choice between good and evil. History has brought about the collapse of a destructive ideology invested in a political and economic system and has thereby liberated a creative health and wealth-producing belief invested in the opposing political and economic system. Where does this notion that there are optimistic possibilities and pessimistic threats in systemic opposition to one another in the processes of our economics come from?

This is another vestige of the enlightenment form of deism which was the source and motivation of Adam Smith's discovery of, and hopeful investment in, the Invisible Hand. In that context we can be optimistic about the interactions between human reasoning and the natural processes of the world because the possibilities of beneficent development are built in to the harmonies of nature and the capacities of human reason by a beneficent Providence. But Skidelsky's optimism for the future is not argued directly from the Invisible Hand of the Market. Rather he discerns the sense and the direction of optimism in the dialectics of history which promote and vindicate the Market. In other words he shares his grounds for optimism about the Market with that development of Enlightenment optimism worked out with regard to economics by Karl Marx.

Paradoxical as this may seem, the evidence is pretty clear. At the end of his first chapter Skidelsky describes the processes by which the breakdown of the post-war Bretton Woods exchange rates system in 1971–3 led, through the four-fold increase of oil prices in 1974 and crises over wages, prices and inflation with accompanying unemployment to: 'The new political economy of the 1980s'.[10] This was focused on

> squeezing inflation out of [the] system of the main capitalist countries by tight money policy ... What was, from one point of view, simply a technical exercise in 'monetarism' was, at a deeper level, a rediscovery of the values of economic freedom.

This point is reiterated early in his seventh chapter on 'The New Political Economy': 'Thus the crucial context of macro-economic stabilisation, supply-side measures, privatisation, deregulation, trade liberalisation and the other reforms of the 1980s was the rediscovery of the value of economic and political freedom'.[11] There is a force at work 'at a deeper level' which manifests itself in the whole gamut of economic measures associated with Mr Reagan and Mrs Thatcher and is more than a technical matter of economics. It is 'the rediscovery of the value of economic and political freedom'. What brings about this deep and important change?

The answer to this is made so clear on the last page of Skidelsky's first chapter that it is worth quoting at length.

> Even so, the speed of Communism's collapse took all observers by surprise. At the beginning of 1989 the 'evil empire' was still intact, if tottering; by 1991 it was all over.
>
> By accident rather than design, the United States, it seemed, had brought about the defeat of Communism on the terms it wanted ... This achievement was bought at a high cost. The ideological obsession of the United States not only destroyed Soviet Communism but damaged Western economies. Permanent macro-economic imbalance was the price it paid for the defeat of Communism. That is why the victory of freedom has left such a disturbing legacy of economic and political problems. But, in truth, there was no other way. It was the very simplicity of the American ideology which enabled it to out-last the sophistries of Marxist-Leninism, and the sophistication of the West's intellectual elites, in remarkable affirmation of Hegel's cunning of reason.

The rise and fall of Communism is part of the larger story of how the world tasted the fruit and came to reject the temptation of collectivism. The shape of the world after Communism will be largely determined by how well we understand, and respond to, this larger movement of history.[12]

This is a vivid example of the perception of a decisive dialectic in 'this larger movement of history'. There is even a direct reference to a 'remarkable affirmation of Hegel's cunning of reason'. It is essential to grasp the 'single organising idea' and the 'very simplicity' by which the presence and significance of a deeper and larger movement of history is revealed, not to the sophistries of Marxist-Leninists, nor to the sophistication of the West's intellectual elites, but to the single-mindedness of such as Reagan and Thatcher. This is a very great matter, for the shape of the world will be determined by how well we understand and respond to this revelation which has been given us by history.

Skidelsky's belief that our history is directed by a decisive dialectical conflict between individualism and collectivism is particularly clearly indicated by an incidental argument which he deploys in a footnote. Here he writes, 'I disagree with John Gray who argues that Hayek was wrong to say that "economic planning and individual liberty were ultimately irreconcilable".'[13] After reviewing a series of points Skidelsky concludes,

> Finally, and most important in the present context, Hayek was talking about the logics of two incompatible systems. He did not deny that they could co-exist up to a point and for a time, but he argued that this co-existence was unstable, with pressure building up to go one way or the another through the accumulation of problems like rising inflation, or structural imbalances, or both. On this point he has been vindicated.

We have, therefore, the dialectic of 'the logics of two incompatible systems' wherein the collapse of communism and collectivism vindicates the proponents of liberal capitalism. How is it established that reality is programmed by a conflict between 'two incompatible systems'? Hegel argued for this and so did Marx but is it believable? Might it not be more appropriate to collaborate together as human beings in facing up to reality as something between a mystery and a muddle which we do well to make sense of by the best possible pragmatic and constantly revised improvisations we can manage. Optimisms and pessimisms may turn out to be neither here nor there – especially if they are matters of temperament or of what one fears most. To surrender to temperament would seem to be a recipe for ultra-subjectivism, isolated individualism and, quite possibly, solipsism. Surely the world cannot really be as I happen to like thinking it is.

Alongside the theoretical point, there is a practical one. How long is Hayek – or anyone else – to be vindicated in their dualistic and dialectical approach by the collapse of communism? Unless one is convinced that the basic theoretical point is real (i.e. there really is an historical dialectic whose thesis and anti-thesis can be consensually understood and pursued), then any vindication depends on what happens next and on what looks like happening after that. I shall take up this point when we come to consider Skidelsky's commendation of the views of Jeffrey Sachs on the shock therapy for the collapsed economies of the communist East and for the developing economies of much of the Third World and especially Africa.[14]

The basic question remains: Why does the collapse of communism guarantee that the liberal approach to the Free Market economy is, and will remain, the politically hopeful way forward for the earth and the majority of its inhabitants? Not only does this presuppose that a dialectical view of reality corresponds to reality indeed. It also pre-supposes that there is a *process* in the ongoing nature of the world which offers some possibility of beneficent progress to us human beings. If we have dispensed with Providence, and perceive grounds for doubting the Invisible Hand, how can we reasonably plump for history – even if we are ignorant of, or are determined to ignore, Karl Popper's devastating dismantling of historicism?

In order to establish that it is feasible to challenge the basic *practicality* of our investment in the current dominance of the Market it is necessary to undermine the theoretical bases of the arguments employed. For, as I am trying to demonstrate, these theoretical ideas inform and guarantee the grounds on which practical decisions and political programmes are adopted in a much more definitive and influential way than 'practical' people usually recognize or admit. In the oft-quoted words of Keynes,

> The ideas of economists and political philosophers, both when they are right and when they are wrong, are more powerful than is commonly understood. Indeed the world is ruled by little else. Practical men, who believe themselves to be quite exempt from any intellectual influences, are usually the slaves of some defunct

economist ... soon or late, it is ideas not vested interests, which are dangerous for good or evil.[15]

We may need to be reminded by another major writer on economics, Karl Marx, that, alas, vested interests can be dangerous too, but the central point is that currently received practices and orthodoxies are never as merely commonsensical as all that.

My next step is to examine the common presuppositions which the proponents of the liberal Free Market economy share with the economic theories of Karl Marx. The theme of this enquiry is 'Can we think again?', but before a wide interest can be aroused for this question it is necessary to demonstrate as forcefully as possible that we *must* think again. Our commonly received political thinking remains firmly restricted within the limits of the Free Market. We are constantly told that in matters economic we have triumphed over Karl Marx and banished his destructive theories from our thinking. In fact we have succumbed to a mutated version of his romantic nineteenth-century optimism about the boundless promises for human prosperity and freedom that are to be derived from the energy of economic production.

Notes

1   F.A. Hayek, *The Fatal Conceit: The Errors of Socialism* (London: Routledge, 1988), Appendix, p. 146.
2   J.M. Keynes, *Essays in Persuasion* (*The Collected Writings of John Maynard Keynes*, Vol. IX, Macmillan/Cambridge University Press, 1972; originally published 1931), p. 36.
3   Derek Fraser, *The Evolution of the British Welfare State* (London: Macmillan: 1973), p. 5.
4   Paul Ormerod, *The Death of Economics* (Faber & Faber, 1994), p. 23.
5   Paul Krugman, *Peddling Prosperity: Economic Sense and Nonsense in the Age of Diminished Expectations* (New York and London: W.W. Norton & Co., 1994), p. 3.
6   Samuel Brittan, *Capitalism with a Human Face* (Aldershot, UK: Edward Elgar, 1995), p. 99.
7   Robert Skidelsky, *The World After Communism: A Polemic for Our Times* (Macmillan, 1995), p. xi.
8   Skidelsky, *Polemic*, p. xiii.
9   Skidelsky, *Polemic*, p. xiii.
10   Skidelsky, *Polemic*, p. 13.
11   Skidelsky, *Polemic*, p. 117.
12   Skidelsky, *Polemic*, p. 16.
13   Skidelsky, *Polemic*, p. 128.
14   See Chapter 11.
15   J.M. Keynes, *The General Theory of Employment, Interest and Money* (*The Collected Writings of John Maynard Keynes*, Vol. VII, Macmillan/Cambridge University Press, 1972; originally published 1936), p. 383.

7 Optimism from the Nineteenth Century – Not for the Twenty-First

My claim that enthusiastic proponents of the Free Market against collectivism in fact share basic presuppositions with Marxists does not mean that I am producing my own version of what Skidelsky calls 'the inexcusable errors of some Western historians and analysts [which is] to treat the values and logics of the two sides as symmetrical'.[1] Skidelsky's 'two sides' are framed by the Cold War stand-off of Stalinist Communism and the USA on behalf of the capitalist world. My own line of enquiry goes back considerably earlier than the years of the Cold War into the ideas of the mid-nineteenth century. I also seek to delve deeper than Skidelsky does into the philosophical issue of how we should view history and the world.

The connection between the original ideas of Marx and the form they had assumed by the time they were claimed (in Marxist-Leninist Stalinism) for the taking of sides in the Cold War can be left as an open question – while the question of assumptions shared between Marx and the marketeers can be pursued on its own merits as a diagnostic probe into the origins of market optimism.

I doubt Skidelsky would admit to a charge of historicism (let alone to any association with Marxism). I am not clear, however, that he can sustain such a rebuttal. Take, for example, the way in which he ends his chapter on 'The New Political Economy'. He is summing up the way in which there has been an increasingly wide perception of

> what Margaret Thatcher also saw: that inflation is a problem in political economy, not just in economics. It is a symptom of state damage, a signal that the relationship between the state and the

economy needs to be changed. In the mending of the state, a cunning of reason was powerfully at work, for the 'accident' that the commercial banks were awash with petro-dollars in the 1970s meant that the collectivised economies of both the Second and Third Worlds could postpone their day of reckoning until the pro-market philosophy has established its intellectual dominance.[2]

In other words the cunning of the Hegelian dialectic saw to it that the fortuitous developments to do with the action of the Oil States in 1973–74 were transformed from 'accidents' (his inverted commas) into part of the meaning and process of the dialectic, allowing the pro-market philosophy to emerge ready to fulfil its dialectic purpose. Does Skidelsky actually mean this or is he pursuing a more pragmatic argument, casting it in a somewhat metaphorical and ironic way in order to highlight a claim that looking at historical developments in the way he recommends is to see that it is 'as if' a version of the dialectic of Hegel and Marx were at work? Presumably this would be parallel to economists arguing that the Market does work 'as if' the Invisible Hand were at work. But both of these suggestions rely for their maintenance on practical observation rather than on the actual existence of an Invisible Hand or an historical dialectic. The critical question is this: Is optimism in the way of the Market something which can be tempered by experiences of what the Market actually delivers? Or do references to 'the Invisible Hand' or 'the cunning of reason' suggest that the apologists for market optimism believe that the Invisible Hand or the cunning of reason are sufficiently real to exert a controlling influence and can be relied upon to do so whatever the current (and therefore temporary) evidence? That is to imply that we should (even, must), act on the conviction that awkward facts (such as persistent market failures, increasing gaps between rich and poor, growth inevitably adding to pollution and so on) will, over time, be shaped by the power of the Invisible Hand or the dialectic of the cunning of reason into delivering a promising and shareable prosperity for more and more of us.

I am not sure where Skidelsky stands. However his claim that historical developments demonstrate that reliance on the Free Market allied to the promotion of liberal and political economic freedom is the only optimistic way forward appears to be uncertainly based. I suspect that this is typical of the majority of the practical and political proponents of liberal Free Market optimism. They like to believe (or really do believe) that there is a sound basis in theory and history guiding their choice for the Free Market. Whereas detailed examination suggests that they read economic theories and make historical interpretations in the light of their optimism about the Free Market. Skidelsky's argument has strong resonances of the Hegelian dialectic in its Marxist form. But in that case his optimism of the Only Way is no more firmly grounded that any of the other expressions of faith in the Market. For the Hegelian dialectic and its materialistic Marxist form are very dubiously founded in both reason and history.

Skidelsky's extended explanation of his position hardly clarifies the situation.[3] Reading it strengthens my suspicion that while Skidelsky presents his polemic for the Market as being largely based in empirical evidence and pragmatic evaluations, nonetheless his approach is fundamentally ideological. He writes, for instance: 'There are plenty of problems. But as the basis of prophecy they reveal little more than the power of dramatic events to unlock the pessimistic imagination.'[4] This power, presumably, holds sway over those who are not enlightened enough to perceive which dramatic events have positive promise in them. The unexpected collapse of the evil empire was, after all, a very dramatic event. For Skidelsky however it would seem to reveal the dialectic recalling economists and politicians to the value and resources of economic and political liberty, setting our feet firmly back on the way of the Free Market – the only optimistic way open to us.

Skidelsky lists some of the obvious problems in national and international politics in regard to which he attributes absolute degrees of hopelessness to his 'pessimists'. He thus underlines his dialectical tendency to turn the problems he is rightly concerned about into the arena of antithetical conflicts between those who are hopefully informed by the cunning of reason and those who are pessimistically traumatized by the threat of events. He continues: 'There is no assurance . . . There is a long history of economic reasoning to suggest that it will benefit all its participants. This ray of hope should not be dismissed out of hand.'[5] Certainly the Market has delivered the most amazing things over the last two hundred years or so. But a ray of hope is not all illuminating; it does not light up every feature of the human, political and ecological landscape through which we have to negotiate our way. Further, as will be shown at a later stage, an examination of the methodology of economic thinking makes this status more doubtful than ever.[6]

Skidelsky, however, rules my type of arguing right out of court in a robust and challenging paragraph which seems to me to be much more like a rhetorical utterance about 'where I stand' than a contribution to any argument about why the rest of us should stand there with him. The tone of this declaration resonates (albeit in more academic terms

than they would use) with the impatience with which practical men
and women of business, industry and finance dismiss critical enquiries
into the workings of the Market. Hence my concern to consider
Skidelsky's argument at such length, for I take it to reflect the
practical impatience of those who both dominate the Market and
insist that it is good for us.

> Apart from short-term/long-term issues being an optimist or a
> pessimist turns out largely to be a matter of disciplinary back-
> ground. Economists are a more cheerful breed than historians,
> political philosophers, sociologists – and priests. This is probably
> because they suffer from almost total historical amnesia – if indeed
> they ever learnt history in the first place. Not only do they believe
> that the Market will sort things out, given a chance, but, like
> engineers, they are problem-solvers, coming to new situations
> equipped with portable science. Economics is almost the last bastion
> of the optimism of the Enlightenment.
>
> By contrast, all the non-economic interpreters of post-communism
> come to it either with sophisticated theories of social structure and
> change or with wide historical culture, or with both.[7]

It turns out, therefore, that being an optimist or a pessimist is a matter
of discipline as well as temperament. Skidelsky's insistent reiteration of
the optimist/pessimist antithesis underlines how dialectical/antithetical
his perspective is. It assists him in designating 'economists' as the
standard bearers in service of the cunning of reason. But who are these
economists? As his citing of the Harvard economist Jeffrey Sachs in
connection with the application of economic shock therapy in ex-
communist countries indicates, Skidelsky is concerned not with the
detailed theoretical enquiries of academic departments of economics but
with the intervening of 'economists' in practical affairs. He is thus
relating his generalization about economists to what Professor Krugman
(Professor of Economics at MIT) in his book *Peddling Prosperity* has
designated 'Policy Entrepreneurs' as distinct from 'the professors'.

In proposing this distinction Professor Krugman (I suspect with some
mischievous intent) starts a significant hare about just where credibility
of economic pronouncements relevant to policy-making lies. I pursue
the distinction at this point in the hope that a discussion of the two
classes of 'economists' will throw light on the difficulties an anxious idiot
like myself experiences in trying to evaluate and respond to theories
about market realities.

Professor Krugman makes the distinction between professors and policy entrepreneurs in an Introduction entitled 'Looking for Magicians'. He writes that in the USA between the end of the War and 1972 everyone

> took it for granted that the economy would continue to deliver an ever higher material standard of living.
>
> In 1973 the magic went away.
>
> Of course it wasn't really that sudden. Acute observers saw signs of an end to the great post-war wave of growth in the late 1960s – and with the benefit of hindsight we can now see that productivity growth, the engine that drives rising living standards, was beginning to sputter as early as 1965 ... For a while it seemed that our economic malaise was the result of a few individual pieces of bad luck: the energy crisis that followed the 1973 Arab-Israeli war, and the 'stagflation' ... of the next two years. It wasn't until 1978 or 1979 that the public began to develop a really deep sense of unease about its economic future.[8]

Reviewing the steady decline in optimistic expectations of the economic future in the USA up to the Clinton election of 1992 Krugman continues:

> Why did the magic economy go away? Hundreds of books have been written on that topic. This isn't one of them ... but let me cut to the chase: the real answer is that *we don't know*. There are a lot of stories out there. Most of them, including the ones that have achieved the widest currency, are dead wrong on logical or factual grounds ... The problem is that 'we don't know' is not a very encouraging answer. It is especially unsatisfying for politicians faced with an increasingly pessimistic and angry electorate ... their jobs depend on finding an answer – not necessarily an answer that is right, but at least one that will convince enough of the voters that they can make things better.
>
> So what do you do when the magic isn't working? You look for a new set of magicians ...

Krugman goes on to argue that in response to this political need for a new set of economic magicians able to conjure up the guaranteed growth (which their experiences since 1945–73 had led people in the West to assume to be the natural and proper road for an economy) a new set of 'economists' emerged who became very influential in political affairs. These he labels 'policy entrepreneurs'. He describes the difference between the 'the professors' and the 'policy entrepreneurs' as follows:

> A professor writes mostly for other professors. If he should happen to write for a wider public, no matter how well and simply he may write, he will always have in the back of his mind the reaction of his colleagues, which will inhibit him from saying things that sound good but which he and they know to be wrong. And lurking behind his words, no matter how simple, are usually concepts that a broad audience does not understand.
> The entrepreneur, however, writes and speaks only for that broader audience. And as a result, his or her writings suffer from none of the professor's inhibitions. They offer unambiguous diagnoses, even when the professors are uncertain; they offer easy answers, even where the professors doubt that any easy answer can be found.[9]

Earlier he states:

> Economists know a lot about how the economy works, and can offer some useful advice on things like how to avoid hyper-inflation (for sure) and depressions (usually). They can demonstrate to you, if you are willing to hear it, that folk remedies for economic distress like import quotas and price controls are about as useful as medical bleeding. But there is a lot they can't cure. Above all, they don't know how to make a poor country rich, or bring back the magic of economic growth when it seems to have gone away.[10]

Professor Krugman provides a cautionary tale about how much assurance we should invest in economic proposals urged as essential for our longer term well-being by economic policy entrepreneurs, the sellers of particular economic ideologies – or, to borrow a term from Krugman, the peddlers of prosperity. This takes us back to Skidelsky's appointing (or anointing) of 'economists' to the role of standard bearers to the cunning of reason.

Skidelsky's chosen economists are much more like Krugman's policy entrepreneurs than professorial economists. 'Like engineers they are problem-solvers coming to new situation equipped with portable science.'[11] This, presumably, is why they are 'a more cheerful breed' for 'they believe that the Market will sort things out given a chance'.

And so these economists can get on with their problem-solving in the manner of an engineer dealing with a faulty hydraulic system. They have no occasion to be anxious, or even pessimistic, about wider problems such as whether structural adjustment programmes reduce resources available for education, health and water supply in developing countries. Their concern is that the 'economic machine' should produce what they call 'wealth' in what they define as the most efficient way. As Skidelsky puts it: 'The economists are concerned with how to get as quickly as possible from a command to a Market economy.'[12] They apparently have no concern with the human costs of getting there, for there is no other way and when the way is travelled far enough all will be well – for all or most. Skidelsky says of this optimism: 'Economics is almost the last bastion of the optimism of the Enlightenment.' This is a revealing remark, especially when one reflects on his exasperated dismissal of 'historians, political philosophers, sociologists – and priests'. He re-enforces it with a dismissive observation: 'The economists and non-economists have almost no point of contact.'[13] For him the economist is down-to-earth and poised to attack obvious problem-solving with his economic bag of tools equipped with portable science. Skidelsky is clear that 'one has to make a choice' and, for economic reasons, the choice must be made for the economy of the Free Market.

On inspection this looks like a circular and deliberately closed argument, one more example of putting one's hope for human progress, prosperity and freedom in the expansion of materialistic wealth production as that process has been developed in the last two hundred years or so. This faith is not 'the last *bastion* of the optimism of the Enlightenment'. It is a variation of the last *vestiges* of the optimism of the Enlightenment which lingers in all the normative theories of economics as a heritage from Adam Smith: a belief that as human beings we have *structural* reasons to hope, work for, and collaborate with processes which promise progress.

The radical Enlightenment soon dispensed with the deistic idea of God (it was too weak, formal and unexciting an idea of God to be worth retaining). The idea of the possibilities of progress being structured into the pattern of things, was invested, on the one hand, in politics with the dynamics of the pursuit of liberty, equality and fraternity (or, in the more cautiously democratic form of life, liberty and the pursuit of happiness). On the other hand and at the same time, economics were invested with its own dynamics in what turned out to be two different ways. First, economics were developed as a normative tradition (and later, via attempts at mathematicizing and generalizing as a quasi-science). In the exciting boom conditions of the nineteenth century the Invisible Hand could be taken for granted and rationalized. Amazing growth was a sufficient replacement for amazing grace.

However, second, there were those to whom it seemed clear that for the majority of people the Invisible Hand did not work. On the contrary it – or rather the industrial and commercial processes by which the economy was being developed – licensed a great deal of exploitation. Perhaps these political and economic thinkers were pessimists because they lacked the insight and patience to wait optimistically for the saving delivery of the progressive operation of the Free Market. This disillusionment with what the political and economic processes were actually delivering for the majority of people in rapidly industrializing Western Europe, together with a great and romantic longing that all human beings should share in a just proportion of the prosperity and freedom which economic production seemed to promise was given powerful and influential expression by Karl Marx.

Marx took over Hegel's idea that human living in the world was an expression of the immanent 'skill (or cunning) of Reason' and of the Spirit (Geist) which was the immanent and true form of God, and thoroughly secularized it. The historical dialectic was at work in the processes of history and it structured them far more efficiently, forcefully and decisively, than any Invisible Hand.

The processes of economic production form the focusing sphere of this dialectical and materialistic process. Hence the Marxists' attempts at an economic interpretation of history and the political belief that if the processes of economic production can be directed and operated according to the immanent laws of the material dialectic, then human prosperity, freedom and justice will be achieved. The deistic god of Providence has been replaced, via Hegel's immanent but universal Spirit and Reason, by the economic working out of the dialectic. The obvious dynamics in practice of nineteenth-century economic production and growth are thus promoted into a secular and material version of ideas of creation, harmony and Providence, notions which go back via deism into biblical doctrines of Theism and an active creator God who wills and works for a fulfilment to creation which catches up human beings into that fulfilment. Marx secularized the kingdom of God while retaining the idea of a progressive possibility built into the structuring of human living and human history in the world.

It may be thought that I am making far too heavy weather of Skidelsky's assertion of the evident superiority of the capitalist and liberal Free Market method of promoting economic production over

that of the Marxist and collective one. He is simply making deductions
from what has obviously happened so far. But he is not. He makes claims
about how one should recognize and interpret what has happened so far
in language laced with ideological judgements. He appears to claim that
his choice is both indicated and vindicated by the 'cunning of reason'
which he himself relates explicitly to Hegel's,[14] just as he declares
bluntly: 'one has to make a choice'.[15] He has chosen a particular way of
looking at the course of events, both political and economic, drawn from
and interpreted by, a provocative ideological mix of the Hegelian/
Marxist dialectic and a strong commitment to the Free Market. The
principal point is that it is an *ideological* mix and, further, that the
ideology is a *closed* one. He corrals the contributions from 'historians,
political philosophers, sociologists – and priests' into a class of 'non-
economic interpreters of post-Communism' and dismisses them. In
other words Skidelsky is in active agreement with Karl Marx that the
only interpretation of history worth having is the economic interpretation of history. He differs only in identifying those who assist the
historical dialectic in the persons of those economic problem-solvers
who enable a market economy to take-off through the liberated activity
of investors and entrepreneurs. The way of looking at the world and
history as in a structured process is the same. The basic faith in
economic production as both the critical energy and the all-providing
producer of prosperity is the same. And the basic hope and end is the
same – the materialistic prosperity of all, sufficient to give them freedom
and satisfaction. Or, as Skidelsky himself puts it:

> The premise of what follows is that *all* the problems thrown up by
> the collapse of Communism, the end of the Cold War, and the de-
> collectivisation of economies will be more tractable if they can be
> dealt with in a context of economic prosperity.[16]

A generation or so ago the judgement was that there is only one way,
Left. Now the movement of history and the structuring of economics
has made it clear that there *is* only one way left – and that is the way of
the Right.

It is politically and humanly challenging to discover that both Karl
Marx and Lady Thatcher share the belief that the economic processes of
production can be relied upon (providing the laws of their structuring
are observed) to produce a materialistic prosperity which will be shareable by all to the freedom of all. Karl Marx however looked to a classless
society beyond the state. Lady Thatcher looked forward to a property-

owning democracy with a minimalist state. Neither utopia is anywhere in sight. Yet the ideologists of both sides, in their time, share the view that there is no alternative. Marxists knew that our freedom and prosperity lay in accepting the necessity of the material dialectic. Lady Thatcher has always known that you cannot buck the Market. Now that enlightenment vestiges of a providential God have disappeared, we are left with the saving knowledge that it is the Market whose service is – or promises to be – perfect freedom.

Notes

1   Robert Skidelsky, *A Polemic for Our Times* (Macmillan, 1995), p. 5.
2   Skidelsky, *Polemic*, p. 140.
3   Skidelsky, *Polemic*, Chapter 9: 'Understanding Post-Communism'; cf. pp. 161ff.
4   Skidelsky, *Polemic*, p. 162.
5   Skidelsky, *Polemic*, p. 162.
6   See further discussion, especially in Chapter 10.
7   Skidelsky, *Polemic*, p. 162.
8   Paul Krugman, *Peddling Prosperity: Economic Sense and Nonsense in the Age of Diminished Expectations* (New York and London: W.W. Norton & Co., 1994), p. 3.
9   Krugman, *Peddling Prosperity*, p. 11.
10   Krugman, *Peddling Prosperity*, p. 9.
11   Skidelsky, *Polemic*, p. 162.
12   Skidelsky, *Polemic*, p. 163.
13   Skidelsky, *Polemic*, p. 163.
14   See p. 76, above.
15   Skidelsky, *Polemic*, p. 163.
16   Skidelsky, *Polemic*, p. 163.

8 What About Realism? Coming to Terms with Optimism and Pessimism

I think I have demonstrated sufficient reason for doubting that the spark of market optimism exists in its own independent reality. Rather it is a Snark, some sort of quasi-metaphysical focusing of an idea which its adherents have come to cherish – because of their temperament, disciplinary training – as protection against what they fear most, or because they have decided to put their money on what the Market has delivered so far. Where should I put my trust? Why not, *faute de mieux*, transfer God and Providence from the motto on a dollar bill to the activity of the dollar itself as the effective symbol of those market operations?

The received views about the workings of the economy of the Market are, in effect, taken as a secular 'revelation'. Orthodox economic arguments have been (knowingly or unknowingly) invested with metaphysical powers. When a CBI document on *Prospering in the Global Economy* states that: 'ultimately the management of macro-economic policy must become politically uncontroversial' and then continues with the phrase – 'in an ideal world ...' that document is making a metaphysical statement. We are not just involved in discussing alternative views of economics, their operations and applications. We are discussing far-reaching commitments and claims about reality.

There is urgent need to acknowledge the inescapable role of moral and metaphysical choices (how we view the world and how we understand our interactions with people within it) in any assessment of economic behaviour. For we seem to be trapped in some sort of economic fatalism. If the Market requires it, then so it must be. If it can be shown that the theories appealed to as the source of Free Market realism are by no means value-free nor fact-neutral, but are shaped by the way their proponents perceive the world and direct their values, then our common collusive bluff is called. We have to think again or, at the very least, we are free to think again.

The idea that the development of economic theory from Adam Smith's discovery of the Invisible Hand and on through nineteenth-century theorizing, model building and mathematizing, has produced a neutral and accurate view of economic operations does not stand up to serious investigation. It is held, for example, that individual freedom is so important that rich men should be taxed minimally, for they must not be coerced, while poor men must be helped minimally for they must not be made dependent. That is the moral aspect, but it is reinforced by the metaphysical side of things. For the way of the world and of human being is held to be such that minimally taxed rich men contribute to greater investment, increasing wealth and thereby prosperity for all, while minimally assisted poor men proceed into employment and on to make their contribution to the eventual wealth and prosperity of all.

The claim is that Free Markets, individual freedom and promising prosperity have been shown to be interdependent through the accumulated tradition of articulated economic theory, based on the structuring of observed behaviour of markets and people. But this claim is false. Arguments about economic policies, about what we can afford and cannot afford in budgets, taxes, welfare payments and so on, are not just about details and adjustments within a universal view of economics and the world. There are assumptions underlying the arguments which are chosen rather than obligatory. The pressure of evidence about the number of people and communities who are losing out at present under this system requires the questioning of these assumptions. Such questions may lead into deeper issues than many people are willing to face – but they are issues about our future, our freedom and our hopes for prosperity. There are prudential grounds – as well as exciting, exploratory and visionary grounds – for being concerned with both morality and metaphysics.

At this stage in my enquiry I need to enter a disclaimer. I am not working through sceptical questions about the grounds for believing in the Market as if it had replaced Providence in order to prepare the way for a triumphalistic argument that to deal with the problems of the Market, restore hope for the future, and face up to our deep social and moral malaise, requires a return to belief in God. In my own theological understanding of God I am quite clear that to introduce God in order to deal with some lack in an argument about the world or ourselves is to make 'god' a function of the world and ourselves, so that he is reduced to one of our arguments and is clearly thereby not God.

I am not investigating the sources of market optimism in order to make a case for God. What I *am* doing is pursuing a secular case against investing optimism in the current operations of the Market on the basis that these operations are inevitable as well as beneficial. My concern is to establish the possibility of changing things. I am not an economic determinist and I do not believe that 'there is no alternative'. I believe the possibilities of human freedom are rooted in something deeper and more realistic than the trading activities of human beings. It is my conviction that to put one's faith in the operation of the Free Market is a potentially disastrous inversion of causality, determination and responsibility. We cannot rely on the Market as if it were Providence or the cunning of history. We have to rely on ourselves with whatever resources – practical, moral, inspirational and spiritual – we are able to discover in and between ourselves. The Market is certainly not the source of a guaranteed future. It need not be the provider of an inevitable fate – unless we collude in allowing it to become so.

The truth of the matter is that all the *theories* of the Market and all the *grounds* for insisting on the alleged necessities of the Market, are human constructs. The attempts at systematic observation and analysis of the happenings of economic productivity which have, over the past two hundred years, built up a tradition and a discipline of economics fall very short of being a 'science' as that term is understood in relation to physics, chemistry, biochemistry and biology – the 'life sciences' as we might say. Economics is not 'a life science'. It is, as Samuel Brittan hints (although he does not follow up the operational consequences of this) much more like philosophy, or even literary criticism.

Economics delivers partial insights and limited explanations of the workings of the Market. When these are shaped into formal explanations which can be taken to point to possible expectations, and are therefore applied to practical decisions, then there is always a normative – and not a scientific or value-free – choice implied. For the choice of the descriptions and expectations which are to be applied is determined not by universally agreed evidence, which tends to be in short supply, but by the political, moral and personal preferences of the economists concerned. They are supported in this by those politicians and citizens who join with them in putting forward the 'economic' advice for political and social application. Applied economic advice depends, as I have already pointed out several times, on such matters as 'what you fear most', where you put 'the onus of proof', and what 'view of the world' one takes.

In his *The Methodology of Economics: Or How Economists Explain*,[1] Professor Blaug shows that despite the aspirations (or even claims) of economists to be 'scientific', economics is nowhere near achieving standards of scientific precision and falsification. Blaug has a particularly telling section entitled 'Biases in Assessing Empirical Evidence' in his fifth chapter: 'The Distinction Between Positive and Normative Economics'. In discussing these biases he writes *inter alia*:

> Samuelson (1948, p. 203) once observed 'at least from the time of the Physiocrats and Adam Smith there has never been absent from the main body of economic literature the feeling that in some sense perfect competition represented an optimal situation'. The modern Invisible Hand theorem provides rigorous support for that feeling: given certain conditions, every long-run, perfectly competitive equilibrium yields a Pareto-Optimal allocation of resources, and every Pareto-Optimal allocation of resources is attainable via a long-run, perfectly competitive equilibrium. Of course this leaves out the justice of the underlying distribution of endowments in competitive equilibrium – and much besides.[2]

Indeed it is 'much besides'. Consider, for example, the argument developed in Paul Ormerod's *The Death of Economics*.

> The model of competitive general equilibrium is regarded as a theoretical, idealised form of the workings of such [mixed] economies. It is this link, made between the transparent success of Western economies and the theoretical economic model, which sustains the intellectual dominance of the model. It cannot be emphasised too strongly that, in practice, the competitive model is far removed from being a reasonable representation of Western economies in practice. By definition, any model necessarily abstracts from and simplifies reality. But the model of competitive equilibrium is a travesty of reality.[3]

Blaug in effect establishes the same point in a detailed and more theoretical way in his later chapter on 'General Equilibrium Theory', but in the chapter I am citing Blaug himself continues:

> Nevertheless every economist feels in his bones that the Invisible Hand theorem is not just an abstract proof of hypothetical significance in the stratosphere of ideas. Somehow, it seems just as

relevant to socialism as to capitalism, coming close indeed to providing a universal justification for the price mechanism as a rationing device in literally any economy. If this is not what economics is ultimately about, why bother with it? It is hardly surprising, therefore, that economists fight tooth and nail when faced with an empirical refutation of a proposition in positive economics involving the assumption of perfect competition. For what is threatened is not just that particular proposition but the entire conception of economic 'efficiency' that gives *raison d'être* to the subject of economics.

Was there ever an economist who came to believe in either socialism or capitalism because of the compelling empirical evidence about economies of scale? For that matter, it is probably not economic arguments at all that turn economists into planners or free marketeers. We can look high and low in the body of received economic doctrine without so much as encountering a well formulated attack on, or justification for, private ownership of the means of production ... The fundamental link between economic freedom and political freedom, however, is rarely discussed, possibly because mainstream economists are embarrassed to admit that what really lies behind their preference for private over public ownership of industry is a definite piece of reasoning in political theory.[4]

Blaug then quotes enthusiastically from Joan Robinson's *Economic Philosophy* (1962).

It is possible to defend our economic system, on the ground that, patched up with Keynsian correctives, it is, as he put it, 'the best in sight'; or at any rate that it is not too bad, and that change is painful. In short that our system is the best system that we have got. Or it is possible to take the tough-minded line that Schumpeter derived from Marx. The system is cruel, unjust, turbulent, but it does deliver the goods, and, damn it all, it is the goods that you want. Or, conceding its defects, to defend it on political grounds that democracy as we know it could not have grown up under any other system and cannot survive without it. What is not possible, at this time of day, is to defend it in the neo-classical style, as a delicate self-regulating mechanism, that is only to be left to itself to produce the greatest satisfaction for all.[5]

Blaug comments: 'I fancy that, wording apart, the four defences Robinson offers do cover the standard view and that the third of them

outweighs all the others for those who "defend our economic system".[6]
He then further adds the very interesting observation:

> Even among the majority of economists who believe in capitalism,
> *free marketeers* of various kinds, there are profound differences of
> opinion on the degree to which income inequalities in our societies
> are remedial by ordinary economic policies. For example, in a
> survey of the views of academic, business, and government econo-
> mists in the United Kingdom, compared to politicians and journal-
> ists, Samuel Brittan (in a publication of 1973) showed that
> economists as a community tend to have distinctive views on
> public policy that set them apart from others in any public
> discussion: they have an appreciation of the functions of the price
> mechanism as a method of allocating resources in accordance with
> relative scarcities and the revealed preferences of consumers that is
> lacking among non-economists. Nevertheless whether a particular
> economist is willing to subscribe to 'the liberal economic orthodoxy'
> frequently depended on whether 'he was prepared to treat the
> question of the allocation of resources on their own merits, in the
> belief that any major undesired effect on the distribution of income
> could be off-set, or more than off-set, by the tax and social security
> system'.[7]

The notion of reliability and objectivity in economic theory and derived
economic decision-taking would seem to be engineered out of a mixture
of naivety, unreflective ignorance, and more-or-less cynical self-interest
which compound into a collusive readiness to take the way things are said
to be going – for it is very difficult to imagine anything else. As Joan
Robinson says, 'the system ... does deliver the goods, and, damn it all,
it's the goods that you want'. Naivety assumes that since economic
production so clearly supports and directs our lives, it must be
structured into the very processes of our world and there must be
people (like scientists in general) who know how that structure works. (It
is beyond me, but it is not beyond 'them'.) Unreflective ignorance is to
do with being too busy and indifferent to do anything more than get to
grips with what one has to get to grips with, without having any time (let
alone capacity, one supposes) to try to get to grips with what is one is in
the grip of. More-or-less cynical self-interest is to accept the (agreed)
fact that we are all motivated (at least to a considerable extent) by self-
interest, with a leaven of gratitude for the received wisdom that self-
interest operating through the economic system works for the best for all.

So we believe in the Market, and we put our trust in the Market, because of what economic production has delivered over the last two hundred years. What more could you want but more of the same, and what else can you expect but more of the same? The state of public consensus was exemplified in the United Kingdom in the way in which the conference of the Labour Party in October 1996 was persuaded to support the liberation of business in order that increased prosperity might be spread round with a little more social sensitivity and sense of fairness than experienced under the neo-classical economic extremism of the right wing Tories. More concern was to be displayed towards the less well off, but there was to be no higher taxation of any kind – or at least no significant *direct* taxation of any kind – for the electorate would not wear it. The electorate's primary concern is their bank balances. (In the jargon – PDI, Private Disposable Income.) The international financial markets would not wear what they would interpret as Labour heading once again for the round of high taxation, higher spending, lower production, lower demand and higher inflation.

The Market rules in political orthodoxy and public esteem because of the prestige of the economic production which has been delivered in the past. The *reality* of the Market is its actual record of performance, production and effect. It all depends on how the economic processes we live by affect us, our communities and societies, and our earth.

This is sufficiently clear but it is not generally entertained as a serious possibility. The whole market-inspired political, economic and social operation is entirely closed and circular. There is no alternative because nobody wants to think about it, and those who dominate received opinion in the media refuse to think about it. When it looks as if the Market is not delivering the performance and the products that won it its original prestige, or when evidence accumulates that its operations are threatening the very life-systems of the earth itself, then it is replied that it only appears to be so if one fails to take into account the beneficent powers of the Market as outlined by, and established through, the economic theories of the Market. There is no readiness to recognize that this is using a set of metaphors derived from the past to interpret the reality of a set of observations and experience which arise in the present.

Even if it could be reasonably shown that this is not closed-circuit thinking, it would still be a very questionable system of thinking. For it involves the paradox of turning what is claimed to be the promise of the Free Market into the necessity of the Free Market. The promise is that the competitive operations of the Free Market will ensure the most efficient degree of productive growth in relation to the most freely chosen possibilities of individual consumption. The necessity is that the Free Market, through competitive production, must maintain a steady growth of goods and services which must find consumers at prices yielding satisfactory profits, or the whole system will collapse. The Free Market can be kept going in a steady progress only if competitive growth is successfully maintained. If there is indeed and indefinitely no alternative to the currently declared necessities of the operation of the Free Market, then it is difficult to see how that freedom of the Market promotes the freedom of individuals. It would seem that the allegedly beneficent market is on course to degenerate into a threatening treadmill. (As, indeed and in practice, it always has been – and continues to be – for a very substantial number of human beings whom the 'market forces' press to the edge of subsistence.) If this is what the evolution we are part of has come to, and no realistic alternatives are thought to be possible, then these economic processes are not merely the expressions of fate, but are arrived at the 'end of history' in that fate. This is in strict paradoxical contradiction to the indefinite optimism invested in the Free Market and expressed (if only by powerful and influential metaphors) in economic theories. How can we possibly go on deluding ourselves about the desirability and possibilities of human freedom?

We need to consider the proper reaction when confronted with the claim that 'there is no alternative' to a collection of *overall* descriptions and prescriptions about the living processes and structures in which we are involved – all the more when this cry of 'TINA' is used to close off argument and divert certain types of evidence. Such combinations of claims must surely alert all our capacities for critical reflection (with which our capacity for freedom is so closely intertwined). The prestige of the processes and performance of economic production cannot possibly warrant such uncritical self-surrender. Atheism should be maintained as atheism, it should not be displaced by a surrender to a force or a necessity which is far less than God would have to be if he were to have any possibility of being God.

My plea is that we should not invest *faith* in the Market. Faith can only properly be invested in persons – and in God if there be one. The purpose of this plea is to gain a serious hearing from the committed practitioners and politicians of the Free Market to the mounting practical evidence that the Market as currently operating has inherent defects which prevent it from working well, and makes demands on the resources of the world which will prevent it from working well into any indefinite future.

Despite the urgency of this type of evidence, I have deliberately devoted a major part of this book to examining the *theories* which enthusiastic Free Market proponents use or imply. I have done this because, to gain a serious hearing for this counter-evidence, one has first to shake the apparently impenetrable false confidence with which the Free Market optimists and politicians have deceived themselves. I hope that a systematic exposure of the underlying weakness of the theoretical claims that are made for the inevitability and beneficence of the Market will get as many people as possible among the voting and thinking public at large to question their collusion with this received wisdom.

A notable handbook, now easily available, which summarizes much of the mass of evidence about the increasingly destructive impact of the operations of the Market system is a 1996 publication by Earthscan, entitled *The Politics of the Real World*. Described as 'a major statement of public concern from over thirty of the UK's leading voluntary and campaigning organisations', it gathers information from leading relief and campaigning organizations including Christian Aid, Friends of the Earth, Oxfam, Save the Children Fund and the World Wide Fund for Nature. The information summarized in this handbook is quite as authentic, well-documented, realistic and relevant to the lives and hopes of millions of people across the world as is information signalled around the Market by the price mechanism. The Free Marketeers and their apologists have no claim whatever on a monopoly of realistic and relevant information affecting our lives and the earth, just as they have no right at all to claim that theirs is the decisive information.

There is well-collated information about such matters as poverty, environment, the continuing existence of slavery, the growth of inequality, the cynical collusion between multinational companies and corrupt governments which slants trade to the detriment of the majority of the inhabitants of too many developing countries. The way in which major trading organizations, lobbyists and all too many politicians write off the information of our major relief and campaigning organizations is a plain human disgrace as well as a perilous piece of imprudence. Our collective task as citizens and as human beings concerned with the future is to gather the courage to examine the evident facts free from the prejudice that the *theories* of the Free Market justify our expectations of this Free Market whatever facts may be in evidence at the present time. The critical issue is whether 'the Free Market' has trapped us all in this dead-end or whether we are the ones threatening ourselves with a dead-end through apathetic acceptance of *current* Free Market orthodoxy. Once you start trading, do you have to trade yourself into vast and increasing gaps between a few wealthy, an increasingly struggling and stressed 'middle class' and a majority of poor with no real hope?[8] Does this have to involve increasingly uncontrollable pollution, and the erosion of communities and the ecological systems of the earth? Is the only (short-ish term) future one in which the rich barricade themselves in fortified ghettos while the poor exist in increasing numbers of 'no-go areas'? Does TINA rule or could 'We' (see later discussion for what the symbol 'We' might point to) so influence and direct our trading and other activities that we can discover ways forward which offer a reasonable chance of a sustainable and shareable prosperity? Must we surrender our freedom to the Free Market as at present understood and commended? To accept this would seem to be the ultimate idolatry – and idols never deliver.

It may be, however, that those who claim 'There Is No Alternative' are right and that we have to come to terms with the strong probability that the TINA enthusiasts are fatalistic TINA pessimists in disguise. It may be that the present form of the Free Market has simply evolved its own momentum and will go on following this momentum however many people, communities and ecologies are crushed in its course. As we saw in Chapter 5, Sir Samuel Brittan in commending 'the human face of Capitalism' sets great store by his understanding of the Market as 'a device which has evolved':

> The true case for the Market mechanism is that it is a decentralised and non-dictatorial method of *conveying information* [my emphasis] ... the view of the Markets as a discovery procedure and co-ordinating mechanism is now common property to many economists, irrespective of their politics.

A 'device which has evolved' may have evolved in a way that we, as human beings, can do nothing about. Indeed, market enthusiasts hold it to be a virtue that we can do nothing about it. If the effects of expanding production across the world at large now show indisputable signs of becoming more threatening than promising, that is too bad. What can *we* do about it? After all 'the most important role of markets [is] as evolving institutions reacting to unforeseen change'.[9] Why assume that evolving process offers human progress – let alone guarantees it?

This may be a metaphysical question but it is also a vital, practical and political question. If you really believe that 'in the processes of evolution' the Free Market ultimately fixes everything, then you will be ready to put your trust in the most efficient fixers and diviners of the

Free Market on offer (and perhaps you will consider that they are perfectly entitled to the rewards they appoint themselves in the way of salaries, share options and pension funds, however out of proportion these may be to what is available to those hanging on the fringes of that flexible labour market required by the Free Market). You might further believe that it is imprudent to sign up to a social chapter or be overly anxious about health and safety at work (just as factory and mine owners and investors back in the early 1800s were clear that to restrict the conditions of labour of women and children in the mines and factories would ruin the country's trade and prosperity). Pursuing this line of argument to its possibly logical conclusion, you might then even conclude that the only 'realistic' thing to do is to bully the unemployed into jobs at near or below subsistence wages – even if the evolutionary processes of the Free Market fail to throw up such jobs in sufficient numbers in the part of the world or area of country in which you happen to live. If you did so conclude, and then gave a few moments of reflective thought to considering both the premise and the trend of your arguments, you would then surely be likely to conclude that 'evolutionary processes' were by no means guaranteed to (or even in aggregate are likely to) deliver good things for most people. At any rate it would be clear that a 'metaphysical' view of the world has a pretty straightforward connection with quite a few physical things which might be held to challenge us in moral and human ways. Is that what Brittan might call 'a pious thought', to be entertained only to be dismissed? Or might we have some *real* freedom to make a difference – if we organize politically – and, at least to some extent, *collectively?*

As I have already hinted there seems to me to be one theoretician and proponent of the Free Market who has made a serious attempt to deal with this metaphysical and practical problem. This is Friedrich Hayek. I propose therefore to examine, through his argument, whether one can restore a plausible case for putting our trust in the Free Market as a device or system which has evolved in such a way as to promise us, by its sheer and mere operation, growing prospects of prosperity and freedom. I believe that examination of Hayek's work throws into relief what I would call the hubris of economic theorists and commentators. This is that in unacknowledged ways they are claiming the right to be the dominant metaphysicians of our time. In practice they exercise the right – a right which received wisdom acknowledges they have – to be definitive about reality, in the sense of what delimits and drives our human lives together. The idea of the Market as a global information system demonstrates this claim in practice. Can this carefully articulated argument make the case that there is indeed no alternative to the Free Market way?

Notes

1   See Samuel Brittan, *Capitalism with a Human Face* (Aldershot, UK: Edward Elgar, 1995), Introduction, p. 17, cited and discussed at page 54 above.
2   Mark Blaug, *The Methodology of Economics: Or How Economists Explain* (Cambridge University Press, second edition, 1992).
3   Blaug, *Methodology*, p. 131.
4   Paul Ormerod, *The Death of Economics* (Faber & Faber, 1994), p. 48; see also Chapter 3: 'Roots of Economic Orthodoxy'.
5   Blaug, *Methodology*, pp. 132 and 133.
6   Blaug, *Methodology*, p. 133.
7   Blaug, *Methodology*, p. 134.
8   See Chapter 13.
9   Brittan, *Capitalism*, p. 268

9 Is a Realistic Optimism Rescued by the Evolution of the Market as an Information System?

The most impressive attempt to construct both an inevitable and optimistic explanation of the alleged workings of the Free Market is the case put forward by Hayek that the Free Market has evolved as an indispensable information system. This powerful theory is referred to succinctly in the reference from Samuel Brittan's, *Is There an Economic Consensus? An Attitude Survey* (1973), which I have already cited as referred to by Blaug. I used this reference to underline my case that economists of all persuasions at least partly choose the policies they urge by reference to their own political and moral choices. I pick it up again now because the passage sets out what it is that differentiates economists from the rest of us who are trying to understand political and economic affairs and indicates what they regard as their most convincing explanation of how it all works.

> Economists as a community tend to have distinctive views on public policy that set them apart from others in any public discussion: they have an appreciation of the functions of the price mechanism as a method of allocating resources in accordance with relative scarcities and the revealed preferences of consumers that is lacking among non-economists.[1]

The price mechanism, working through the networks which form the Market, conveys the information required by those active in economic production in order that they may deliver products which will persuade people to buy those products at prices which will generate sufficient profit to keep the system going. As I have already cited from Brittan, this information must enable the economic system as a whole to:

> coordinate the activities of millions of individuals, households and firms; obtain information about people's desires, tastes and preferences; decide which productive techniques to use; and create incentives for people to act on such information.[2]

So it is the price mechanism which reflects, and is then reflected back into, the wages paid for production activities, other costs of production (which include the costs of obtaining capital to finance productive means); what consumers will pay for the product; what will serve as incentives to get people into work and persuade consumers to be customers who pay sufficient prices; encourage industrialists, entrepreneurs and innovators to develop new products and methods of production; and pay the interest which capitalists require as an incentive to invest in enterprises which they believe show sufficient evidence of being sustainable and profitable. It is prices which link all these things together and balance them out.

This concept of the mechanism of pricing and prices acting as 'bits' of the information which integrates all the myriad of interacting factors is a concept of elegant and powerful simplicity. It has the apparent advantage that nothing mysterious or metaphorical (such as the historical dialectic) is required to explain how the pricing mechanism is structured and structuring. It is held to have evolved. As Brittan states: 'To a liberal the Market is not just a piece of machinery to manipulate but a device that has evolved.'[3] Thus the Market is not just a set of happenings it is, in some sense, a given. What has 'given' us the Market, in the first place, is the particular purposeful activities of particular human beings. As particular human beings have busied themselves producing and trading, they have developed networks which have exploded into the rapidly increasing complexities of the global operations which constitute modern economic production. The interactions of all the various purposive activities of human beings in producing, trading and financing have evolved this 'device' which, through the price mechanism, structures networks, operations and choices. It does so in such a way as to produce overall results which nobody chooses. (Nobody chooses them in aggregate but solely at the level of particular transactions.)

So the Market is an unconscious and unchoosing 'device' which has evolved its own ways of working. Or, to put the matter more precisely and accurately, 'the Market' *is* the totally unconscious and unchoosing 'device' that has evolved. It may look therefore *as if* the Market has its own 'wisdom' and *as if* the Market has its own purposes and rules. However these are simply evolved dynamics which work because they grew out of the workings of production, trade, industry and finance, the particulars of which (but not the overall effects and processes of which) were and are human purposive activities. There is nothing human or purposive about the Market. It is simply a given evolutionary (and, therefore, evolving) dynamic network. Perhaps this is the plausible substitute for the now impossible notion of Providence. Nobody meant to do it. What they meant to do was trade and make a profit. What emerged was 'the Market'; and the way the Market has evolved is by the price mechanism.

As I pointed out in Chapter 5, for Hayek Adam Smith is the conveyor of a 'secular revelation' about the way things are. ('Smith's work marks the breakthrough of an evolutionary approach.')[4] Thus Hayek argues for his views on the Market from a fully developed evolutionary worldview in which he holds that all our important understandings of the rules and realities of law, morals and economics, have developed 'between instinct and reason'. This, indeed, is the title he gives to the first chapter of the summary of his views, *The Fatal Conceit: The Errors of Socialism*.

The flavour of his fascinating and closely argued theory is given by a section heading in this first chapter 'Mind is not a guide but a product of Cultural Evolution, and is based more on imitation than on insight or reason.' He argues that human beings do not think up their understandings of how the world works and of how society should work (law and morals) by the power of direct and intuitive reason (and certainly not by any reasoning powers that might reflect some ultimate mind or reason behind and at work in the universe). Rather we develop ways of living together, of thinking about the world and ordering the societies which emerge, as it were, by instinct. Our reason then enables us to see that this is the way things are and should be. In all this we can only respond and not initiate. The Market has evolved out of trade (which according to Hayek is 'older than the state') and the laws, requirements and workings of the Market are what we come to discern as having so evolved. Thus to discern and comply with the evolved (and evolving) structure of the Market is to comply by reason with the 'freedom of necessity' (a phrase borrowed from J.B. Haldane, a professor of a scientific discipline who wrote as a Marxist) – and therein is our freedom. Hayek is a passionate proponent of the freedom of the individual. How his thinking relates this immensely valued gift of individual freedom to the blind workings of the evolutionary happenings which have produced 'the Market' is not clear. One might be inclined to think that the coincidence of evolution and the gift of freedom is so beneficial as to verge on the 'providential'. But it is clear that, for Hayek, to entertain such an idea would be neither scientific nor rational.

One cannot go very far into Hayek's work before discovering that his theories of economics are intimately bound up with 'ways of looking at the world', and 'what he fears most'. He feared socialism and collectivism so much that he apparently conceived the notion of having a grand international symposium that would settle the matter. The editor of *The Collected Works of F.A. Hayek*, W.W. Bartley III, reports the matter thus:

> In 1978, at the age of nearly eighty, and after a life-time of doing battle with socialism in its many manifestations, Hayek wanted to have a show-down. He conceived of a grand formal debate, probably to be held in Paris, in which the leading theorists of socialism would face the leading intellectual advocates of the Market order. They would address the question: 'Was Socialism a Mistake?'. The advocates of the Market order would argue that socialism was – and always had been – thoroughly mistaken on scientific and factual, even logical grounds, and that its repeated failures, in the many different practical applications of socialist ideas that this century has witnessed, were, on the whole, the direct outcome of these scientific errors.[5]

Two things are to be noted. First, the approach remains sharply dialectic. There are two opposing views of reality of which the socialist view is 'a fatal conceit' and a superstition, while the liberal Free Market view is scientific and realistic. Second, the two ways of looking at the world are both conceived of as total. One must be totally false and the other totally true. That we human beings can expect to have such a comprehensive grasp on the reality (or the realities) of the world and ourselves, is surely, a perilous presumption. The free marketeers, as human beings, do well to fear the tyranny and distortion of a *total* socialist view as forced into the service of a Stalinist tyranny. But should we not equally fear the tyranny and distortion of a *total* Free Market view which attempts to force us to submit to that view of the

Market? 'No' is the apparent answer of the Free Market enthusiasts, for nobody is coerced (or coercion is reduced to the minimum) by the evolved activities of the Market – in which we (all?) exercise our freedom of choice and through which we (all?) obtain the means to exercise our freedom of choice. The obvious question which arises here is 'who are *we*?'. Certainly not the majority of the present inhabitants of the earth (see further investigation in what follows). Nonetheless the proponents of the Free Market do seem to claim actual universality for this individual freedom of choice, if not now, at least in prospect.

Hayek sets out a clear theoretical basis for his approach to the Market, prices and freedom. The tone and logic of that basis is well worth investigating as it is pretty evident that all the Free Market apologists and politicians share the *working assumption* of Hayek's theory of the Market as an extended information system working through prices. Whether or not his *theory*, as a comprehensive view of the world and humans living in it, is shared by most Free Market proponents – or whether they would accept it if they had considered it in detail – is another matter. Brittan, who has considered Hayek's thought with sympathy, is firm in his preference for the working assumptions rather than the theory. The point at issue – to put it in terms of the order in which I have developed my investigation and argument – is: does evolution fulfil the role which eighteenth-century Providence used to supply to the extent that we are forced to accept that economics effectively is 'the last bastion of Enlightenment optimism', as Skidelsky urges? Or are we looking at a reasonably reasonable provisional 'as if', which will have to be modified as soon as enough counter-facts to the hypothesis accumulate? Do we, therefore, read the world and ourselves in terms of that form of the Market theory which has most public consensus now, or must we perpetually struggle to read the Market theory in terms of ourselves and the world? Is the scope of our thinking about the world, including our thinking about the Market, determined by the Market? What of freedom then?

The moral implications of this last question are particularly clear with reference to Hayek's formulation of his theory, as can be seen from the following passage:

> continued obedience to the command to treat all men as neighbours would have prevented the growth of an extended order. For those now living within the extended order gain from *not* treating one another as neighbours and by applying, in their interactions, rules of

the extended order – such as those of several property and contract – instead of the rules of solidarity and altruism. An order in which every one treated his neighbour as himself would be one where comparatively few could be fruitful and multiply.[6]

This is a challenging point of view (which as Hayek points out goes back to David Hume and other eighteenth-century thinkers) and raises issues so central as to deserve a book to themselves. I am however endeavouring to open up fresh thinking about the Market and this type of approach by investigating what proponents of the Free Market actually say and the implications of the language they use. The aim of the enquiry is thus to discover and evaluate how *authoritative* Free Market talk is, and hence what binding effect it has on the conduct of politics and the pursuit of economic production.

The essence of Hayek's evolutionary argument for the Market is that we now live in an 'extended order' which is decisively different from the primitive communities in which we were habituated to face-to-face ideas such as solidarity, altruism, or love of the (tribal) neighbour. It is, he held, the developments of trading and economic production which have enabled and expanded our civilization. In an early exposition in *The Fatal Conceit* he describes the type of development that economic processes have brought about:

> It is no accident that many abstract rules, such as those treating individual responsibility and several property, are associated with economics. Economics has from its origins been concerned with how an extended order of human interaction comes into existence through a process of variation, winnowing and shifting far surpassing our vision or our capacity to design. Adam Smith was the first to perceive that we have stumbled upon methods of ordering human economic cooperation that exceed the limits of our knowledge and perception. His 'invisible hand' had perhaps better have been described as an invisible or unsurveyable pattern. We are lead – for example by the pricing system in market exchange – to do things by circumstances of which we are largely unaware and which produce results that we do not intend.

A little later he continues:

> All this is possible because we stand in a great framework of institutions and traditions – economic, legal and moral – into

which we fit ourselves by obeying certain rules of conduct that we never made, and which we have never understood in the sense in which we understand how the things that we manufacture function. Modern economics explains how such an extended order can come into being, and how it itself constitutes an information-gathering process, able to call up, and to put in use, widely dispersed information that no central planning agency, let alone any individual, could know as a whole, possess or control.[7]

This is a clear statement about the necessity of the Market, its inscrutability from the point of view of any one or any group of us (including any government) and its consequent inescapability as the evolved framework of the extended order within which we must, perforce, operate. Later, when he is indicating why any form of socialist or central planning or regulation is in theory, and in practice, quite impossible, Hayek writes:

The order of the extended economy is, and can be formed, only by a wholly different process [different that is from the attempted processes of planning] – from an evolved method of communication that makes it possible to transmit, not an infinite multiplicity of reports about particular facts, but merely certain abstract properties of several particular conditions, such as competitive prices, which must be brought into mutual correspondence to achieve overall order. These communicate the different rates of substitution or equivalents which the several parties involved find prevailing between the various goods and services whose use they command. Certain quantities of any such objects may prove to be equivalents or possible substitutes for one another, either for satisfying particular human needs or for producing, directly or indirectly, means to satisfy them.[8]

Thus everything is sifted by the price mechanism which expresses, if not equivalent *values* at least equivalent *valuing* – and the measure of this valuing is money. This is why money (in some form or another) is so absolutely central to the whole economic process. Contrary to the cynical observation that we are in danger of knowing the price of everything and the value of nothing, it is only through prices that the economic system as a whole evaluates and works. For as can be seen from the opening of the paragraph I have just cited, this 'evolved method of communication' transmits 'not an infinite multiplication of reports about *particular* facts, but merely certain *abstract* properties of ... [my emphasis]'.[9]

This is vital. The Market cannot and does not deal with particular facts, it operates on abstract properties. Yet all human beings (except, possibly we may wonder, the international jet-set of business commuters) live 'in particular' with all their (our) particular characteristics, connections, communities and environments. We are not mostly concerned with 'abstract properties'. Our lives are built on concrete happenings and needs. It is this aspect of the Market and of the price mechanism which presumably explains why the writings of economic commentators so often do not seem to be talking about the majority of real people in what common sense might perceive as the 'real world'. For instance, economic talk assumes most people to be in possession of property and savings which they can invest. It also conceives of a species of sub-contractors – the workers who must not get too much by way of wages lest they upset the 'efficient' workings of the Market. And then there are non-contractors, 'the poor', who are burdensome and, in underdeveloped countries often have to be displaced from impoverished living on their own lands to languish in the growing suburbs of overcrowded and underserviced cities while they wait for the Market, in some indeterminate future, to take hold of their localities and finally suck them up into some share of prosperity. The dominating role of money in all this probably explains the convention in economic and financial writing of referring to financial markets without inverted commas, while references to the 'real' economy tend to wear the inverted commas. Economic writers and financial commentators know where the real power lies. In contrast they verge on indifference about the 'real' world where most people live, experience, rejoice and suffer.

However, this may all be the inevitable result of evolution. The great and glorious merit of this evolution, according to Hayek, is that the system as it has evolved sets the individual free to pursue his or her private choices. (Whether these individuals, able to exercise freedom *in* the Market as well as *through* the Market, constitute an actual majority in the (real or 'real') world is empirically another matter – which will be considered later.) Hayek is typically clear and trenchant about this great virtue of the evolved market.

> Each person has his own peculiar order for ranking the ends that he pursues. These individual rankings can be known to few, if any, others and are hardly known fully even by the person himself. The

efforts of millions of individuals in different situations, with different possessions and desires, having access to different information about means, knowing little or nothing about one another's particular needs, and aiming at different scales of ends, are coordinated by means of exchange systems. As individuals reciprocally align with one another *an undesigned system of a higher order of complexity* [my emphasis] comes into being, and a continuous flow of goods and services is created that, for a remarkably high number of the participating individuals, fulfils their guiding expectations and values.[10]

This is a particularly lucid statement of the reason why passionate and worried liberals plump for a theory of the Free Market which purports to show that the Market must work as Hayek says it does. The Market allows for, and protects, these acts of choice of atomic individuals in their carefully protected, private and differentiated identities. One does not have to know about, still less be concerned about, other individuals in their private and protected choices. The Market gathers it all up and, despite all the 'differential scales of ends', achieves results which are 'coordinated by means of exchange systems'. This is the pearl of great price which lies hidden at the heart of the Market and which liberals claim to value above all other things. The Market, as it has evolved, promotes and protects the freedom of choice of each and every individual.

But this undergirding and underlining of the supreme value of private individual liberty is not the only reason for the fierce defence of the Free Market. The Market is an effective delivery system – 'a continuous flow of goods and services is created that, for a remarkably high number of the participating individuals, fulfils their guiding expectations and values'. This appeal to the obvious *results* of the process links up a combination of Hayek's argued way of looking at the world and his moral preferences (including what he fears most – namely coercion or tyranny over individuals) with what he claims the system actually delivers. In this, I would suggest, he is at one with all the other theorists of the Free Market. What is held to validate any particular economic theory is not the force inherent in the theory as such, but the power and prestige of what the Market has delivered, or is believed to have delivered, in the last two hundred years. What the Market has delivered and can be relied upon to continue to deliver is described and evaluated in accordance with what the particular proponents of the particular theory prefer, cherish and hope for.

Brittan's sympathetic evaluation of Hayek supports this view. He is critical of Hayek's evolutionism because he judges that if everything is determined in an evolutionary way which can only be picked up, so to speak, after the event, by human reasoning responding to what has happened, there are insufficient grounds to support moral and political preferences for one particular system, or against another. But we do hold strong preferences and Brittan shares Hayek's. He writes:

> Competition between social systems may lead neither to liberal results nor even to survival of the fittest, unless 'fit' is defined in terms of ability to capture the coercive powers of the state. So, as Gray puts it, [John Gray has been previously referred to by Brittan as giving a sympathetic account of Hayek's theory] one may have to choose between Hayek's 'evolutionary endorsement of man's random walk in space' and his critical analysis of twentieth century thought and practice.
>
> My own choice is unhesitatingly for the latter. I was first attracted to Hayek by his concern, voiced in *The Constitution of Liberty* 'of that condition of man in which coercion by some by others is reduced as much as possible'. Hayek's writings have asserted the case for general rules over discretionary authority. They have exposed the misleading identification of a liberal democracy with a divine right of a temporary majority. They have shown the domination of both the political and economic market place by interest-group struggles is a source of evil and instability. They have explained why pecuniary rewards neither can, nor should, reflect merit. These important and controversial assertions were made before Hayek became so taken with evolutionism; and for a great deal of the time one can forget the unsatisfactory evolutionist or instrumentalist roots of his concern for liberty.[11]

This underlines that we are dealing, in theories about the Market, with 'as if' statements supported by reasons of a sort but which do not amount to decisively established theories. They are accounts of the world and of economics which are preferred by their exponents only partly because of what they hold to be empirically observable. Moral and political concerns play a powerful part in the way in which they hope to see their theories interpreted and applied. Brittan, as can be seen from the quotation above, declares his rejection (or setting aside) of Hayek's theoretical evolutionary grounds for his critical analysis but very much accepts and endorses that analysis for practical purposes and with regard to the Market working through the price mechanism as 'a device which has evolved'.

A problem lurks here. If, as Brittan does, one puts aside 'the unsatisfactory evolutionist or instrumentalist roots of [Hayek's] concern for liberty'[12] where does that leave the description of the Market as this device which has evolved? Surely it ought to be regarded as another of those 'ways of looking at the world' which are 'neither falsifiable propositions nor just political judgements'.[13] Wherever the theoretical idea or structuring model came from, and however useful it has proved to be *so far*, there always remains the critical need for judgement about the appropriateness of the model now and for the future.

In contrast to this strictly provisional, pragmatic and critical approach, Hayek's evolutionary theory has the apparent attraction of claiming to be a description of the way things have evolved derived from the use of reason and scientific thinking. It appears to be so real and accurate a description of the way the 'Market' has evolved in structuring and working that it is clear we must follow those ways of structuring and working in any rational economic behaviour. Further, what we can hope for from that behaviour is limited and defined by the ways of structuring and working which have emerged.

Socialism, for instance, is a 'fatal conceit' arising out of romantic and ignorant readings of the evolution of human society. It may be that to claim that the 'screw of history' (or the 'cunning of reason') has turned decisively against all socialist and collectivist ideas is an injudicious attempt at historicism – all forms of which Karl Popper (a great friend and correspondent of Hayek's) has shown to be unscientific and logically untenable. But an *evolutionary* way of reading the world and society is a much more sound and decisive matter. If one has discerned the direction of evolution and discovered within that the structuring which has produced so much prosperity out of the human propensity to produce and trade, and at the same time, has discovered that conformity to the evolutionary rules protects and promotes individual freedom, then one has apparently firm grounds for optimism.

Hayek is offering in a scientific-sounding formula an account of the expectations we can invest in economic activities. The system has evolved to deliver and so it will deliver – if we conform to the patterns of working which have evolved. This, so Hayek's development of the observational theory argues, requires the show-down with socialism, because socialism is the source of such innumerable and dangerous errors. This show-down is required to preserve the proper ways for pursuing evolutionary based optimism which evolution thus far has produced.

Thus the understanding of the Market and the price mechanism as a 'device which has evolved' is not just a useful model for looking at one aspect of economic affairs. It is a required and scientific way of looking at the world as economic activity. If the economic rules are not rigorously adhered to then something worse than the current conditions, if not something disastrous, will come about in penalty for going against, not so much 'the wisdom' of the Market but – something much more basic and simple – the evolution of the Market. The challenging point about Hayek's trenchant analysis is that his developed evolutionary theory of the Market and the price mechanism is overtly 'metaphysical'. 'Metaphysics' is 'the philosophical discussion of the nature of reality'. Hayek's discussion of the Market concerns the 'nature of reality'. This is doubtless why Brittan, who claims to be much more pragmatic about economic theorizing, rejects the 'evolutionism' while hoping to retain the detached, analytical ideas. Brittan is persistently cautious about espousing big ideas which threaten to explain too much. In his chapter on Hayek in *Capitalism with a Human Face* he comments:

> Hayek's defence of the Market is ... subtly different from that of many other economists.
> ... This is alright so long as we are free at the last resort to judge the outcome and do not feel bound to welcome institutions simply because they have survived.[14]

Brittan aims to be persistently pragmatic about the Market, judging it by its results. This is wholly consistent with his qualification that the price mechanism is 'a device which has evolved – *imperfect and capable of much improvement*' (my emphasis). But can Brittan really maintain this pragmatic stance? Is it sufficient to justify the weight which both he and Hayek put upon the efficiency and necessity of the Market as this evolved information system? How is this evolved device really working? Does examination, for example, of the financial markets[15] persuade one that they are the products of an assuredly beneficial evolution, unless one already has a strong faith that the Market is a basically beneficial process (which one believes to be scientifically and philosophically justified)? Is the evolved device a happy accident or an unhappy fate – or is 'evolved' too strong a word with too deterministic and, therefore, possibly fatalistic undertones?

In relying for his prescriptions about our responses to the Market on the idea of the Market as a device which has evolved for collecting, passing on and co-ordinating information, it would seem that Brittan has arrived at a 'way of looking at the world' which at least verges on being metaphysical owing to the way it works by determining how we should interpret the evidence.[16] It is very doubtful, therefore, whether in practice Brittan is entitled to distance himself from Hayek's 'evolutionism' – and simply rely on its conclusions without accepting its theoretical construction.

This ambivalence about the status of Brittan's claims for the Market highlights the case for claiming that all apologists for the Free Market as the essential dynamic for our prosperity and freedom are involved (often implicitly far more than explicitly or intentionally) in making claims about the nature of reality – both as it is experienced in the workings of human experience and activity in the world and as expressed in human nature. Thus it is, in effect, a metaphysical approach. The Market is not merely a means of operation, it is a definition of how we may and must live. A useful *modus operandi* has been overpromoted into being an inevitable *modus vivendi*. That is to say that the Market is being treated not as a subordinate *assistance* to living but as a dominant *way* of living by which we are constrained and directed.

Hayek's exposition of the Market is of central diagnostic significance for an enquiry into what drives the Market, what we can rely on it to produce, and how far we are bound to follow its prescriptive trends and laws. As Brittan says,

> Hayek tried . . . to embed his economic teachings in a wider view of Man and Society . . . It is not surprising that there are gaps and contradictions in his wider social philosophy, as in that of everyone else who has tried to construct such an edifice.[17]

Hayek makes it quite clear that he *is* expounding the Free Market 'in a wider view of Man and Society' while other economic commentators generally refuse to acknowledge – or are seemingly unaware – that they are doing the same.

The reason for persevering in excavating these unacknowledged presuppositions in theories of the Market is to make the case that we are confronted with market apologists who make too all-embracing claims for the Market. They are assuming 'a wider view of Man and Society'. The vitally important corollary to this is that, in practice and effectiveness and most importantly of all in completeness, there are 'gaps and contradictions' in the expositions of market theories and consequently in the claims which are made for them and the prescriptions drawn from them. Economic activity does not define the world of nature and of human activity, and economic theories do not even definitively describe economic activity.

This may sound like a truism. But as my examination of the language of economic commentators has shown, it is a truism which is neither acknowledged nor observed. Currently received economic theories *are* assumed, at least implicitly, to describe the way the world is, and the pattern of economic and political activity. This is so, it would seem to me, even with so reasonable and cautious a thinker as Sir Samuel Brittan when it comes to describing the status and effects of what he calls the 'hard core economic doctrines'.[18] Hence the prestige and political dominance of the Market mantra, even if such as Professor Krugman maintain that this is the peddling of prosperity by economic magicians rather than paying serious attention to the cautious work of the professorial economists. If, however, it is recognized that there are 'gaps and contradictions' in all this talk of the economy and all its practical applications then, logically speaking (and so, it is to be hoped, practically and politically speaking), TINA is dethroned. It is not true that 'there is no alternative'. Neither inevitability nor guaranteed beneficence are built into the Market way. The only obvious truth is that it has become the fashion, a fashion sustained by considerable momentum or inertia, for some very powerful persons to maintain that there is no alternative. But this rests more on decisions about ways of looking at the world, about hopes and fears and about interests (self-interest, as Adam Smith was clear), rather than on proven and established metaphysical and scientific discernment of underlying 'Reality'.

The assumption that the Market is simply common sense may be, indeed, 'common' but it is neither good, realistic, nor hopeful sense. It is a metaphysical and ideological assumption. To bring this theoretical, but important, enquiry down to earth, I next propose to consider the merit of the 'efficiency' of the Market measured by its capacity to preserve and promote future and shareable human welfare and prosperity. Let us consider the accounts of how the Market works in practice.

Notes

1 Mark Blaug, *The Methodology of Economics* (Cambridge University Press, second edition, 1992), p. 134. See above, p. 95.
2 Samuel Brittan, *Capitalism with a Human Face* (Aldershot, UK: Edward Elgar, 1995), p. 59. See above p. 63.
3 Brittan, *Capitalism*, p. 270.

4   F.A. Hayek, *The Fatal Conceit: The Errors of Socialism* (London: Routledge, 1988), p. 146.
5   Editorial Foreword to *The Fatal Conceit*, published as a new work to initiate the series of Hayek's collected works in 1988.
6   Hayek, *Fatal Conceit*, p. 13.
7   Hayek, *Fatal Conceit*, p. 14.
8   Hayek, *Fatal Conceit*, p. 86.
9   See above.
10 Hayek, *Fatal Conceit*, p. 95.
11 Hayek, *Fatal Conceit*, p. 121.
12 Brittan, *Capitalism*, p. 121.
13 Brittan, *Capitalism*, Introduction, page 17; cf. my earlier discussion in Chapter 5.
14 Brittan, *Capitalism*, p. 115.
15 See Chapter 11, Sections 1–3.
16 E.g. the theory tells us how to discern what is 'efficient' as a contribution to human well-being. See next chapter.
17 Brittan, *Capitalism*, p. 119.
18 Brittan, *Capitalism*, p. 17.

10 'Evolution' – Not as Hopeful as all That

In 1973, Samuel Brittan identified a consensus between economists which differentiated them from politicians, journalists and the rest of us:

> Whether a particular economist is willing to subscribe to the 'liberal economic orthodoxy' frequently depended on whether 'he was prepared to treat questions of the allocation of resources on their own merits, in the belief that any major undesired effect on the distribution of income could be off-set, or more than off-set, by the tax and social security system'.[1]

In my present enquiry into the implicit claims of economic commentators to give definitive and all embracing descriptions of 'reality', two points are significant here.

The first arises from the notion of treating the allocation of resources on their own merits. This refers to the consequences of having 'an appreciation of the function of the price mechanism' similar to that of Hayek. The questions which are to be 'settled on their own merits' are questions of *allocation* of resources. What is involved in settling such questions 'on their own merits'? I think it must imply leaving the Market to work according to the price mechanism alone. But what is 'meritorious' about the price mechanism? The meritorious feature of prices is held to be that they enable the Market to work 'efficiently'. This would appear to mean that the Market is the most effective means of distributing limited resources and meeting the needs and wants of people according to their ability to pay. This process also multiplies incentives to extend these operations, stimulating production so that increasing numbers of needs and wants are met.

The basic model is very simple. Once we have moved beyond simple bartering of object or service in exchange for object or service, then I trade with you because you have produced something that I want or need and I give you in exchange something ('money') that you can use both to pay you for your cost of production and to leave you with the best possible surplus (profit); which profit you then exchange in order to meet some of your own wants and needs. And if you are inclined to be an entrepreneur, you can invest in further production and trading activities. Transactions are effected through the price which balances out what I am able and willing to pay with what you need and hope to receive. This basic type transaction is then thought of as multiplied expansively across the world in ever various forms involving the production of forever diversifying goods and services. The motor of this expansion and diversification is due to the fact that the payments for the costs of production plus the making of surplus 'money' in profits, fund wages and returns on capital which enable more individuals to become increasing consumers and thereby purchasers of additional goods and services. As part of the same process, enterprising persons make use of savings to put on to the Market various new and innovative types of goods and services which generate new demands. Hence the never-ending growth of the whole multiplication and diversification process in ways which cannot be foreseen but are responding to one another.

This vast process is both unsurveyable and unforeseeable as a whole but, providing that the price mechanism is left to operate on its own merits, it results in the most efficient allocation of resources (which are themselves being multiplied by the very efficiency of the process). The process itself does this without any need for, or possibility of, any set of persons or institutions improving on this. Indeed, the price mechanism cannot work on its own merits unless trade is free. So the only proper action for organizations such as governments is to remove barriers to free trade.

It cannot be too strongly emphasized that this simple modern model of the Market is taken as being literally and universally true over all human communities and environments, and timelessly true into the indefinite future. The whole edifice is built on my trading with you through the price mechanism. The evidence for the existence and power of this assumption about the world of human living and transacting is clearly articulated in innumerable *obiter dicta* of Free Market commentators and practitioners. A type specimen quotation turns up in a 'Comment and Analysis' article in *The Financial Times* of 25 November 1996. In it Michael Prowse reflects on six years in Washington, lauding the economic achievements of the USA. In moving into his concluding argument about the superior commitment of the people of the USA to the libertarian way of running society he observes:

The market after all, is nothing other than a network of voluntary transactions between individuals. Trade occurs only if both parties expect to benefit from the transaction. It is thus by definition welfare enhancing.

Here we have a complete worldview encapsulated in an *obiter dictum*. ('After all' we all know and accept this, do we not?) In fact, this statement confronts us with a moral stance which is specifically claimed to be the most valuable or reasonable available. Prowse's article contains the moral protestation: 'Libertarians, contrary to the popular caricature, are not selfish atomists. They are better characterised as passionate believers in social co-operation and community.' He then continues with a critique of the coercive activities of governments from a libertarian stand-point. Such a stand-point, the author argues, requires 'continuing consent' from the governed. He concludes: 'I make a contribution to your welfare if and only if I agree to do so. And vice versa. What more adult way can there be of running society?'

I do not cite Prowse's article here in order to take issue with his political argument about libertarianism and government. It looks, *prima facie*, as if the form of political structuring which he commends would hardly be feasible – except possibly in a society of altruistic anarchists miraculously supplied with the resources to meet their reasonable wants and needs. The likely correspondence between his libertarian views and practical politics is not the issue. I draw on this article because it presents a concise example of how a simple model of the Market, based on individual trading transactions, is asserted in combination with a strongly held moral and political stance. This illustrates my thesis that theories about the Market, no matter how much their proponents strive to make them strictly descriptive, always have a strong prescriptive element in them drawn from the theorist's moral commitments and preferences.

This must call in question the validity and scope of the *authority* of any theory. Such a simple model must exclude too many of the complexities of the real world. It cannot be realistic of us to rely on such a model to provide us with any inescapably necessary set of rules about economic behaviour, or any set of guarantees of results, or any promises of indefinite continuity of systemic behaviour.

Introducing evolution into the argument is of little help on the issue of the authority and scope of economic theories and models, despite the forcefulness of Hayek's metaphysical and moral arguments, and despite the apparently matter-of-fact arguments of Brittan for the inevitability of the Market as an information system in promoting economic growth. Consider further the claims about the 'merits' of the price mechanism, and the 'efficiency' which results in the allocations of resources, in light of the fact that the whole concept of the information system depends on the basic model and unit in the system being transactions of exchange between individuals, measured and effected by prices. (As described by Adam Smith in *The Wealth of Nations* and unquestioned by so many 'received' economic and financial commentators of whom Michael Prowse in *The Financial Times* may be taken as typical.)

Take the quotidian experience of shopping in a supermarket. Does one feel like a free and independent individual entering into a trading transaction with another free and independent individual? As you hand your debit card to the cashier are you confident of your money passing as a neutral and free unit of exchange which will, sacramentally and surely, and in the aggregate of all transactions, statistically ensure that the transaction will be 'by definition welfare enhancing'? My personal impression is that supermarkets surround me with messages designed to entice me – possibly even trick me – into buying. I understand that there is a considerable 'science' involved in contriving sights, sounds and smells so as to encourage customers to buy. Most of the choices on offer involve items so irrelevantly differentiated that personal choice is reduced to petty objects. It is about the generation of want, not the meeting of need.

Not, that is to say, if one seeks to preserve a distinction between 'needs' which are not freely chosen and 'wants' which are a matter of will and preference. This is a difficult distinction to preserve. Consider for example the controversial nature of attempts to define a 'poverty' line and the evident psychological and social fact that when nearly everyone around you appears to be able to fulfil a particular range of 'wants' then you do 'need' to be able to join in if you are to feel yourself a proper member of the society which defines reality and expectations for you. This is one social reality which is doubtfully registered in the messages of the Market information system. Nonetheless it is a basic feature of the current operations of the Market that its very maintenance relies on it multiplying wants, while, its very nature which operates by money, means that it is less and less likely to respond to messages about real and basic needs. The only individuals who count in a trading transaction model are those with access to money. It is only through money that they can register, even remotely, effective messages as far as the Market is concerned. This no doubt explains why the International Monetary Fund and others feel justified in enforcing structural adjustment programmes on poor countries which make poor people worse off, at least for the time being. (How long is the long run if you are starving?) The poor must wait until they gather capital which will give them access to the Market. They are called upon therefore to suffer in hope – their suffering not being a quantity which can be registered in the Market information system.

To take another example, it is not at all clear to me that the ordinary shop-lessees in the local trading centre experience themselves as free and independent individuals entering into a series of 'welfare enhancing' transactions with other individuals as they are involved in the renting and maintaining of their shops. (I leave entirely out of account the full-time and part-time waged employees in such a centre. We will come to them in a later chapter. Wages, after all, are a cost and not an investment.) Lessees, for example, are at the mercy of a take-over of their particular complex by some new cash-rich, or credit-worthy business. Overnight their terms of tenure and prospects can be altered. They have to negotiate trading deals with large suppliers who have greater resources than they, and even if a local bank manager attempts to be accommodating in the hope of longer term prosperity, he or she is at the mercy of instructions from on high laying down fresh computer calculated rates of credit-worthiness and return, so bankruptcy can loom at the press of a computer key. No doubt theoreticians can fit all this into a *model* of aggregating individual transactions. But it simply does not 'feel like it'. Still, as writers in *The Economist* are inclined to remark, economics is at its most interesting and exciting when it is counter-intuitive. Whatever it 'feels like really' it is all part of a much more encouraging ball-game which 'enhances welfare by definition'.

It is important not to allow my doubtless superficial impressions to lead me into romantic and impractical rhetoric. I waive therefore, for the time being, impressionistic statements about what it feels like and move on to a more soberly logical analysis of what is involved in talk about the merits and efficiency of the Market as an information system operating via prices. It may, however, not be entirely improper to register the possibility that if this apparently impersonal way in which market emporia such as shopping malls are actually run is, in fact, 'a network of voluntary transactions between individuals' and that 'it is by defini-tion welfare enhancing' for human beings at large, then it is a quite remarkably miraculous coincidence. For this outcome is not produced by 'Providence' nor by the 'Historical Dialectic', and the idea that 'two hundred years of normative economics' adequately replaces such metaphysical notions will not stand up to investigation. It may be that blind evolution has produced this welfare enhancing, individualistically and transactionally based 'mechanism' by chance. Of course, it could not literally be a mechanism, for that which evolves is an 'organism'. The Market, therefore, will have to be a process and not a mechanism. This means that it too must evolve. And that is a major reason for doubting whether what has happened in the past can be any sure, or even likely, guide to prospects in the twenty-first century.[2] Next, however, I propose to consider the internal logic of an information system generated from trading transactions between individuals in the form of exchanges enabled by prices.

The major flaw in the logic attributed to the Market information system as described by both Hayek and Brittan would seem to be that the basic operating unit of this system is a transaction between individuals, while the way in which the Market transmits messages (*viz.* by prices) is an almost total abstraction from the personal reality of each of the individuals involved in those transactions. This is underlined by the fact that individuals without access to money cannot take part in the Market. Therefore the price mechanism is not a truly universal mechanism. And to treat it as such is to exclude a large part of the present population of the earth from the equation. The immediate and timeless point is that the mechanism, in accordance with its *modus operandi*, has to treat individual persons wholly impersonally and in its own money terms. How can such an abstracting operation be relied upon to promote the well-being of individuals in general and in their various particularities? Presumably, because of the Invisible Hand and because individuals are relied upon to be the best judges of their own welfare and prospects. If they follow their self-interest, all promises to be well.

This is to make the theory of the Market as an evolved information system depend for its validity and promise on the theory of the Invisible Hand. It is not, as Hayek appears to claim and Brittan may seem to suppose, that the evolutionary theory of the development of the Market decisively replaces the role hitherto played in optimistic market theory by the Invisible Hand (or rather, as Hayek says, by Adam Smith's intuiting an unobservable and invisible pattern which is discovered to be the evolutionary pattern). The theory of the Market as an information system does not therefore succeed in rescuing any reasoned optimism about the Market. Any hope we may reasonably invest in the Market will still have to depend on how we evaluate and extrapolate what the Market delivers. The Market as information system may explain *how* the Market delivers, but it can say nothing at all about whether the deliveries of the

Market are, overall, good and hopeful for us – still less whether we can *rely* on the Market to go on delivering good and hopeful things for us. We may guess that the Market goes on spreading prosperity and freedom, or we may hope that it will, but there is no firmly based theory to underwrite our optimism.

This brings us to another weakness. If, as it seems we must, we can look only to present and future deliveries of the Market to support any hope which we may invest in the Market, then we are relying on the accumulation and aggregation of the results of the individual trading decisions which constitute and motivate the Market. But what compelling evidence is available to show that the accumulation of particular and discrete 'goods' adds up to overall, increasing and sustainable 'good'?

The famous example is the motor car. The advent of the motor car revolutionized transport, trade and family life. But as a car becomes essential to increasing numbers of people, it develops into a burdensome necessity. In ever more families husband and wife must work hard enough to be able to maintain what have now become these necessities of life. Add to this the threat of urban gridlock and mounting pollution and we are presented with an example of the way that individual trading decisions in a networking market are not, by definition, conducive to welfare in any long run, either for individuals separately or for all of us together. Hirsch puts this succinctly in introducing the discussion of 'positional goods' in his powerful analysis of why continuing economic growth cannot automatically enhance everyone's standard of living or, indeed, continue indefinitely: 'The choices offered by the Market opportunities are justly celebrated as liberating for the individual. Unfortunately individual liberation does not make them liberating for all individuals together.'[3] There is no earthly reason why, cumulatively and in aggregate, individual transactions should amount to overall good – unless the Invisible Hand is really a very firm and beneficent fist (the hand of a providential God?). It all depends on how things work out.

Further, if everything in and through the Market is worked out by exchange transactions through the price mechanism expressed and effected through money, what are we to make of the amazing explosion in the money and financial markets over the last twenty years or so? Are these a huge aggregation of individual trading transactions depending on the absolutely free choice of particular individuals, and can they continue to be construed on this model? *Prima facie* it seems to be beyond belief that the global financial markets can be understood on Adam Smith-type models. Are the seven major firms said to dominate dealings in the global derivatives markets guided in their control of Market information by the Market's capacity to be an unprejudiced information system based on individual trading with individual? Who controls the information system and at what costs to both controllers and dealers? This question will be considered further in Chapter 12, but its obvious existence further calls into question the assumed optimism of theories of evolved information systems. Meanwhile it should be noted that Adam Smith suspected merchants of a tendency to arrange monopolies if they could. Also, at the present time there is a growing concern about mergers and a search for suitable anti-competition regulation. Suspicions, therefore, of the type I am raising are nothing new.

Relying on such a system to produce allocation of resources 'on their own merits' is not, as far as one can see, to rely on a dynamism which is by nature 'meritorious' for human beings – or for most of us over a longer run. The term 'merit' refers to the uninterrupted working of the information system and has no inherent notion of wider or human value. Being 'prepared to treat questions of the allocation of resources on their own merits' merely means being ready to let the system work as it will. This is not a statement of the case for welcoming *laissez-faire* (that is to say, establishing the case that we can be optimistic about what it will allow to be delivered), but simply a description of the workings of *laissez-faire* with, at most, the implication that we can do nothing about it. This is not optimism but fatalism. The picture is that we have generated an organic-like mechanism – the Market – about which we can do nothing except succumb to it. The Market does not shape decisions 'on their merits', it simply brings them about. Whether there is any merit in the results of these decisions is quite a different matter. As so often, when one looks closely into market apologia one is confronted with the muttering of mantras rather than facts. Or, perhaps better, the facts are noted, selected and read in the 'light' of the mantras so that the whole operation is, so to speak, talked into a meritorious reading.

If there is no inherent wider merit in the manner in which the information system of the Market influences decisions and transmits the effects of those decisions, there is a correspondingly limited and diminished meaning to the *efficiency* with which the Market is alleged to bring about the allocation of resources. For, once again, it is the *allocation*, and not the nature or impact of either the resources or their distribution, which is effected by the messages of the Market information system. There is no information passed about the nature of resources themselves, nor how their production, distribution and use affects particular persons and places. All such things – vital to the living and prospects of actual people – the Market has no means of registering. Thus the notion of market 'efficiency' within economics is a particular, specialized and limited one. It refers to efficiency in terms of allocating and circulating resources within the Market system of economic production so that the system continues to expand in production, consumption and profit. Constant exhortation from current politicians in the UK informs us that the first priority must be to excel in competitive productive growth. Everything else must be subordinate to this, including, for example, working conditions, safety regulations and minimum wages for those in work; social security, health and family support for the unemployed and the aged.

This present climate of opinion is in contrast with Brittan's 1973 assessment of the consensus of economists.[4] At that time he reported that a particular economist's readiness to subscribe to the 'liberal economic orthodoxy' (about the allocation of resources on the merits of the price mechanism) frequently depended on whether he also believed 'that any major undesired effect on the distribution of income could be off-set, or more than off-set, by the tax and social security system'. In other words he observed a strong tendency among economists to ally their understanding of the Market as an independent and freely operating information system with a belief that 'a major undesired effect' of the working of this system could be off-set by government fiscal action outside the Market so to speak. The awareness of the need, and the possibility of, such compensating action is, of course, an admission that the Market operating as an information system does not necessarily deliver results that are 'meritorious for' all either immediately or even in the longer term, without compensatory action from some other source. In 1973 it was still possible for economists to believe that the information system of the Market could safely be left to work 'on its own merits' for 'any major undesired effect on distribution of income' could be dealt with in other ways. But in 1973, or thereabouts – as Krugmann and many others have pointed out – 'the magic went away'. The effects of the amazing growth of the Market which made it possible to rely on the Market working 'on its own merits' *and* in addition produce sufficient surplus to deal with 'any major undesired effect', were evaporating. With hindsight, economists in 1973 were still too easily optimistic.

In the Introduction to his 1995 publication *Capitalism with a Human Face*, Brittan updates his previous views (published in 1973 and 1990) commenting that:

In both surveys the majority of respondents took every opportunity
to show that they were opposed to anything like a minimal state
approach, to endorse the slogan of more equality and to reject cuts in
government spending. There was something goody-goody in the
economists' attitudes [in 1973].[5]

Even if it can still be maintained that it is, first, possible to describe
'capitalism with a human face' and, second, that there is no alternative, it
is still necessary to be clear that the belief up to 1973 in the possibility of
off-setting major undesired effects by other means was, at the time,
politically correct, but it appears to have turned out to be economically
disastrous. This is why Skidelsky and many others argue so fiercely that
the pre-1973 political correctness has to be replaced by the 'realistic' late
1990s political correctness determined by economic correctness.

I am writing this book to protest against any claim that there is such a
thing as guaranteed economic correctness, and that to link such a claim
to a belief in congruent and deducible political correctness is to grossly
compound a metaphysical and moral error. To do so is to surrender
humaneness and hope to a threatening view of our interactions on this
earth. It is to suggest that one, and only one, set of possibilities can be
correctly understood and responded to in a rigidly definitive way for
good and all. The populist economic commentators are attempting to be,
and are too often allowed to be, the authoritarian dogmaticians of our
times.

The internal coherence of the theories which are supposed to link up
into the overall authoritative claims to prescriptive knowledge is, often,
very questionable. It may be that in the Golden Age (or Golden Spasm)
which arose after the war of 1939–45 and ended around 1973, it was
possible for economists to combine their awareness of 'market failures'
in promoting increasing prosperity *for all* with a belief that any major
undesirable result could be corrected from elsewhere for the time being.
This would allow the maintenance of the faith that *in the longer run* the
Market as information system would indeed indefinitely deliver the
goods for more and more. So economists as liberal citizens, democratic
human beings and humanely decent colleagues and neighbours could
rest assured, and assume (with the rest of us who do not understand
economics but just put our hopes in the Market), that all would turn out
reasonably well if we all persevered.

When, however, the magic of growth falters – what then? It seems
that today's economists in general have forgotten that they, or their
predecessors, were ready, twenty or twenty-five years ago, to agree that

major undesired effects of the workings of the Market did exist but that
they could be – if not corrected – at least ameliorated. Does it make no
difference to the case for the optimism of the Market theories that since
1973 this shared belief in correctional possibilities has turned out to be
false and that much currently received Market theory accepts this
falsity? In particular – and most critically – it appears to be widely
concluded that it is *not* possible that 'any major undesired effect on the
distribution of income could be off-set . . . by the tax and social security
system'. This is surely fatal to any faith in the Market as a guaranteed
source of *optimism* – where this optimism is held to extend across the
globe in a utilitarian and democratic way. (That is to say when the theory
of optimism is held to be humanly universalizable because the Market
process will produce both 'the greatest good for the greatest number'
and the maximum possibilities of freedom for the greatest number.) If
'any major or undesired effect upon the distribution of income' cannot
be off-set by other means within the power of a government and its
people then this hope would seem to be hopeless anyway – for income is
essential to taking part in the Market.

The direct connection between relying on the price mechanism in its
market form for economic intercourse, and issues of power and
participation in political and social intercourse, is brought out cogently
by the philosopher Alastair MacIntyre in his discussion of 'Liberalism
Transformed Into a Tradition', towards the end of his book *Whose
Justice, Which Rationality?*. For example, he writes:

> In the markets . . . it is only through the expression of individual
> preferences that a heterogeneous variety of needs, desires, and goods
> conceived in one way or another are given a voice. The weight given
> to an individual preference in the market is a matter of the cost
> which the individual is able and willing to pay; only so far as an
> individual has the means to bargain with those who can supply what
> he or she needs does the individual have an effective voice. So also in
> the political and social realm it is the ability to bargain that is crucial.
> The preferences of some are accorded weight by others only in so far
> as the satisfaction of those preferences will lead to the satisfaction of
> their own preferences. Only those who have something to give get.
> The disadvantaged in a liberal society are those without the means
> to bargain.[6]

In 1973 many economists thought that a sufficient power to bargain,
albeit at a minimal level, could be maintained by some redistribution of

income through fiscal means to those suffering from any 'major undesired effect on the distribution of income'. This is now ruled out. As the financier, philosopher and philanthropist George Soros has said, *laissez-faire* ideology, by declaring governmental intervention the ultimate evil, has 'effectively banished income or wealth distribution'.[7] Mature market economies – and most notably in the USA and the UK – have developed what J.K. Galbraith calls 'the war against the poor'.[8] There is an assumption that such economies, relying as they do on competitive production, cannot afford to allow workers to retain any capacity to organize in order to protect their wage-rates, working conditions, pension rights or health benefits.

In 1996 Galbraith wrote with reference especially to the USA:

> Nothing could be more obviously a threat to the well-endowed than responsibility and associated expenditure for the poor. To this end in the United States we have just emerged from an intense legislative orgy over welfare. The result was legislation involving a devastating deprivation of the unfortunate. No one, or anyhow not many, wanted to say they were against paying for the poor; that would be too candid.
>
> The case was that our dole persuaded people that they did not need to work; that women, many unmarried, were avoiding toil by giving birth to children; and others were just resting. But the truth was never far from sight. Those who mounted the attack were speaking for the fortunate who simply did not want to pay. And, indeed, the need to lift the tax burden from the hard-working middle class was amply emphasised.[9]

We have a similar situation in the UK. *The Times*, for example, carried a leader commenting on Mr Clinton's signing of the slightly amended Republican Bill to cut down drastically on welfare rights and payments under the triumphant heading: 'End of the New Deal'. The detailed regulations of the Job Seekers' Allowance introduced in 1996 were persecutory and aimed at forcing idle shirkers into jobs no matter at what wage. Such regulations do not have the appearance of measures designed to assist fellow-citizens into work and out of the misfortune of unemployment, to the benefit of them and their families as a contribution to the welfare of all of us. They are being forced to join in on the economy at a level well below any possible 'power to bargain'.

As Galbraith wrote:

The attitudes here cited are present in all the fortunate lands. There are concerned and compassionate people who reject them, along with the silent poor. Perhaps it is time to bring them out into the open – to seek the therapeutic value of clear speech. In the modern economy let us say simply that the rich do not want to pay for the poor; that unemployment is necessary and good; that recession can be tolerated, certainly by the many who do not suffer as compared with the smaller number who do. Even mild inflation affects the many as compared with unemployment, which affects the relatively few, and there is this fear it will get out of hand.[10]

This last reference to inflation refers to the currently accepted necessity for governments and central banks to exercise control through interest rates on the money supply in order to maintain a balance between the capacity to produce goods and services, the demands for those goods and services which people have the money to satisfy by price and purchase, and the numbers employed, together with the wages which are paid to those who labour to provide the goods and services. One of the tell-tale signs of this balance getting out of control, and so threatening inflation, is the unemployment rate dropping too fast. Thus we are repeatedly told that too sharp a fall in the rate of unemployment is *bad* news for the market – in this case the Market which consists in the financial markets who, as distinct, from the actual producing and delivering markets (i.e. the 'real' economy) do not need inverted commas. It is clear where the actual power lies over who should have what degree of bargaining power.

Now, it may be that the Market as 'an evolved device' is bound to work like this. If this is indisputably and irrevocably so, however, it is a very severe challenge to any optimistic faith in the Market in the utilitarian and democratic sense to which I have referred above. For it looks as if minimal wages are both inevitable and 'desirable' for those who have nothing but their labour to give them access to the Market processes. It should be no great surprise to discover that this is so. Adam Smith himself was not noted for his optimism about the lot of labourers.[11] Nor is it entirely evident that Ricardo's 'iron law of wages' which, together with the prognostications of Malthus, earned economics the name of the 'The Gloomy Science', does not continue to resonate.

The theory of market optimism is, of course, that by making the rich richer, more wealth will be created which will trickle down to the poor – who, after their initial exclusion, will eventually end up less poor. Some of this trickle-down has happened to some extent in some parts of the world as a result of the amazing growth of the nineteenth century and the post-war Golden Spasm up to 1973. But evidence is accumulating which provides strong empirical grounds for concern about the *distribution* of the wealth produced.

The evidence shows that the wealth created by the current market operations is being sucked up rather than trickling down, and that the gaps between the rich and poor, both between and within countries, is in the aggregate, growing. On the one hand we have the evidence which, for example, leads a commentator such as Victor Keegan to write:

> People have felt bad during a period when most of them have never had it so good, partly because their comparative wealth improvement has coincided with an unprecedented worsening of the wealth of those at the bottom of the scale.[12]

Some of the evidence for this with reference both to the UK and the USA will be considered in Chapter 12. Keegan adds: 'Wealth and income distribution haven't been off the agenda for the past seventeen years, it is just that the entire emphasis has been on redistributing wealth from poorer to richer people.' On the other hand, the prospects for most (or even many) of the late-developing countries entering as fully equal participants in the global market dominated by the OECD countries and their allies is very remote.

Thus, across the world developed economies are 'doing well', and some (a small minority of) developing countries are 'doing better', but everywhere an increasing minority of people in developed countries, and still a majority of people in developing countries, are doing worse. Labourers must work at the lowest possible wages and the poor outside the market are sheer burden.

This is not to be wondered at. It is built in to the very concept and construction of the Market as an evolved device; evolved to work as an information system. By the nature of the system information is conveyed by prices expressed in, and responded to, in money terms. What counts in the Market are those who have the money to express and enforce their *wants* – no matter how exotic, specialized or particular they are. People who have *unmet needs* but no money are simply non-entities as far as the Market information system is concerned. People desperate for money are either wage slaves as they often are in Third World countries where everything from Barbie dolls through designer trainers to sugar are produced at bare subsistence wages for immensely profitable sales in developed countries. Or else they are outside the statistics and subject only to aid from famine and medical charities while the structural adjustment programmes of the IMF and the like deprive too many poor peasants of the poor living they might have had on their own lands. Of course this is all in the expressed hope of eventually drawing them into market growth and market prosperity. The empirical evidence is poor, but the official hope of market and development agencies is strong.

As the investigations of this book so far show, the theoretical grounds for this hope are weak to the point of non-existence. What matters is not how the Market is supposed to work, but how it actually works. Here the evidence is increasingly alarming – if it is not assessed through eyes and minds already dominated by market mantras.

A striking example of the distorted and strangely inhuman view of the world held by the Market faithful would seem to be the way in which Singapore and Hong Kong are held up as leading examples of the hope we can invest in the Market economy. Yet both are entirely atypical of countries in the world at large. They are small enough and limited enough to be much more like a multinational corporation than a normal country. To set either of these concentrated commercial areas up as stars and models for economic development in the future seems to underline, in a most alarming way, how proponents of the Free Market ignore the real world and why they put 'real economies' in inverted commas.

Quite apart from wider metaphysical and moral questions about what happens if one puts one's hope in evolutionary optimism allied to evolutionary determinism, there are strong grounds for doubting that the Market as an evolved information system holds out realistic hopes of ever-increasing, ever-improving and ever more democratic ways of economic production, consumption and shared prosperity. Money, the dynamic of the information system, is not interested either in human needs (as distinct from endlessly multiplied wants), nor does it have any way of reconciling and responding to what the expanding (or even exploding) production methods are doing to people, communities and the earth. The ideas of 'merit' and of 'efficiency' which are made much of in the theory of the Market as an information system are simply tautologous references to the way the system in fact works and have no necessary connection with what is meritorious, even on a utilitarian definition, for human beings, nor with what is efficient for men and women to help more and more of us to live shareable, sustainable and enjoyable lives on an earth which is both globalized and physically limited.

Optimism is therefore a matter of faith or of self-interested fiction. The faith is, allegedly, supported by Adam Smith's secular revelation concerning the Invisible Hand, reinterpreted as the discernment of an evolutionary force. This patterning force offers us the best we can expect from our lives as producers, traders and consumers. Whether this force is sufficient grounds for general optimism about the results of our obedience to its workings is a proper matter for empirical observation but not for faith. The possibility of our being confronted with a self-interested fiction arises because the people who are most adamant about the necessity of observing the evolutionarily developed rules of the Market seem to be those who most benefit from it. There are, surely, grounds for a cautious and critical scepticism when the argument being put forward seems to be: The case for allowing us to make as much money as we can is that in the longer run this will enable all of you to share in making as much money as you can.

It is a matter of observation that this 'self-interested fiction', if it indeed be such, is maintained by people who can command enough money to give themselves some protection from a money-less poverty which forces them out of the system altogether. Once one ceases to be impressed by the prestige of the mantras deployed, in face of actual facts, the whole theoretical construction becomes increasingly unbelievable and, alas, increasingly unhopeful.

In order to pursue this in accordance with my method (that is by examining actual language employed 'economically') my next chapter considers the degree to which hopes about Third World development are a case of market enthusiasts from the developed world being hopeful at other people's expense. Once freed from the constraint of believing that the present market system must be the product of the most promising evolution we can expect, it seems increasingly difficult to believe that the antics of global financial markets are bound to be a reliable part of a universal, beneficent, utilitarian and democratic way of living. Has the Market, in truth, evolved as inescapable fate or is it a human and powerful artefact capable of being influenced and directed to truly human purposes, wherein profits are related to both persons and the sustainability of the earth? This fundamental question is basically a political, and not an economic, one. That is, it is a matter of individual and corporate choice and will about how we should be governed and with what aims. It is not a matter of blind faith in economic orthodoxy to be put into free practice by the economic experts and business operatives.

Notes

1 Brittan quoted by Mark Blaug, *The Methodology of Economics* (Cambridge University Press, second edition, 1992), p. 134 (cited p. 95 above).
2 See Chapter 7 above.
3 Fred Hirsch, *Social Limits to Growth* (London: Routledge & Kegan Paul Ltd, 1977), p. 26; and see argument of whole book.
4 See pp. 117f above.
5 Samuel Brittan, *Capitalism with a Human Face* (Aldershot, UK: Edward Elgar, 1995), p. 17.
6 Alasdair MacIntyre, *Whose Justice, Whose Rationality?* (London: Duckworth, 1988), p. 336.
7 Reported in *The Guardian*, 18 January 1997.
8 See *The Observer*, 26 September 1996.
9 J.K. Galbraith, *The Observer*, 26 September 1996.
10 Galbraith, *The Observer*, 26 September 1996.
11 See, for example, *The Wealth of Nations* I, 1, viii ('Of the Wages of Labour').
12 *The Guardian*, 20 January 1997 (see further p. 201).

11 Being Hopeful about the Market at Other People's Expense

In his *The World After Communism*, Skidelsky presents one of his economic heroes. He introduces Jeffrey Sachs, a 'thirty-five year old economist from Harvard', as a pioneering economic problem-solver in a chapter entitled 'The New Political Economy'. The introduction has tones of the revelatory, if not of the messianic. I have already discussed the basic weakness of Skidelsky's dialectic optimism, but I wish to follow up its practical application in the particular ideas and activities of someone whom Skidelsky clearly regards as an important standard-bearer. For, as I have already said, I consider that Skidelsky articulates with revealing frankness the presuppositions which underlie so much of the continuing optimism of the enthusiasts of the Free Market. The 'Sachs Case' illustrates how the expectations of the Free Market are extended to cover the whole world, every one in it and the indefinitely extensible future of all of us and our descendants.

> In July 1985 ... Jeffrey Sachs went to Bolivia to act as a financial adviser to the main opposition party (ADN) which was expecting to take power after an election victory. He had been asked to prepare an economic programme to stop the forty thousand percent per annum hyper inflation then raging in the country. In two weeks he and a local team drew up an emergency plan for rapid disinflation, based on analysis of the major hyperinflations of the 1920s. Let Sachs take up the story:
>
> 'During the two weeks I attended a cocktail party at which a middle-aged man came up to me to ask me about my ideas. I told him about the idea of a decisive "fiscal shock" to end high inflation. He said that Bolivia needed much more than a stabilisation programme ... In sum it needed a decisive ... reduction in the role

of the state in the economy which would come in a master-stroke just like stabilisation.'[1]

Sachs then says that he thought he was having his leg pulled so that he would reveal himself as a 'free-market extremist'. He continues his story:

'I really didn't guess that evening that the man, Gonzalo Sanchez de Losada, would soon lead a true economic revolution in new democratic Bolivia, with consequences for many other countries ... I learned that "shock therapy" can work in a democracy, but that it takes active management and executive dynamism to make it work ... Our work in Bolivia in the first few years involved fundamental tax reform; the establishment of an emergency social safety net programme (the Emergency Social Fund); the first ever debt reduction programme under IMF auspices ... ; Central Bank reform; closure of Bolivia's loss making tin mines; an overhaul of the tariff system; and so forth.'

Of this Skidelsky comments:

Sanchez de Losada had realised what Margaret Thatcher also saw: that inflation is a problem in political economy, not just in economics ... Within a few years the service of Sachs would be required in Poland and Russia, and the new political economy would become truly global.

Here then is the way forward – it is the way for everybody; it is the only way and it is the promising way. But what actually happened? Bolivia's Free Market operations were not sufficiently successful to appear in a survey ranking international growth prospects, reported in *The Times* of 14 October 1996. Bolivia does not feature on the international map accompanying the report, being part of a blank in Central South America covering Bolivia, Paraguay and Uruguay. One of the encouraging items in Sachs' own description of 'our work in Bolivia' was the reference to 'the establishment of an emergency safety net programme (the Emergency Social Fund)'. *The OXFAM Poverty Report* (published 1995) cites World Bank documents of 1991 and 1994 which read:

In Bolivia, the Emergency Social Fund (ESF) sought to off-set the effects of the unemployment caused by adjustments, providing the equivalent of one-third of public spending by 1991. However, over half the beneficiaries from this programme, which focused on construction work, already had a job; and the poorest regions of the country received least funding. Another way in which the programme failed to reach the poorest was that only one percent of the jobs created went to women. These failures reflect a wider failure to make ESF funding available to the poor. But perhaps the biggest failings were that the programme was able to reach only a small proportion of the unemployed, and that it came to an end before any sign of recovery had occurred.

I find the last sentence particularly significant. There seems to be practically overwhelming evidence that whatever good intentions are initially built into structural adjustment programmes and the like, they are soon dropped and the poor are the casualties.

The Oxfam Report further comments:

> Drastic wage reductions also have the effect of reducing demand for local producers, undermining growth prospects and deepening recession. The World Bank itself has acknowledged that this was one of the reasons for the failure of Bolivia's adjustment programme in the 1980s.[2]

This is an example of a pretty general observation by respectable aid agencies such as Oxfam and Christian Aid, conclusions supported by quotations from the UN, World Bank and IMF documents. The premise of shock therapy and of structural adjustment programmes is no jam today (hence the shock), but always jam tomorrow. For the years documented so far, not only is jam never on the menu but very many poor people are deprived of even the jam-less and thin crusts they had. The international financial community sees to it that jam is preserved for the outside investors. Nonetheless, as *The Economist* observed in a report of 13 January 1996 on a study held to come near to proving that economic freedom promotes both liberty and prosperity: 'these things take time'. Why should the poor believe this? Why should anyone believe it when the theoretical basis is so shaky and the concrete results so poor? It is a matter of faith. Facts are to be explained, or ignored, so as to fit that faith.

We now know from the United Nations *Human Development Report* (published in 1996) that, as the headlines put it, 'Richest 358 people own as much as half the world'. Far from demonstrating the famous trickle-down theory, the evidence is for a 'sucking up' of wealth to the rich and super-rich. It was already well-known (although not much attended to) that the richest 20 per cent of the world's population had access to over 80 per cent of world income. The latest evidence makes it clear that the situation is getting worse. Between 1960 and 1991 the poorest 20 per cent of the world's population saw their share of wealth fall from 2.3 per cent to 1.4 per cent, while the top 20 per cent (us) head for 85 per cent – with the remaining 14 per cent or so distributed between the remaining 'middle' 60 per cent.

From the purely trading and market point of view, much of this evidence is set out in *Globalisation in Question*, by Paul Hirst and Graham Thompson in their chapter on "Trade, Foreign Direct Investment and International Inequality'. The authors base their arguments on charts of IMF, UN and other data, largely drawn from 1993 and earlier. The material should be considered in detail by anyone who wants to make a serious assessment of the value and 'reality' of various types of information (see further Chapter 12 on financial markets). Why should statistics like these (and others in documents such as *The OXFAM Poverty Report*) be considered any less significant indicators about the state of the world and the lives of people than statistics of money flows, interest rates, and capital markets, highlighted by economic commentators?

Discussing two tables setting out investment flows and populations 1981–91 and global distribution of trade 1992 (exports only), respectively, Hirst and Thompson write:

> on the basis of these admittedly rough and ready calculations, between 57 and 72 percent of the world population is in receipt of only 8.5 percent of global Foreign Direct Investment. In other words nearly two-thirds of the world is virtually written off the map as far as any benefits from this form of investment are concerned. The question is, for how long can this kind of severe inequality continue? What is more, this inequality is paralleled by the case of trade.

They then summarize the figures they have set out on the global distribution of trade showing that the trade between the main trading blocs (USA and Canada, EU and EFTA, and Japan), together with the ten most important developing countries, amounts to between 84 and 79 per cent of world trade in 1992. Their comment is that this 'again demonstrates an incredible inequality in terms of the populations involved'. They present a further table to indicate the persistence of inequality in the world distribution of income.

> This distribution changed little from the 1970s to the 1980s. Looking at the global distribution of income more generally ... on the basis of the two measures indicated this has become more unequal rather than less since the 1970s. All these measures go against the sentiment that benefits to the less well-off nations and regions will 'trickle down' as investment and trade are allowed to follow strictly Market signals. Inequalities are dramatic, remain stubborn to change and indeed have grown since the 1970s [p. 69].

The authors then refer to 'the practical economic and political objections to the continuation of these trends':

> With an increasingly interconnected international system, the majority of the world's population excluded from prosperity, even greater political, social, environmental and therefore economic disruption of the world economy can be anticipated ... Greater disruption in and by the 'periphery' now tends to have more immediate consequences within the 'core' and the 'core' itself is not immune from many of these trends; it 'imports' the consequences of poverty. The pressure on Europe and the USA of migrants fleeing conflicts and poverty is obvious. Any new migration and its containment constitute a major new security risk, and this is likely to be exacerbated by the continuing reproduction of extreme inequality in the distribution of wealth on a global scale [p. 70].

Hirst and Thompson summarize this particular part of their discussion:

> There must be some question as to whether the existing situation, analysed above, is sustainable even in its own terms in the long run. How can a 'global system', however partial in its truly internationalised features, manage when two-thirds of its population is systematically excluded from the benefits of that system, whilst the limited prosperity it generates is increasingly concentrated among the already employed and successful in the wealthy fourteen percent of the world and its few client states [p. 72].[3]

A summary form of equivalent information is given in the UN report. It presents the information that while there has been 'a dramatic surge in economic growth in fifteen countries since 1980 ... Economic decline or stagnation has affected one hundred countries'. Nine countries are reported as having per capita incomes lower than they were ten years ago. There are even worse off countries, nineteen in all, where incomes are less than they were in 1960 or before. As the UNDP administrator comments: 'The world has become more economically polarised ... if present trends continue, economic disparities between industrial and developing countries will move from inequitable to inhuman.'

None of these data appear to be taken into account by Sachs. In *The Economist* article entitled 'Growth in Africa: It Can be Done',[4] he is described as 'an outspoken critic of the IMF' and he refers in his article to 'the dreadful policy errors of the past [and] the mutual complicity of Africa and donor nations'. Sachs is clear that 'a fresh start requires a thick line drawn under the past', and recommends that, 'as with other forms of assistance, debt cancellation should be deep, phased over time and conditional on fundamental reforms'. But here comes the rub. His 'fundamental reforms' require steady and rapid opening up to unrestricted trade in the Free Market, a policy which so far has very uncertain results indeed – and most certainly very uneven ones.

Thus Sachs' article states:

> The best evidence of the failure of the IMF and World Bank in Africa lies in the programmes themselves. Institutions have actually been targeting low levels of growth per head throughout Africa ... even though worldwide evidence shows that market-oriented poor countries can grow faster than richer countries.

No account is taken of how far the 'worldwide evidence' is typical globally. However if you have sufficient confidence in the Market it is not a question of what is typical but of what is significant. Sachs suggests that: 'The evidence on cross-country growth suggests that Africa's chronically low growth can be explained by standard economic variables linked to identifiable (and remedial) policies.' He then summarizes a previous article he wrote with a colleague from the Harvard Institute for International Development on 'Sources of Slow Growth in African Economies'. This appears to be a typical econometric study, producing a table allocating factors with numerical values alleged to contribute to Africa's growth short-fall, and distributing values to points such as 'lack of trade openness'; 'low saving rates'; and 'highly distorted domestic markets'. A value is also assigned to the difficulties arising in Africa because of 'land locked-ness' and 'natural resource dependence'. Sachs triumphantly concludes: 'Once these factors are taken into account, there is only a small (0.5) residual or unexplained puzzle to Africa's growth.' It seems difficult to put much confidence in this sort of use of figures to arrive at satisfactory policy decisions which impact on people and places.

Another *Economist* article, entitled 'How Poor is China?', reinforces suspicion of the arbitrary nature of numerical values attributed to matters like 'growth' factors and 'development' factors.

> In its recent poverty report [on China] the World Bank has made two important changes. First it has raised the income level below which a Chinese is deemed to be poor from $0.60 cents a day to $1 a day. This has had the effect of increasing the number of Chinese deemed to be poor from fewer than one hundred million to well over three hundred million. Second, the report has lowered estimates for Chinese income per person, measured on a purchasing power parity (PPP) basis which adjusts for the local cost-of-living. The Bank's 1996 World Development Report puts Chinese GDP per person, measured on a PPP basis, at around $2,500 in 1994. The new report puts the figure at $1,800. This change shrinks the estimated size of the Chinese economy dramatically.[5]

What are we to make of predictions and policy recommendations based on statistics and evaluations of this nature? Sachs is confident that:

> successful growth will depend, more than anything else, on economic integration with the rest of the world . . . Aid works when it is limited in time (and thus is not a narcotic) and, is part of an overall market-driven growth strategy.

The issue of how far it is possible to rely into an indefinite future on 'a market-driven growth strategy' is critical and will be discussed in Chapter 13. The point at the moment is Sachs' confident dependence on the ability of market-driven growth to solve all problems if only it can be set free to work. The evidence would seem to be very dubious except, possibly, in a small number of cases. Even in those successful cases the evidence of benefit to a majority of the people concerned is not unambiguous. As a symptom of this one may cite the title and subheading to an article in *The Economist* of 13 April 1996: 'South-East Asia's Wealth Gap – most economists believe that in East Asia increased wealth has led to increased equality. That is not how many people in the region see it.' There are similar reports from, for example, both China and India about the immense strides made by some in becoming very wealthy while the gap between even the middle class and the vast numbers of poor becomes greater and greater.

The 'on/off' nature of the actual concrete hopes which market-led development offers to what are statistically referred to as 'the lower deciles' of the world's population is well illustrated by the recent financial and economic history of Mexico. It was Mexican default on foreign debts payments in August 1982 which triggered off the world-wide debt crisis among LDCs (Less Developed Countries) which soon involved dozens of developing countries, including major economies like Brazil, Argentina, Nigeria and the Philippines. The tale of the incompetence, incomprehension and mistaken forecasts of the World Bank in relation to all this is documented, for example, in *Faith and Credit: The World Bank's Secular Empire* by Susan George and Fabrizio Sabelli, and especially in Chapter 4, 'False Prophecy'. This 'financial disaster' is, for example, described in an article by Anatole Kaletsky in *The Times* of 2 February 1995 as '[condemning] the whole of Latin America to a "lost decade" of economic depression and culminated in loan losses worth far more than the combined capital of all the big American banks'.

I am not concerned with the whole story here but with the particular history of Mexico. It is worth noting however, for further consideration below, that the 'lost decade' of development is explicitly admitted in an article in 1992 by Lawrence Summers, then the World Bank's chief economist, and cited by George and Sabelli: 'This lesson is well learnt now, but the cost of delay has been to put development on hold in many of these countries.'[6] The particular issue I am raising is that of who bears what costs in these ups and downs of international investment and struggle for development. An article in *The Economist* of 11 May 1996 in its International Section under the heading of 'Mexico: Fighting Poverty with a Credit Card' indicates, in a matter of fact way – where costs fall.

> Being poor is no fun anywhere but particularly not in volatile Mexico. The economic crises of the 1980s were hard on the poorest who saw their share of the pie shrink nearly a fifth from 1984 to 1992. By 1992, though, there seemed to be hope.

So here we are again. Never jam today, even less jam for the time being, but – persistently – hope. In 1996 Mexico remained a frequent subject for economic commentators because in December 1994 Mexico found itself back in acute crisis, referred to in the heading of a further *The Economist* article of 23 December 1995: 'Mexico's financial crisis began with a botched devaluation, culminating in an international bail-out plan led by the United States Treasury.' The plan worked – at least in the sense that there were no serious knock-on effects in financial markets across the world. With reference to other developing countries, confidence in Mexico's own financial viability was more or less restored and everybody (in governmental and financial circles) was able to breathe again. *The Economist* would publish an article on 24 February 1996 entitled 'Half-Way There in Mexico'. This was followed up in *The Economist* of 22 June 1996 by a 'box' in the Finance and Economic section entitled, 'Mexico's Debt Hat-Trick'. This was illustrated by a sketch of a Mexican determinedly shovelling dollars out of a large sombrero into the top hat held by a pleased looking Uncle Sam. Everything was clearly working fine.

Meanwhile *The Economist* published a letter in their edition of 30 March 1996 from a correspondent, one Adam Morton, which the sub-editor entitled 'Up-Side Down'.

> In 'Half-Way There in Mexico' (February 24) you emphasised the beneficial consequences of Mexico paying back $2 billion of the 'bail-out loan', as well as $750m in interest after a further DM 15m had been borrowed on the Euro-dollar market at premium rates. Primary among such benefits, you argue, has been that the 'bail-out' has yielded a profit to the lenders. Thank Heavens. You overlook the fact that the G7 nexus, involving the IMF, the World Bank and the Bank for International Settlements, has provoked the worst recession in Mexico since the 1930s.

The writer then listed a series of figures about further payments and borrowing in which Mexico will be involved and concludes:

> They will have to borrow a further $20 billion during 1996 just to balance the servicing of its existing debts. In sum the G7 nexus (and *The Economist*?) is maintaining a fiction of repayment to declare the PSO rescue a 'success', which in reality is destroying Mexico's industries and exacerbating social misery.

A month later (27 April 1996) the magazine carried a letter from Kevin Watkins, the compiler of the 1995 *OXFAM Poverty Report*. The core argument states:

The case for a bold initiative on multi-lateral debt is self-evident. Repayments to multi-lateral creditors now absorb around half of the debt repayments from the world's poorest countries, or some $3 billion annually. These transfers are beyond the fiscal and export capacity of around 30 poor countries ... They are also destroying human development prospects. Uganda's government spends more repaying multi-lateral creditors than on health care. This in a country where one child in five dies before its first birthday, because of diseases that are largely preventable. In Zambia, repayments to the IMF during the first half of the 1990s amounted to ten times government expenditure on basic education.

Watkins then refers to proposals that the IMF and World Bank are showing signs of producing, but indicates that:

eligibility for relief under their proposals includes compliance with two consecutive IMF programmes. Few countries would qualify. Those that can will have to wait for up to six years, when what is needed is debt reduction now.

The reply from the IMF printed on 11 May 1996 reads like a mere set of counter-assertions, but includes the sentence: 'But we now know that the international community has no appetite for a quick fix.' Who are this 'international community'? How do their concerns relate to local and national communities such as Mexican peasants or the struggling Mexican middle-class whose debt burdens have become incapable of repayment through the ups and downs of the peso and fluctuations of credit policy?[7] It would seem most likely that the 'international community' concerned is the international community and the 'investment community' named in *The Economist* article of 23 December 1995 mentioned above. This is a 'By Invitation' article contributed by Lawrence Summers, Deputy Secretary, now Secretary, at the US Treasury. This is the same Lawrence Summers who was chief economist at the World Bank and whose confession of errors over the 1982 onwards Third World debt crisis I have already mentioned. As 'deeply involved in the [Mexican 1994/5] bail-out' Mr Summers responded to *The Economist*'s invitation to 'draw lessons from Mexico's troubles for other emerging countries'.

The author is remarkably sure of himself given the ups and downs of the history of the relationships between the World Bank, IMF and developing countries. But it is a splendid (or depressing) example of the confidence of an utterly faithful free marketeer. I wish simply to draw attention to three tell-tale phrases which reveal the tone of his argument as Summers sets out ten lessons which 'can now be distilled'. His sixth lesson is 'the need for greater openness'. This is because 'full disclosure will attract capital by reassuring the investment community'. This goes with: 'in future the international community will have to explore the possibility of orderly work out arrangements for situations in which debt cannot be paid'. 'International community' clearly equals 'investment community', so it is in this community in which all our future hopes and indeed all our futures are 'invested'. However, as Summers' tenth lesson shows all is – or will be – well.

> There can be no substitute for continuing the work of economic integration if the momentum of reform in the developing world is to continue ... there is nothing going on in the world today that is as hopeful for humanity as the trend towards market institutions in the developing world.
>   Or, finally, none of these ten lessons represent a radical departure from past knowledge. In detail, Mexico's crisis may have seemed to belong to the twenty-first century. In basic substance, it points out eternal verities of finance.

The simplest and crudest versions of the Market, now plainly equated with global financial markets, is as beneficial and as guaranteeing as Providence. I find it somewhat suspicious that Mr Summers' article is illustrated by two photographs of children. One depicts small girls sitting at school benches, heads bent over their work with fierce concentration. The caption reads: 'I must not run a big deficit'. The other picture shows cheerful small boys and girls playing in a sunny street lined by scruffy shacks and is captioned: 'happy but poor'. Who is deceiving whom and who garners hope from 'the eternal verities of finance'? *The Times* article of 2 February 1995 written by Kaletsky to which I have already referred, is entitled 'Why Mexico Has Done the Market a Good Turn'. It is, at times, pretty fiercely critical of 'the investment community' and points out that 'the G7 Governments, led by Washington, have tried to protect their financiers from the con-sequences of their own stupidity by conjuring up vast rescue packages'. Evidence once again of the tendency to rescue the rich, leaving the poor to pay. But Kaletsky draws a lesson of hope from all this.

> The unexpected benefit of the Mexican crisis lies in its timing. A recession is now certain in Mexico and probable in most of Latin

America. [Indeed he was right, and I have already quoted evidence to that effect.] There should also be a sharp slow-down in other developing countries. This will come at a handy time for the rich industrialised countries of Europe and North America, just as it did in the mid-1980s. Flagging demand in the Third World should counteract inflation, weaken commodity prices, and reduce the pressure for higher interest rates in Europe and the US ... The long-suffering people of Mexico will find this no consolation, but the incompetence of their governments may have done the rest of the world a good turn.

No doubt this comment is meant wryly rather than cynically. Nonetheless the observation presents a disturbing example of the *obiter dicta* of economic commentators which expose, if they do not give away, the 'Market game'. 'A recession is now certain in Mexico' and 'this will come at a handy time for the rich industrialised countries ... just as it did in the mid-1980s'. There is no consolation in all this for 'the long-suffering people of Mexico' but a second-time around good turn for the rich industrialized countries in which the commentators and we ourselves overwhelmingly reside. Does this not echo and underline the case made by Galbraith in drawing attention to 'the war on the poor' that recession is no bad thing for those of us who are comfortably off.[8] Market prosperity is exposed as having no direct positive effect on human prosperity in general. It is highly selective and accompanied by adverse effects on many actual human beings. At the present this still includes the majority of contemporary human beings – if the UNDP (and other) reports on the growing gap worldwide in wealth distribution have any truth in them. To acknowledge but dismiss these large scale adverse effects *en passant* in a mere *obiter dictum* is neither an honest nor a compassionate way to offer commentary on what the Market is, how it works, and what it offers us.

It is not an honest commentary because it lays claim to 'the unexpected benefit' and to '[doing] the rest of the world a good turn' balancing these statements with reference to the costs which have been inflicted on those who cannot take part in the Market and the unrestricted power which the rich world has (especially if organized by Washington) 'to protect their financiers from their own stupidity'. Yet Kaletsky is a commentator who is constantly praising the US economic performance, presenting it as *the* model for hope for market growth and prosperity into the future. It looks as if, like the Market itself, he has no interest in, or concern to make judgements about, anything but the profit-making and taking effects of the activities of those who by their control of money supplies effectively decide what the Market delivers, where, and to whom. He thus appears on examination to be a mere market follower, rather than the critical and analytical commentator on the Market which so many of his clear and incisive articles lead one to hope that he is.

The effects of the Market are not being honestly described and assessed – assessed that is to say, in open and overt relation to the admitted relevant facts. (It is acknowledged, for example, that the people of Mexico are 'long suffering'.) The type of *obiter dicta* which I believe to be exemplified in this particular comment on the Mexican crises seem not only to ignore these people (a considerable majority of human beings in this world and a considerable minority among those living in the rich countries) who are too poor in money terms to play any positive or free part in the Market, but also positively to discount and discard them. They are unheeded ciphers while we are hopeful players in the Market's game. The question arises as to whether this is not a stance lacking in humanity and compassion.

Of course, this may just be the way the world is. Kaletsky probably takes it for granted (as one might say 'as gospel truth'), as does Jeffrey Sachs and many another proponent of the untrammelled Free Market, that there is no alternative. The one and only way out of poverty is clear – get the Free Market going, then there will be jobs, then there will be wages. Then (and only then) will these poor people register on the Market and count in a democratic society by virtue of their purchasing power. That is to say they will have some access to, and some control over, at least some money.

It becomes clear that it is very naive to accept the repeated assurance of the money-makers of this world that the way they make their money is the one and only way of prosperity for all of us. As I have already remarked, the very sound of a suggestion such as, 'what justifies my making and taking large sums of money is that this enables all the rest of you to have some hope of making some money, at any rate in the longer run, and if you suffer the necessary hardships en route' ought to put reflective persons on their guard. If one has any acquaintance with the history of ideas one will surely recognize that versions of this argument have been around ever since persons with power and wealth have felt the need for some justification of their power and legitimation of their wealth. But, then, as Skidelsky observes, economists suffer from almost total historical amnesia – if indeed they ever learnt history in the first place.[9]

Perhaps the naivety of economists over the power carried by control over money is a mere matter of ignorance of history. Or, more likely, as the investigations of my previous chapters show, there has been a widely shared and genuine belief that whether by Providence, or enlightenment intuition, or historical dialectic, or evolutionary luck, the Market has emerged to neutralize power and so ensure that unconstrained self-interest and unregulated competition, turns out – on aggregate – to do well for people, societies and the earth. Once, however, one looks seriously at these ideas, their history and their logic, it becomes obvious that such a belief is alarmingly close to a superstition, blatantly overoptimistic and, in all probability, sustained by a collusion between the self-interest of those who now do well out of the Market with the self-deceit of those who hope to do well out of it.

It may be that we cannot shift the power of our financial lords and masters but there is absolutely no reason why we should either respect or commend them; and even less reason why we should trust them. Thirty millionaires created overnight by the rejigging of some merchant bank or other institution of 'financial services' must be a con-trick of breath-taking proportions. To relate it to Adam Smith's views about the Invisible Hand in the Market looks as if it is as intellectually despicable as it is morally cynical. But I doubt if either intellect or morality come directly into it. It is much more simply the case that people who can buy their way into positions of financial power make all the money they can out of it. Why not? Individual self-interest rules. It is merely a useful common fiction – as and when fitful bursts of moralizing or practical anxiety break out – to dress it up in a thin version of an economic theory whose detailed origins are unknown to most and whose lack of compelling logic is completely ignored.

So the game goes on clothed with respectability (one, as Dean Inge of St Paul's remarked back in the 1920s, of the Seven Deadly Virtues – Respectability is a virtue which achieves not only wealth but knighthoods and life peerages). It is in some respects a profitable game. But in other respects it is a threatening and dangerous game which uses as stakes and cost-bearers the lives and environments of multitudes of poor people across the world.

If examination of the facts persuades us that the faith in the Market is not only false but a force which licenses myriads of activities which are quite as likely to have harmful effects as good ones, then one is bound to raise the question as to how far those who confidently promote such activities are acting dishonestly, promoting immorality or lacking in compassion to a degree which is criticizable, if not culpable. We are up against issues of what is true about our world and our interactions, what is possible in that world, and what we are responsible for in these respects. It is not just a matter of working the mechanisms of the Market in functional efficiency or of acting as well as you can on what everyone takes for granted is commonsense that you should be doing. There seems to be at least a *prima facie* case for suspecting that there is something twisted and distorting about the 'common' sense which we are supposed to share concerning the 'Market'.

This means that in pursuing issues to do with whether we can think again about markets, politics and people, it is impossible to avoid raising issues of honesty, morality and compassion which are implied by the ideas and proposals put forward. It is my hope that this can be done while avoiding any moralistic or personally censorious attack on particular individuals. It is, presumably, a simple matter of human respect and mutuality to give actual market proponents and operators the benefit of the doubt and assume they are acting in about as much good faith as all the rest of us seek to do. The actual moral disposition of any particular person is the responsibility of that particular person. But, acting in good faith is no guarantee that the faith is either good in its contents or moral in its effects. The raising of issues about honesty and compassion, truth and morality, cannot therefore be avoided. This difficult and uncomfortable issue of personal morality and responsibility with regard to market claims and market operations will be pursued further in Chapter 15. Meanwhile there would seem to be a moral challenge properly raised by a comment on a financial debacle involving developing countries and putting the blame on 'the incompetence of their governments'. Is it really all the fault of these incompetent governments? Has the international investment community no share of blame, and no responsibility? Especially when, as I explore in my next chapter, the international markets seem to operate on limited and selected information, with considerable incoherence and under the dominance of powers who control nominal sums of money out of all proportion to the sums used in the transactions of the 'real' markets and in the daily lives of communities.

Notes

1   Robert Skidelsky, *The World After Communism: A Polemic for Our Times* (Macmillan, 1995), p. 138.
2   Kevin Watkins, *The OXFAM Poverty Report* (UK and Ireland: OXFAM, 1995), p. 98.

3   Paul Hirst and Graham Thompson, *Globalisation in Question* (Cambridge: Polity Press in association with Oxford: Blackwell Publishers, 1996), pp. 68–72.
4   *The Economist*, By Invitation series, 29 June 1996.
5   *The Economist*, 12 October 1996.
6   Susan George and Fabrizio Sabelli, *Faith and Credit: The World Bank's Secular Empire* (Penguin, 1994), p. 83.
7   Referred to, for example, in a *Guardian* report of 18 March 1996: 'Mexican Debtors Demand Relief'.
8   See pp. 193f. above re. Galbraith's article in *The Observer*, 26 September 1996.
9   See above, p. 83.

12 Markets, the Control of Money and the Realities of Power

Financial Markets – Theory and Practice

In assessing the role of the international investment community – as represented by the global financial markets – in promoting prosperity in the less developed countries, I would like to focus on the views of Mr Summers.[1] Mr Summers was once chief economist of the World Bank which, together with the International Monetary Fund, acts as a financial intermediary between the world financial community and the developing countries. As a respected voice of this investment community he writes, as we have already seen, with assurance of the 'eternal verities finance'. He is clear that, 'there is nothing going on in the world today that is as hopeful for humanity as the trend towards market institutions in the developing world'.

I have been arguing that this hopefulness is not self-evident – especially *for the time being* – to the vast majority of the inhabitants of developing countries. Market institutions' delivery of benefits into the future depends on how enduringly true 'the eternal verities of finance' are. Mr Summers is assured that they can so deliver. He thus expresses the same faith in 'the Market as Providence' that I was tracking in *The Economist* supplement of October 1995.[2] I have been examining descriptions of the Market machine or organism and the various grounds on which it has been claimed that this mechanico-organic Market can be relied upon to work consistently to promote generally increasing prosperity and freedom. I believe I have demonstrated that the descriptions are insufficiently coherent and the grounds insufficiently compelling. The compulsion driving the Market is the power and prestige of the market operators and the faith in what market operations have delivered so far. It is not the Market's inherent logic, its scientifically perceivable dynamic, nor its guaranteeable promise. Mr Summers typically expresses a faith he has read into economic happenings. It is indeed, as Samuel Brittan says, a way of looking at the world. Once this way of looking at the world is claimed to be, in its essential details, an inevitable way of looking at the world, we are well on the way to being diverted from a hopeful faith into a fatal conceit.

In order to underline the urgent need for a radical rethinking of our commonly accepted approach to the Free Market, I propose to examine how the operations of the investment community are described and evaluated by those who comment upon them, and take part in investing in them. The transactions which take place in the financial markets underline to the nth degree that the data on which the price information system of the Market operates take no account of people, use (save the use of making money out of money for the operators in the Market), or the future (save the very short-term 'futures' of financial instruments). So the data-deficiency of the whole market system (with regard to the real world, real humanity and real prospects) is glaringly underlined. Far from neutralizing any distorting or overcentralized power in market operations at large, the financial markets actually concentrate and exert a self-interested power of their own. Ultra-rapid responding, multi-programmed, computers show no signs of having an omega factor relating to general beneficence built into their programs to go with the beta factors about risk.

The financial markets form networks which can force decisions about the value and application of money via the activities of a small – and increasingly amalgamated and conglomerated – number of institutions and people who operate in and on a market of their own. Current evidence suggests that the power of the Market is running in the reverse direction to that claimed by economic orthodoxy. It is not guided by the purchasing power of the masses of individual choosers or enterprise operators. It is the concentrated power of the operators in the financial markets which determine how, when, and to what extent the would-be purchasers have opportunities for access to the money which everyone requires if he or she is to transact in the Market. Everything turns on the availability of money.

The information system of the Market works through *prices*. For prices to mean anything, there has to be a medium which is generally accepted as a comparative standard of value, a means of exchange at the prices comparatively valued and a store of value for future transactions. This medium is 'money' in its various forms. So the way money is operated is absolutely central to the way the information system which is the Market actually operates. This central question of the way money 'works', or is 'worked', is therefore crucial to the issue I am pursuing, *viz*, What grounds are there for the conviction that the markets operate benignly overall and with the guarantee of increasingly shared prosperity?

Who or what, in reality, controls the availability of money? And who or what controls the controllers? The answer to these two questions appear to be that the financial markets control the availability of money and no one controls the financial markets. Indeed, as *The Economist* so proudly claims in the Supplement I considered in Chapter 2, this is all to the good. For the financial markets are the wisest guides available to us in the literally vital matter of setting the Market free to promote our prosperity and freedom. Consider therefore how the markets exercise this universal trusteeship.

In order to keep in mind as far as possible actual people and places where this trusteeship of the financial markets resides, I return to the case of Mr Summers and the eternal verities of finance versus the ordinary inhabitants of a developing country. It should be noted that in the Mexican debacle of 1994/5 the 'eternal verities of finance' did not exercise an inescapable discipline on Mr Summers' colleagues in the financial markets of the USA and its allies among the Group of Seven leading economic countries. As Kaletsky wrote in *The Times* of 2 February 1995: 'The Seven Governments, led by Washington, have tried to protect their financiers from the consequences of their own stupidity by conjuring up vast rescue packages.'[3] Governments in the developed world, therefore, can intervene when it helps financiers to protect their funds. However, any government's direct intervention to help the poor in developing countries to gain access to small funds which might help them to begin to enter the Market is frowned upon, if not forbidden. Under the eternal verities of finance, as in other regards, there is one law for the rich and another for the poor.

An apologist for the Free Market and, in particular, for the global financial markets might well dismiss this as superficial sentiment. Subsidies can never be sufficient to set the poor up in enterprises which could be viable in today's markets. Such subsidies only reinforce the poor's dependence on hand-outs, while imparting no hope of entry into the economic transactions in the Market wherein hope solely resides. Help to keep the capital of financial institutions largely intact is justified because it is this capital which, when properly invested, provides the rising tide of enterprises able to flourish in this economic world of interactive global markets.

This is one way of looking at things. But it is also worth noting for further consideration that the fact that the markets cannot sustain small-scale, local enterprises with a low rate of return on investment may be one of the decisive pieces of evidence that the markets as at present organized (i.e. dominated by demands for high, short-term returns on capital invested) are increasingly useless for – and indeed hostile to – precisely those types of economic development required if *most people* in the world are to have a chance of joining in market activities which will both better their lot and enable an indefinitely sustainable level of economic activity.

I leave that issue for my final chapters. Meanwhile, consider the common theory of the markets and their relations to economic activity. In the over-all market scheme of things, the financial markets are concerned with general allocative efficiency. It will be remembered, that according to the famous definition of Professor Lionel Robbins, economics is the science that studies the allocation of scarce means among given but competing ends. The 'scarce means' with which the financial markets are concerned is capital. The 'given but competing ends' are the aims, purposes and productions of various corporations, firms, institutions and individuals who require supplies of capital to fuel their varied economic activities or set up new enterprises. The 'real' economy (that is the vast network of producers of supplies of goods and services which provide the jobs, and the wherewithal for the livelihood of all of us) is crucially dependent on obtaining sufficient allocations of money as initiating, working and developing capital.

The financial markets therefore play this critical role at the heart of the whole economic system in the provision and distribution of capital across the world. Money, of course, is neither an unlimited, nor free, resource. How, therefore, is money to be distributed? Obviously in the most profitable way, that is in a manner which brings about the best profit for the suppliers of capital (i.e. interest/return on the lending or investing) and the best possible profit for the entrepreneurs of, and investors in, the enterprises of the 'real' markets. Providing such distribution can be done efficiently, this will tend to produce maximum economic growth because capitalists will make enough money on their capital returns to have more to spare for further investment, while entrepreneurs will have more money to spare for developing their businesses, retain profits for themselves and their investors, as well as employing more people, improving wages and so on. The theory depends on the money available being used in the way which will produce the maximum possible growth at all possible levels.

Only enterprises which can plan and then deliver sufficient profitability on the capital invested in them are able to compete successfully in the financial markets for sufficient capital to keep going, extend the range of the business or start up further enterprises. Just as the 'real' market is the means to allocative efficiency in the wealth-producing, 'on the ground', so the financial markets are the means – parallel and similarly operating means – for capital and money. This assumption that the very term 'Market' licenses the assumption of Adam Smith-type reliance on the operations of 'an Invisible Hand', transferred from the limited markets of the eighteenth century to the globalized financial markets of the end of the twentieth century, seems to be completely unwarranted by observation.

However, current economic orthodoxy (at any rate that peddled by politicians and their supporting economic gurus) assumes that the financial markets have developed (like the 'real' markets) as an evolved information system working by price – that is to say by the pricing and prices of money as this is developed by financial services and financial markets through the determination and manipulation of interest rates. Two things are required of the operations of the financial markets to discharge the basic and archetypal market function for the efficient allocation of capital. First, the market must produce prices (i.e. interest rates) which reflect what lenders of capital want – or need – to receive. For example, it is commonplace for market commentators to point out that mutual and pension fund managers (who are currently providing more and more of the funds available for investment in stocks, shares and bonds) must have results (returns) which improve steadily, are above the average rates of interest-receiving and are short-term returns because results must constantly show on the listings of their fund's results.

The prices (interest rates) will also reflect what borrowers of capital are ready to pay and the transactions of the financial markets will both convey and react to the relevant information. This last point is very important, for it touches on the question to be taken up shortly as to how far the financial market 'massages its own messages' (i.e. influences its prices through its own expectations or reactions).

Besides the role of the markets in the pricing, and therefore the allocation of, capital there is a further influential function to be performed. In order that the information which is relevant to pricing may be available in such a way that the prices themselves may be realistic, comparable and efficient, the free markets must also provide the means for the price signals (which inform the markets in international trading in the 'real' markets) to be interchangeably comparable. That is to say, not only must money be the means of exchange, but in order to be an efficient means of exchange the various denominations which are given to units of money in the currency systems of the world must also be either equivalent (literally 'equi-valent' means 'equally powerful' which, in the case of currency and prices, means equally powerful in purchasing power), or easily comparable by some other standard of reference. Unless such equivalent and comparable signals are available, capital will be 'mis-invested' or mis-directed. The people or institutions investing will not have accurate information about the real worth of what is being produced in one economic context (or country) in strictly comparable terms to what is going on in other economic contexts (or countries). Thus the 'comparative advantage' (between, say, cheapness on the one hand, or greater cost but wider range of usefulness on the other) of one set of goods or bundle of services in one country (or trading zone) with that of another will not be realistic. The transactions of exchange and trading will, therefore, not achieve allocative efficiency and the world as a whole will not be getting 'value for money'.

But, we are told, the world *is* getting value for money, for the financial markets, by and large, allocate capital in ways which produce the best possible contribution to more and cheaper production and trading. Thus profits and returns steadily rise over time along with market sales and the widening of distribution. This efficient and steady growth in products is the very essence of the Market and how it supplies us all with the promise of benefiting from this ever-expanding access to the Market. It is in this way that Mr Summers' 'eternal verities of finance' refer to that which will *eventually* co-opt all and sundry into the Market and provide jobs for all. The process takes time; it is uneven and uncertain, but it will eventually work and there is no equivalently satisfactory alternative. Interfere with this process and interrupt its steady progress towards its all embracing destiny and 'we' recede from our goals of prosperity and freedom for all. That, therefore, is how the financial markets discharge the trusteeship 'invested' in them for ensuring the optimum use of capital towards the ultimate benefit of all.

In working this beneficent circle of capital and trade, the markets inevitably exercise influence over the fiscal possibilities of governments. For all governments now exercise whatever powers they have over the trading and living activities of their respective nations, within the global markets wherein the deregulated circulation of capital and financial assets takes place. This means that financial markets – and most notably the foreign exchange markets – will (particularly by determining exchange rates) make great differences to the possibilities open to governments by way of such matters as balances of trade, fiscal options (how governments can spend, raise money and borrow) and interest rates. This may appear to be restrictive and coercive, but we are told it is healthily so.

The case for the wisdom of financial markets is that the two processes I have just outlined (for allocations of capital and for producing, through exchange markets, a balancing-out comparability of trading transactions) produce justly comparable conditions for international trading by producing prices which are realistic, comparable, and efficiency-promoting. All this happens by the various actors in the 'real' Market who need capital interacting with the operators in the financial market. Prices are thus produced – in the form of interest rates and currency exchange rates – which enable the most effective dealings in capital for enterprises and the growth in economic production of all kinds on which we all depend.

Thus the financial markets provide in their own sphere (that of capital and money) what all markets, according to economic orthodoxy and the Market mantra, are believed to produce. The markets produce appropriately denominated prices which enable the maximum efficiency of production, consumption, jobs and prosperity. The financial markets facilitate the circulation and allocation of money throughout the world and at all levels, through the Market's means of collecting and circulating information about the demands, needs and availability of money. The information comes together to fix prices of money, prices of financial dealings in all sorts of financial instruments, and prices for facilitating the whole process. Again, therefore, like all markets the financial markets are involved in the operations of innumerable individual transactions of self-interest in such a way that these market operations transmute the transactions of self-interested individuals into aggregate effects which benefit all – in this case through the efficient allocation of capital. The physical and metaphysical successor to Adam Smith's Invisible Hand, the Market's evolved information system working by prices, thus maintains its beneficent guidance.

Observation makes it extremely difficult to believe this. It looks as if the financial markets fix and manipulate the prices in the interests of their own operators in an increasingly self-contained and self-determining way. It does not look as if the financial markets *facilitate* the formation of prices as emergent effects of individual transactions as they take place. Rather the various groups of operators in the financial markets seem to *make* prices. In practice the financial markets are not price-enablers, they are price-fixers. What they fix is the price of money. They, therefore, have powerful control over the availability, allocation and, indeed, the very creation of money. In so far as this turns out to be so, then there is not much hope of our benefiting generally from the 'wisdom' of the markets. We are much more likely to be exploited by those who operate the markets.

The obvious reason for doubting that the current financial markets can be playing the role of wise and beneficent guides of the global economic activities of all of us on our shared and common earth is that, statistically, their transactions are dominated by speculative efforts to make money out of transactions which are concerned purely with money. Ingenious minds are always devising new types of financial instruments which they can bet on, or deal in, to provide hedges against the way things turn out. All this provides investment opportunities for sufficiently funded experts to play the markets in ways which will add to savers' money-denominated capital without this capital ever being involved in any 'real' wealth creating activities at all. There is nothing productive about these activities which directly adds to the goods and services which are available to human beings across the globe for the enhancement of their day-to-day affairs and for the provision of employment to more and more people.

The foreign exchange markets are held to play a decisive role in administering the 'wisdom' of the markets. Consider, therefore, the type of statistics commonly reported about transactions in the Forex markets. That is to say, in the markets (of which the biggest is still located in the City of London) which deal exclusively in exchange operations concerning the values and parities of national currencies – i.e. the pricing and processing of FOReign currency EXchange. The 'Forex' markets, which are among the biggest of any kind of market in the world, are the means whereby payment is made between one country and another.

Let me pick up one example of these statistics that I have already quoted from the *Survey of the World Economy* published in *The Economist* in 1995.[4] A panel entitled 'Masters of the Universe' illustrated how by 1995 the value of daily foreign exchange trading was vastly greater than that of reserves in the Central Banks of the world. The wry title 'Masters of the Universe' went alongside an immensely hopeful exposition (practically a gospel) of the role the exchange markets played. I want now to look at these Forex statistics in a little more detail. They certainly highlight the domination of the Forex markets. But once it becomes clear that there are no sufficient theoretical reasons for taking this market dominance as guaranteeing beneficence the question to consider is: Does it seem likely that those vast sets of transactions in the exchange market are *in practice* beneficent and look as if they can be relied upon to remain so?

How is the power of the foreign exchange markets related to trading in the 'real' markets where wealth other than financial wealth (i.e. the sort of wealth that people can actually live by) is produced? It is generally agreed that the vast majority of transactions in the Forex markets are not directly related to trading transactions in the 'real' markets – that is to say they are purely transactions involving money, out of which money is gained (or lost).

For example, in his 1995 book *When Corporations Rule the World*, David C. Korten cites from *The Death of Money* (1993) by J. Kurtzmann:[5] 'A daily figure between eight hundred billion dollars to one trillion dollars is changing hands each day in the international currency markets.' In Autumn 1995 *The Economist* cited data from an April 1995 survey 'from the World's central banks' whereby:

> It is ... possible to make a good guess at how much money is sloshing around in the currency markets. The ten biggest financial centres have seen trading volumes grow by an average of 47% since April 1992, when the last survey was carried out – slightly faster than the 42% increase seen over the previous three year period.[6]

That is to say, that the business of the financial markets is a booming business showing remarkable increases year on year. Later the article continues: 'Since [1983] trading has exploded twenty-fold spurred by fancy new financial instruments and increasingly powerful computers and telecommunications.' I shall be considering this further indication of the immense and self-generated expansion of the financial markets when I discuss derivatives and other financial instruments shortly. Meanwhile in the exchange markets alone *The Economist* states: 'Using this growth rate suggests that the total net daily currency trading has jumped to about 1.3 trillion dollars, from 880 billion in 1992.' Towards the conclusion of its reports and comments *The Economist* adds the information that: 'Only 7% of London's foreign-exchange transactions and 17% of New York's involve non-financial companies' – although it tends to play down the significance of this. Other commentators, however, treat this small proportion of the transactions which involve 'non-financial companies' (i.e. go directly outside and beyond the financial markets) as highly significant. Thus Korten reports from Kurtzmann that:

> Most of the eight hundred million dollars in currency that is traded
> ... goes for very short-term speculative investments – from a few
> hours to a few days to a maximum of a few weeks ... That money is
> mostly engaged in nothing more than making money.

Further, Kurtzmann estimates that 'for every one dollar circulating in
the productive world economy twenty dollars to fifty dollars circulates in
the economy of pure finance – though no one knows the ratios for sure'.
Kurtzmann then claims that, even allowing for the uncertainty, the
'eight hundred billion dollars to trillion dollars [which] changes hands
each day [is] far in excess of the twenty to twenty-five billion dollars
required to cover daily trade in goods and services'.[7]

Similar comments on the disproportionality between the internal
financial market trading and the trading in 'real' markets, or in the trade
directly between these markets and the financial markets, are common.
Thus Philip Stephens, commenting on financial events in Nigel Law-
son's chancellorship in 1984/5, writes: 'But the world was entering an
era in which massive capital flows across the foreign exchanges were
becoming *divorced from the underlying trade patterns which once determined them* [my emphasis].' He illustrates this by commenting: 'In this
dawning world of hot money less than 5% of foreign exchange
transactions were linked to longer term patterns of trade.'[8] While in
August 1995 *The Economist* could comment that: 'the value of foreign
exchange trading is now seventy times bigger than that of world trade'.[9]

If this is taken for granted then it would seem very difficult to have
confidence that the financial markets are serving the 'real' markets and
promoting the 'wisdom' of allocative efficiency as the orthodoxy theory
of market beneficence maintains. The markets appear to be pursuing
their own special interests, focused on making money out of money.

A reasonable diagnosis of *practice* (as distinct from a theoretical hope
based on faith in the Market mantra) would seem to be much nearer that
set out by John Grieve Smith.

> International Markets are not exercising the function of channelling
> investment efficiently between countries. Movements of capital
> involving real resources are swamped by purely financial transac-
> tions that are speculative in the sense that major investment funds
> are now held in whatever currency and country has the best short-
> term prospects and are subject to transfer by instant decision. The
> Bank of International Settlements' triennial survey of foreign
> exchange turn-over in April 1995 showed a fifty percent increase

since their 1992 survey. Turn-over had reached 1230 billion dollars per day and foreign trade only accounted for 3.5 days' turn-over a year, the rest was accounted for by capital movements, mainly short-term. The problem is to prevent these short-term transactions rather than trade payments of real investment, dominating the determination of exchange rates.[10]

The financial markets are not interacting with the real markets in producing exchange rates which reflect conditions in these markets; rather the financial markets' own transactions are the weightier determining factor.

Money 'Sloshing Around'

It is not simply the disproportion between the money traded in money markets and the money negotiated for 'real' trade purposes which cast grave doubts on the claim that financial markets operate with beneficent and allocative efficiency. There are also a number of more detailed aspects of the operations of the financial markets which add greatly to the volatility of the prices evolved from the process. (The prices concerned here are the exchange values of currencies and the rates of interest applicable in capital markets.) These features of market transactions operate to intensify the degree to which the financial markets react to their own processes. Thus strengthening the evidence that the financial markets are 'a law unto themselves' which inflict their prices on the 'real' markets. They do not operate as part of a mutually interactive process between the 'real' markets and the financial markets out of which prices emerge.

There has been an immense development of *secondary* markets dealing with financial instruments *derived* from the primary assets with which financial markets deal, *viz.* shares, bonds and currency. These secondary markets and, in particular the use of derivatives, are not confined to dealings on the currency exchanges, although they are particularly and obviously influential – and, indeed, notorious with regard to the Forex markets. They are increasingly diversified with regard to all manner of financial transactions from hedging against the effects of unfavourable changes in interest rates to turning mortgages or bad debts or the assets and liabilities of bankrupt companies into securities which can be traded in specialized markets by anyone with sufficient know-how and capital to cover the likely occurrence of bad risks until the good risks pay off. As Anton Kaletsky puts it: 'The only qualifications to play this game are a smattering of economic knowledge, plenty of self-confidence and a big credit-line.'[11] Kaletsky was writing about a particular juncture in the currency game but his remarks seem applicable to the steadily increasing number of games set up by secondary operators in financial markets. The more the bewildered outsider seeks comprehension in this 'rich' variety the more it seems incredible that anything should control or guide in such a game of games other than the determination of all players to make as much money out of the money 'sloshing around' as they possibly can.

To return, however, to a more systematic line of enquiry, in 1997 Don Atkinson contributed an article to *The Guardian* referring to the Lombard Street Research's January Review:

> Most defences of financial markets are expressed in terms of the improvement in resource allocation achieved in the primary markets ... But they say less, or nothing at all, about how society gains from secondary market activity.[11]

If such a point is raised from 'Lombard Street' itself, there must be some grounds for questioning how far the actual current operations of the primary markets as operated by the secondary financial markets fulfil the roles relating to 'allocative efficiency'. I persevere therefore in considering the apparent effects of the secondary markets and particularly those operations to do with derivatives.

In *The Economist* survey examined in Chapter 3 there is a revealing comment about derivatives in the article 'Back to the Future'. 'Transactions using derivatives cost, perhaps, only one tenth as much as those in the underlying cash markets, giving market players another set of potent weapons with which to attack governments.'[13] This is aggressive language but there is no harm in this for *The Economist* because governments are liable to be economically unwise while financial markets are, by definition or by faith, economically wise. But what actually goes on in these 'transactions using derivatives [which] cost, perhaps, only one tenth as much as those in the underlying cash markets'? Gambling. What began as a form of insurance ('hedging') for investors against a fall in share prices has exploded over the last decade into a set of specialized financial markets which have a more-or-less self-contained life of their own and are operated by those who work in them with the sole purpose of making money out of money. What began as financial 'services' to trade, industry and investment in the 'real' markets has developed into an expanding financial industry with its own concerns which dwarf the original service element.

The description of these secondary market operations as 'gambling' is common practice among financial commentators and journalists, regardless of their particular political or economic perspective. A typical example can be found in an article in *The Economist* towards the end of 1996. Entitled, 'Cruising in Neutral', with a sub-title which starts: '"Hedge Funds" are now synonymous with gambling', it is primarily a discussion about a new type of hedge fund which claims to be market neutral. It is useful for the purposes of my brief excursion into the mysteries of derivatives because it opens by summarizing the situation:

> Were he alive today, Alfred Winslow Jones, a pioneering Wall Street investor, would be delighted and saddened in equal measure. Fifty-odd years ago, Mr Jones launched the world's first hedge fund, so-called because his investments were partly hedged – or insured – against a fall in share prices. Since then, the industry that he spawned has grown mighty, managing about three hundred billion dollars for wealthy individuals and institutions ... It has also become wayward. Until recently, the most celebrated modern hedge fund managers were as likely to multiply their bets in the currency and capital markets as they were to hedge them.[14]

It is this 'multiplying of bets' which has provided the heady excitement to derivative market operations and increasing concern among those who are concerned for the effects of these markets on the financial and trading affairs of the world at large.

One of the reasons why derivative trading is a source of worry is indicated by Ruth Kelly in her chapter on 'Derivatives – A Growing Threat to "The International System"' in *Managing the Global Economy*.[15]

> There are two main reasons which give [to hedge funds] much more financial clout than other funds of their size. First, they take highly leveraged positions in the market, that is they borrow up to fifty times the amount of their capital from banks in order to take aggressive bets. Second, by using derivative products, the power of that money is magnified, because only a small fraction of the notional cost, or face value, of a derivative contract is needed up front. In other words, hedge funds can take huge bets in which way a market will move without putting up much of their own cash. If

they get it right they can even reinvest the profits, helping to maintain the momentum of the original movement. The trouble comes when they get it wrong.[16]

Taking 'highly leveraged positions' is a feature of secondary financial markets which needs to be faced up to in any assessment of whether there are any reasonably assured grounds for looking to the financial markets for overall 'wisdom' or 'trusteeship'. As J.K. Galbraith points out, there is nothing new in 'leverage'.

> All financial innovation involves, in one form or another, the creation of debt secured in greater or lesser adequacy by real assets. This was true in one of the earliest seeming marvels: when banks discovered they could print bank-notes and issue them to borrowers in a volume in excess of the hard-money deposits in the banks' strong rooms. The depositors could be counted upon, it was believed or hoped, not to come all at once for their money. There was no seeming limit to the debt that could thus be leveraged on a give volume of hard cash. A wonderful thing. The limit became apparent, however, when some alarming news, perhaps of the extent of the leverage itself, caused too many of the original depositors to want their money at the same time. All subsequent financial innovations have involved similar debt creation leveraged against more limited assets with only modification in the earlier designed. All crises have involved debt that in, in one fashion or another, has become dangerously out of scale in relation to the underlying means of payment.[17]

It has always been a feature of financial markets to be speculative and to play games with money. Each new variation makes money for a while, for the better informed and luckier players until the speculative bubble bursts because the nominal sums of money created are too far out of proportion to anything cashable or liveable upon, in the 'real' world beyond the markets.

Thus, hedge funds and derivatives in general are, in Galbraithian terms, simply another set of developments of 'the same old game'. They are now even causing alarm bells to ring among the financially orthodox because they 'take highly leveraged positions' and because the debt they nominally incur 'has become dangerously out of scale in relation to the underlying means of payment'. This feature of the derivative markets is magnified by the arrangements whereby 'hedge funds can take huge bets in which way a market will move without putting up much of their own cash'. This is, so to speak, leverage upon leverage.

A rough measure of the disproportion involved may be obtained from a 1995 report of the Bank of International Settlements.[18] The report is not on the totality of derivative trading but only on what the reporter describes as 'the exotic and *unregulated* over-the-counter (OTC) derivatives market [my emphasis]'. (That is the report does not refer to the regular exchange-based trade in derivatives which – at the time of the report – was larger than the OTC trade.) The report 'Showed that the notional amounts of the contracts on a typical day was 40.7 trillion dollars, but, of that, only 1.7 trillion dollars was at risk.'[19] The proportion of 1.7 trillion dollars to 40.7 trillion dollars presumably gives some indication of the extent of at least the stage one leverage involved in these operations. It is also, I think, a further indication of the highly leveraged nature of the transactions involved that, as my initial quotation from *The Economist* on hedge funds reported: 'The industry ... has grown mightily, managing about three hundred billion dollars.' The figures I am putting together are not strictly comparable for they are organized for different purposes from differing parts of the 'industry' referred to. But I suggest they serve to give some indication of the problems involved in claiming direct causative connections between transactions in the financial markets and the conditions of transactions in the 'real' markets. Here, in one section of the financial markets alone, it looks as if one 'industry' with a manageable capital of 300 billion dollars is 'multiplying [its] bets in the currency and capital markets, in relation to operations which, daily, put 1.7 trillion dollars at risk in relation to contracts referring to notional [i.e. primary market] values of 40.7 trillion dollars'. Suppose all these denominated sums had to be turned into cash, where should we be? Yet this virtual reality, virtual money, set of games is supposed, in theory, to assure the ultimately wise guidance of the overall financial and economic system. The vastness of the figures involved hardly guarantee that the operations express 'wisdom', nor that the efforts are beneficently 'wealth-creating' in the longer run for all.

This point about disproportionality can also be put in relation to trading in the 'real' markets rather than from the perspective of speculation in the financial markets. Two illustrative examples occur in Kelly. She writes of the growth of the outstanding derivative contracts in exchange-trades and OTC contracts combined:

> The notional value quintupled to an estimated 8 trillion dollars at the end of 1991 from 1.6 trillion dollars in 1987. That is equivalent

to an increase from 35% of US GDP to 140% US GDP. In 1994 those numbers are even greater.[20]

One may compare also her comment when writing about the 'frenzy on the world's financial markets' at the beginning of February 1994:

> On the trading floor of Liffe, the London Futures Exchange, dealers were overwhelmed with orders. Prices crashed . . . On that same day, trading on Liffe hit an all-time high of £300 billion – roughly equivalent to half of the UK's annual gross domestic product.[21]

Further, it is noted by Korten that the 'total value of outstanding derivatives contracts was estimated to be about 12 trillion dollars in 1994 with growth projected to 18 trillion dollars by 1999'.[22]

In 1993 *The Economist* estimated the value of the world's total stock of productive fixed capital to be around 20 trillion dollars. In the statistics of its trading transactions, the derivatives market (like the foreign exchange market in which it is extensively, but not exclusively, involved) is much more concerned with itself than with the trading and operating of the primary assets on which its bets are placed. This would appear to underline a point made by Keynes. Philip Stephens, for example, comments: 'Keynes demonstrated that in a modern, credit-based economy, money was as much an instrument for speculative investment as a means for facilitating transactions in the real economy.'[23] The principal practical point at issue (and this has important political implications) is whether the proliferation of financial market activities has now reached (or passed) the point where in our present 'modern, credit-based economy' money 'as an instrument of speculative investment' has developed a dominating position which not only controls the price of money in the real economy but also threatens the healthy development of that economy.

The immediate threat, which is not infrequently referred to by financial commentators and by reports emanating from various supervisory or professional bodies, is the basic threat that arises from all leverage – *viz.* whether the markets are habitually and increasingly incurring the risk of debts that have 'become dangerously out of scale in relation to the underlying means of payment'.[24] As Kelly writes of the 1994 bond market crash:

> Concerns were triggered that, if hedge funds suffered heavy loses by playing in the market the 'wrong' way they could start to default on

their bank loans – and that, if the funds could not settle their debts, could spark a chain-reaction affecting the whole financial system.[25]

So far nothing worse has happened than the collapse of Barings and various comparatively minor crises (although not 'minor' for the principal participants involved) including some local authorities both in this country and in the USA. We may just be witnessing normal financial speculative win and lose. Although this is not, perhaps, the visible conduct one would expect from financial markets exercising wise trusteeship over the global economy.

The systemic risks involved in all this, however, are serious. A third leader in *The Financial Times* in summer 1997 entitled 'Global Risks' expressed these concerns.

> Central Bankers around the world are becoming nervous ... The Bank of International Settlements ... worries that the frothiness of the markets could have systemic consequences.
>
> ... The former head of the Federal Reserve Bank ... warned that the growing complexity and integration of financial flows would make it much harder to manage shocks such as the 1987 stock market crash;
>
> ... Now comes a report from the Group of Thirty, a top financial think-tank, which explores the scope for limiting systemic risk in a world where the larger financial institutions and markets have outgrown national accounting, legal and supervisory arrangements. Improvised crisis management, it argues, will become more difficult against that background.[26]

However, it reported, 'Leading global institutions ... see no threat to their own survival or that of their counterparties.' The writer thinks this 'looks complacent' and points out various difficulties before ending up with what is surely a very sinister give-away remark. (As I have sought to indicate at various points, it is the *obiter dicta* of financial commentators and experts which are significant. When they are not consciously expounding the official theories and mantras of the Market their incidental remarks are much more revealing.) 'Since many global players are likely to be deemed too big to fail if threatened with insolvency, tax payers of the world are heavily at risk.' This remark is all the more disturbing because there is increasing evidence that tax payers are tending to 'disappear'. People and companies who are part of the globally mobile elite are said to be moving outside the scope of national taxation leaving the ordinary, rooted populations of the world (the workers and the rest of us) to bear the burden. But, leaving this dimension aside, it is sufficiently alarming to learn that *The Financial Times* does not expect the financial markets to handle the risks they create but assumes that they may have to rely on tax payers to bail them out. Clearly the financial markets do not exercise promising economic wisdom. They exploit risk-taking for profitable money-making to the limits where tax payers in the real markets – the very same who are supposed to put their hope for a prosperous future in the guidance of these financial markets – will have to pay up for their failures. Perhaps we should expect this. The tax payers of the USA had to bail out the collapsed Savings and Loan Associations which 'were allowed to retain a highly effective access to government funds through public guarantee of their deposits'.[27] We have already noted the USA organized bail-out in the Mexican crisis of 1994 – again at the expense of the taxpayers of the countries concerned. The financial markets are aligned on financial brigandage not on providing beneficent guidance for the world economy as it effects all of us. (While I have been writing this book, events have moved on to underline all this. See especially Chapter 14.)

We have to be clear about this. People able to reach the levers of power have always tended to use them for their own advantage. Why should it be any different when the levers of power have come to rest with those people who control money? Adam Smith himself had a cautious view of merchants and market dealers.

> The interest of the dealers, however ... is always in some respects different from, and even opposite to, that of the public. To widen the market and to narrow the competition, is always in the interest of the dealers. To widen the market may frequently be agreeable enough to the interests of the public; but to narrow the competition must always be against it, and can serve only to enable the dealers, by raising their profits above what they naturally would be, to levy, for their own benefit, an absurd tax on the rest of their fellow citizens. The proposal of any new law or regulation of commerce which comes from this order ought always to be listened to with great precaution, and ought never to be adopted until after having been long and carefully examined, not only with the most scrupulous, but with the most suspicious attention. It comes from an order of men whose interest is never exactly the same with that of the public, who have generally an interest to deceive and even to oppress

the public, and who accordingly have upon many occasions, both deceived and oppressed it.[28]

Adam Smith might have been somewhat disappointed by the present political love affair with Business. Nonetheless the grip of the Market myth and mantra are firm. The power of the comptrollers of money is growing as the global banks and corporations amalgamate and increasingly detach themselves from particular localities and national states.

In case these last observations should be taken to be mere anti-market rhetoric, and in order to gain a clearer view of the pathologies of current market behaviour so that ideas might be provoked about getting it back on course for what it is worth, consider two further features of the financial markets. These are the intensifying degree to which market operations are computer-driven and the way in which market operations are increasingly influenced more by their own expectations than they are by the wider world of economic activities in general.

The role of computers and, therefore, of computer programmers, in running the financial markets is briefly indicated by a short piece from *The Economist* in August 1995 entitled 'Is Monte Carlo Bust?'

> Wall Street is often likened to a casino. In one respect at least the jibe hits the mark; security firms spend tens of millions of dollars every year on systems employing a complex mathematical technique, known as the Monte Carlo Method, to run models for valuing derivatives.[29]

The article reports two mathematicians who believe that 'they have found a new technique that is faster than the standard one'. The method was original developed by atom-bomb scientists as 'a way of tackling problems that defy simple calculations'. It involves running large numbers of data simulations through a sufficiently complex computer and then correlating and analysing results to 'reach a solution that has a low enough margin of error to be of use' (i.e. apply the formulaic computer-procedure and your guesses will be more reliable than just guessing).

> In finance we are told such computerised simulations are a standard approach to valuing all sorts of derivatives, as well as mortgage-backed securities that contain complex options. Indeed multi-tranche, mortgage-backed issues, some of which have lengthy maturities, are among the hardest financial instruments to value

because they face the biggest uncertainties across a large number of variables. How might interest rates move? How many mortgage-holders will chose to pay back their loans early if they do?

The mathematicians featured believed that they had found a more accurately predictive method than the Monte Carlo one. It still required further testing but the promise of their method, according to the article, had already caused 'a fierce battle among several finance houses for [one of their] services'. Why? Because, if I understand these complex matters rightly, the speed at which reasonably reliable predictions can be reached and acted upon is of the essence of profit-making in the financial markets. For example, in commenting on arbitrage trading Korten observes:

> The margins are narrow, but the action is essentially riskless, and when large sums of money are involved, the strategy can be quite profitable. The key is to act before anyone else notices the same opportunity. Speed is so important that one firm recently spent thirty-five million dollars to buy a super-computer simply to gain a two second advantage in arbitraging stock futures in Tokyo.[30]

Note the amount of money involved in updating computers. You have to have command of a lot of money to make a lot of money. Size is of the essence if you are to produce the speed which is of the essence to produce the profits. Power over the world's markets and the allocation of capital which will, it is alleged, promote the enterprises which provide the jobs which are to give money-access to markets to ordinary people, is thus in the hands of the computerized money-makers. Further, the decisions which implement this power are taken with the help of computers which are working on data abstracted from human and local realities. This abstraction is heightened by the speed with which vast sums of money are switched around the world between the various assets traded. The primary concern is not long-term investment in enterprises producing opportunities for wealth at ground level. All that matters is profit-taking in the monetary manipulations.

This is well-described in a summary passage from Korten's chapter on 'The Money Game'.

> These computer programs are not trading stocks, at least in the old sense, because they have no regard for the company which issues the equity. And they are not trading bonds per se because the programs could not care less if they are lending money to Washington,

London or Paris. They are not trading currencies, either, since the currencies the programs buy and sell are simply monies to be turned over in order to gain a certain rate of return. And they are not trading futures products. The futures markets are only convenient places to shop. The computers are simply ... trading mathematically precise descriptions of financial products (stocks, currencies, bonds, options, futures).

... Which exact product fits the description hardly matters as long as all the parameters are in line with the description contained in the computer program. For stocks, any one will do if its volatility, price, the exchange rules, yield and beta (risk co-efficient) fit the computer's description.[31]

Thus money rules both the making of money and its allocation. The more one finds out about how the financial markets actually work, the more one is forced to conclude that the operators in these markets do not offer us the beneficence of an open and free market, but rather a closed and vicious circle of manipulations powered by money.

The Concerns of Mr Soros – Blasphemy, Revolution or a Glimpse of the Obvious?

I consider the threat from the laissez-faire side more potent today than the threat from totalitarian ideologies. We are enjoying a truly global market economy in which goods, services, capital and even people, move around quite freely, but we fail to recognise the need to sustain the values and institutions of an open society.

This statement that the financial markets as at present operating are more to be feared than trusted was made by the financier, George Soros, in a forceful article entitled 'Capital Crimes' published in the *Atlantic Monthly* for January 1997. The reaction to this article, not least in *The Economist*, was one of such shock and condescending dismissal that, with my own acquaintance with the history of disputes in Christian doctrine I felt the article merited being referred to as the 'blasphemy of Soros'.

Mr Soros is world-famous in financial circles as the Arbitrage and Hedge Fund specialist who won the tag of 'the man who broke the Bank of England'. His Quantum Fund is reputed to have sold 10 billion dollars worth of British pounds in September 1992, so substantially contributing to the devaluation of the pound on 'Black Wednesday' when the UK was forced out of the Exchange Rate Mechanism of the European Monetary System. His fund is estimated to have made one billion dollars out of those dealings. He is thus an almost legendary figure, who is granted his own headlines such as, for example – from the *New York Times* – 'When Soros Speaks, World Markets Listen' (10 June 1993), and 'Rumours of Buying by Soros Send Gold Prices Surging' (5 November 1993).[32]

In his *Atlantic Monthly* piece Soros argued that while the enemy to openness, freedom and generally shared prosperity in our world used to be the communist system, derived from Marxism, we now face a new danger.

> Although laissez-faire doctrines do not contradict the principles of the open society the way Marxism, Leninism or Nazi ideas of racial purity did, all these doctrines have an important feature in common: they all try to justify their claim to ultimate truth with an appeal to science.

He then refers to Karl Popper's influential work on *The Open Society and its Enemies*, observing that Popper was able to show decisively that 'a theory like Marxism does not qualify as a science'. Soros continues:

> In the case of laissez-faire the claim is more difficult to dispute, because it is based on economic theory, and economics is the most reputable of the social sciences. One cannot simply equate market economics with Marxist economics. Yet laissez-faire ideology, I contend, is just as much a perversion of supposedly scientific verities as Marxism-Leninism.

Soros presses his critical analysis home to the very heart of the theory of the financial markets as the information system which secures allocative efficiency for capital. This highly successful practitioner in the markets has indeed become a blasphemer against the faith of the Market. His critique is focused on the interactions of supply and demand as the mechanism by which the Market fixes the *prices* which are the essential means of conveying information for efficient market transactions. He writes:

> The condition that supply and demand are independently given cannot be reconciled with reality, at least as far as the financial markets are concerned – and the financial markets play a crucial role

in the allocation of resources. Buyers and sellers in financial markets seek to discount a future that depends on their own decisions. The shape of the supply and demand curves cannot be taken as given because both of them incorporate expectations about events that are shaped by those expectations. There is a two-way feed back mechanism between the market participant's thinking and the situation they think about – reflexivity.[33]

In the introductory general argument of his article Soros states that his more general reflections have led him to observe that in human thinking, other than the strictly scientific, 'there is a two-way connection – a feed back mechanism – between thinking and events which I have called reflexivity. I have used it to develop a theory of history.' This rather sweeping claim has led some of those who feel him to be blaspheming against market truth to dismiss Soros' more focused and practical criticism of the current workings of the financial markets as the product of an over extended philosophical imagination. It is important to notice therefore that immediately after admitting to 'a theory of history' he goes on: 'Whether the theory is valid or not, it has turned out to be very helpful to me *in the financial markets* [my emphasis].' In other words his criticism of the Market is based on close practical experience. To accept their force does not require any positive or negative decision about his more general theory.

He states the ('blasphemous') conclusion of his practical analysis thus:

> If the supply and demand curves are not independently given, how are market prices determined? If we look at the behaviour of financial markets, we find that instead of tending towards equilibrium, prices continue to fluctuate relative to the expectations of buyers and sellers. There are prolonged periods when prices are moving away from any theoretical equilibrium ... In the absence of equilibrium the contention that free markets lead to the optimum allocation of resources loses its justification. The supposedly scientific theory that has been used to validate it turns out to be an axiomatic structure whose conclusions are contained in its assumptions and are not necessarily supported by the empirical evidence. The resemblance to Marxism which also claimed scientific status for its tenets is too close for comfort.

The reiteration of the claim that the approach to the world of political, social and economic affairs of the current *laissez-faire*, or neo-classical, orthodoxy bears an uncomfortable resemblance to Marxism is of great practical and political importance. It is, I would argue, a true claim and highlights the fact that the deification of the Market by proponents of the Free Market mantra has become, in principle, as much an ideology as Marxist-Leninist communism was. That is to say, it has become an ideology to be enforced on everybody because it is alleged that in the longer run it profits everybody by way of both prosperity and freedom.

I suspect that the ruthless insistence on 'free trade' is the most immediately threatening example of this ideological enforcement. Free trade is being pursued through the international organizations, by the big battalions of the USA and the economically dominating countries, so that the big corporations are free to make money wherever they can, regardless of what it does to communities and environments. Free trade as interpreted and pursued by the World Trade Organization (WTO – taking over from the organization of GATT, the General Agreement on Tariffs and Trade) seems to work on the principle that 'we are free to make money out of you under totally free conditions on the excuse that sooner or later even you will profit'. Comparative advantage is reduced to the comparative efficiency of money-controlling computers in enabling the making of comparatively more money. The conditions of global trading are utterly different from those of the early nineteenth century when Ricardo developed his theory of 'Comparative Advantage'. It is difficult to believe that rooting the current ruthless pursuit of total international 'free trade' in the allegedly established doctrine of 'Comparative Advantage' is any better than relying on an anachronistic shibboleth.[34]

As a small diagnostic symptom to urge one on in investigating scepticism about free trade there is the tone of the remarks with which Paul Krugman ends his chapter on 'The Economics of QWERTY' in his *Peddling Prosperity*. QWERTY, readers will recognize, is the first half of the top letter line of the standard typewriter keyboard. It is also the designation given to a possibly important theory which suggests, as Krugman puts it:

> a different way of thinking [that] rejects the idea that markets invariably lead the economy to a unique best solution, instead it asserts that the outcome of market competition often depends crucially on historical accident.[35]

Thus, the QWERTY keyboard of the first typewriters has carried over to all keyboards – computers and otherwise. It is has become so established it is deemed far too difficult (i.e. expensive) to change, although the QWERTY pattern is now considered inefficient for modern keyboards.

This theory, as Krugman indicates, is potentially highly subversive of much market lore. He gives careful consideration to critical points raised and ends his Chapter 9 with comments entitled, 'Bold Ideas, Cautious Policy recommendations'. These are significantly diagnostic whatever the standing of 'the economics of QWERTY' might be. Krugman comments, 'Yet when it came to actual policy applications, the professors were cautious'. The first reason Krugman gives for that caution is:

> 'that while an acknowledgement of the importance of QWERTY refutes the *near-religious faith of conservatives in free markets*, it is not at all easy to decide which direction the government should pursue [my emphasis]'.

Thus, Krugman says, economists remain somewhat timid about pressing the issue. This, he says:

> may ... have been ... a bit of a relief. ... Although most economists are not doctrinaire believers in laissez-faire, an acknowledgement of the power and effectiveness of the market as a mechanism is a central part of the professional identity even of liberal economists. So they are understandably reluctant to come out too brashly against letting markets have their own way, especially when it comes to *the almost sacred principle of free trade* [my emphasis].[36]

Note the language. I strongly suspect that wrestling with the problems of the Market and our future will require a good deal of 'blasphemy' on the subject of free trade. At least, Professor Krugman's somewhat ironical use of religious-sounding language suggests that he too is aware that much economic orthodoxy verges on being an ideology or faith. There seems therefore to be good grounds for being suspicious about absolutizing arguments about free trade. If there is strength in the argument that the financial markets are increasingly dominated by direct money-making considerations in their distribution of capital resources, then the implication is strong that the trading operations promoted by the Market are not likely to be enterprises chosen to promote broadly beneficial free trade. The Market is much more likely to be promoting enterprises which give high money rates of return – not those which provide cash and prosperity (including jobs) for people on the ground. Such people and their localities do not feature on the computer screens of the Market traders.

Achievements under the Market so far have been remarkable. Although the costs have been tremendous in human suffering and the despoliation of environments, most of us would agree that living conditions for most people in the world today are vastly better than in, say, 1847, let alone in 1797. As Skidelsky puts it in his remarkable second volume on J.M. Keynes, *The Economist as Saviour*: 'The classical economists' endorsement of capitalism was based on their belief, which Marx shared, that it was the first wealth-creating system in history.'[37] This goes with the poignant fact that by the middle of the nineteenth century it looked as if it might be possible to free every human being from the natural fate of a life which was, as Hobbes put it, nasty, brutish and short. The messianic expectations which both Marx and liberal capitalists entertained of the productive possibilities which capitalism was making possible, are not to be wondered at. But the crucial issue is not what happened in the nineteenth century, but what we may anticipate will happen in the twenty-first century in the light of what is happening now. This is why the exposure of the ideologizing of the Market mantra into a fatal conceit is of such central importance. Can we possibly rely on a metaphorical phrase fashioned into a pseudo-theory of the Invisible Hand and transmuted into a quasi-organic theory about an evolved global information system to *guarantee* our receiving the best possible prosperity from the present operations of the Market into which the 'first wealth-creating system' in the world has now developed?

The inward-looking nature of the current operations of the financial markets is highlighted by the 'blasphemy' of Soros. Soros argues that the operations of the financial markets have developed to a point where they are fixated on their own money-making affairs and too exclusively driven by the battle for the survival of the fittest. The effects of this are threatening to an open society interested in increasing prosperity and freedom. There is no recognition of the need to take account of 'a common interest that ought to take precedence over particular interests' and so act to check excessive inequalities of wealth accumulation and apply pressure in favour of some redistribution of wealth. Likewise there is no understanding that 'co-operation is as much a part of the system as competition'. The slogan of 'survival of the fittest' distorts this fact. Thus Soros fears that the openness and so progress of our society 'is liable to break down'.

He diagnoses the source of this threat as lying in the way in which the ruling '*laissez-faire* ideology' has taken on a resemblance to Marxism which is 'too close for comfort'. What is of political importance here is his characterization of the uncomfortable similarity between Marxism as an ideology and current *laissez-faire* market economics. It resides in the dialectical mistake of insisting that reality (both practical and theoretical) has to be understood in terms of conflicting 'either/ors' which are held to delimit the practical possibilities of actual processes and events.

Soros makes the point most clearly:

> Laissez-faire ideologues like to argue that the breakdowns [in the Market] were caused by faulty regulations, not by unstable markets. [But this] fails to explain why the regulations were imposed in the first place. It side-steps the issue by using a different argument, which goes like this: Since regulations are faulty unregulated markets are perfect. The argument rests on the assumption of perfect knowledge: if a solution is wrong, its opposite must be right. In the absence of perfect knowledge, however, both free markets and regulations are flawed. *Stability can be preserved only if a deliberate effort is made to preserve it* [my emphasis].

Or later:

> The laissez-faire argument relies on the same tacit appeal to perfection as does communism. It claims that if redistribution causes inefficiency and distortions, the problems can be solved by eliminating redistribution ... but perfection is unattainable. Wealth does accumulate in the hands of its owners, and if there is no mechanism for redistribution, the inequities can become intolerable.

Such a critique of the 'totalitarian' or 'ideological' error of a dialectical approach, whether economic or other, as I have already said, has important practical and political consequences. As Soros himself writes, 'I can agree that all attempts at redistribution interfere with the efficiency of the Market, *but it does not follow that no attempt should be made* [my emphasis].'

Soros's experiences of the financial markets, and his observations of the world at large, have led him to repudiate the current market faith as a narrow and exaggerated ideology. (Although he does *not* repudiate the Market as a way of doing what it is importantly capable of doing.) He points to the need for action 'outside' the Market, presumably to some extent by government initiative (national and international), which will serve to promote 'social' efficiency – even if these things clash with economic efficiency. This is a direct attack on the Market mantra doctrine that 'there is no alternative', and suggests (although by the merest hints) that alternative, corrective action has to be taken (with reference in particular to some redistribution of wealth) in order to preserve social stability.

No wonder, therefore, the writer of the fifth leader in *The Economist* of 25 January 1997 (mockingly entitled, 'Palindrome Repents') is so deeply shocked that s/he appears to react to Soros' extended argument without having read it with care. Examples of this leader writer missing the point or 'protesting too much' occur in the last paragraph of the leader. First, 'Far from laying claim to some "ultimate truth" of their own liberals in politics and economics are sceptics who want to limit the power of any government to impose some version of truth on its people.' This is to assume that it is beyond all question the case that 'liberals' do not attempt 'to impose some version of truth'. They simply commend what is obviously, indisputably and for all time true, regardless of what happens as time unfolds. The leader writer goes on to quote Hayek: 'Economic control is not merely control of a sector of human life that can be separated from the rest; it is the control of the means for all our ends.' In which case it is surely proper to investigate how money, the supreme means of pursuing our ends under market conditions, is actually distributed through the financial markets? It is not only 'liberals' who are bothered about power. One of the central contemporary issues is just who holds power, in what ways, and in what markets.

Finally this leader concludes: '[Hayek] would have been horrified by the "uninhibited" pursuit of self-interest that is currently running riot – but only, thank goodness, in Mr Soros's imagination.' This seems to be a rather weak and rhetorical flourish with which to finish a brief review of a seriously argued case. We might point to those dealers and City executives pursuing their six figure bonuses. That surely comes close to 'the uninhibited pursuit of self-interest that is currently running riot'. Is it all merely in 'Mr Soros's imagination'? As so sober and reliable an establishment figure as C.A.E. Goodhart writes,

> It is often said that markets for assets which provide no services in use other than their expected pecuniary return are driven by two emotions, fear and greed; observations of such markets indicate that both of these emotions feed on price volatility.[38]

Why such protests, then, when a market practitioner points some of this out?

The most likely interpretation of the evidence would seem to be that the financial market influences itself and plays its own games. The situation is summed up by Ruth Kelly in her article on 'Derivatives: A Growing Threat':

> John Maynard Keynes pictured the operations of the speculative market in his *General Theory* when he likened it to a beauty contest. In the 1930s, a favourite British pastime was for readers of tabloid Sunday newspapers to rank pictures of young women in the order which they believed they would be ranked by a 'celebrity' panel. In other words, they won not by using any subjective judgement about the merits of the beauty queens but by guessing correctly who other people would choose. Imagine the situation in which the view of one of the celebrities leaked out – it would probably be sufficient for most of the readers to vote the same way. In the same manner, the key to playing the markets is not what the individual trader considers to be the virtues or otherwise of any particular policy, but what he or she believes everyone else in the market will think. In this context hedge fund managers such as George Soros can provide a beacon in the dark around which other players can rally. If Mr Soros says publicly that he is going to bet against the Franc – as he did in July 1993 – the large fund managers have to protect the value of their portfolios. They change their asset allocation in accordance with the Soros prediction the Franc will fall out of the ERM and so make it self-fulfilling. As the IMF Report puts it: 'while the hedge funds acted as market leaders, the real financial muscle was provided by institutional investors (mutual funds, pension funds, insurance companies) and by non-financial corporations'.[39]

What these financial movements do to the allocation of capital for beneficent wealth-production in the real world is anybody's guess.

The response of the Market faithful may still be, 'but it works'. Of course it works. But it does not work either according to the theory, or for the steady beneficence of all and sundry. To confirm this, let me bring in the testimony of Charles Goodhart in his book on *Money, Information and Uncertainty*.[40] He is reviewing what he calls the 'Turbulent Float', i.e. the behaviour of the currency markets after the final collapse in 1973 of the Bretton-Woods system of exchange rates controlled by reference to the US dollar linked with the gold in Fort Knox.

The subject takes the form of an enquiry into the empirical evidence for the truth of the basic theory I set out earlier, *viz.* that the operation of the foreign exchange markets brought about *equivalence* in the exchange value of various currencies in relation to the purchasing power of those currencies in their respective countries, so that *prices* could properly interact as signs of comparative value for money in international trading. The theory is focused on the phrase: *Purchasing Power Parity.* (The currency exchange rate reflects and indicates the 'purchasing power parity' – that is the equivalence – of each currency in their respective countries. Thus PPP indicates what, for trading purposes, each currency is 'really' and comparatively worth.) Reporting the evidence from studies of this in actual practice, Goodhart writes: 'Rather than finding evidence of stable, long-run, proportionality between exchange rates and prices, we were unable to reject the hypothesis that they tend to drift apart without bound.'[41] His own comment is:

> While it remains, a priori, almost impossible for me to believe that LOOP and purchasing power parity (PPP)[42] can be infringed beyond some limit, such ranges remain apparently far wider under a regime of flexible exchange rates, allowing greater fluctuations in real exchange rates, than most would have been believed likely or *even possible ab initio.*[43]

What Goodhart is saying is one more version of something common in economic discussions, that is that the economist goes on believing that the underlying workings of the Market system *must* be *as if* such and such a law or theorem were true, even though empirical evidence so far (especially when worked out in detail) contradicts, or at least fails to support, this 'as if'. I have come to regard this feature as the 'Ptolemaic nature of orthodox economics'. In medieval times astronomers observed that the orbits of stars and planets did not conform to the official Ptolemaic theory of a geocentric universe. However the theory was official and therefore true. Consequently official theorists had to spend their time working out explanations which enabled them to maintain that the heavens operated *as if* the basic and official theory were true, even though empirical observation suggested otherwise.

Goodhart comments that attempts at what I would call 'saving the appearances' is not helpful: 'Instead, something is thought to have gone very wrong with the working of the flexible exchange rate system itself.'[44] He goes on to comment on, 'major misalignments in real exchange rates' in the latter half of the 1970s and during the 1980s to the effect that 'the enormous dislocation, disruption, and loss of valuable resources in the form of both human and fixed capital appears to have been a major failing in the working of the economic system'.[45] This leads on to his discussing how this all happened. In the course of this he observes:

> Increasingly, however, during the last two decades the barriers to capital flows, whether by official constraints (exchange controls) or from the natural limitations of information and transaction costs, have been tumbling. As a result, the volume of transactions in the foreign exchange market representing speculative capital transactions have increasingly become a large multiple of the volume related to visible and invisible trade. The foreign exchange market shifted from basically responding to current account flows to reacting to asset holder's decisions on which currency in which to hold their *stock* of wealth.[46]

This would appear to support the conclusion that capital and foreign exchange markets do not perform the 'translation' role for currency and economic activity which the theory of the allocative efficiency of financial markets claims for them. Rather the financial markets determine themselves with regard to their own financial transactions. The determining factor is money-making and the relation to wealth-creation at large is incidental and, on the evidence, not beneficial – it is merely random. The markets are not wise, merely irresistible, and the freedom of the Market is at least as likely to be for the disturbance and disruption of trade and commerce as it is for its beneficial promotion.

As a footnote I would refer to an article in *The Economist* discussing the effectiveness of ideas such as PPP. Its conclusions include 'in practice PPPs have proved a poor guide to exchange rate forecasting. Currencies can deviate from their PPP for long periods.' An attempt was made to establish an alternative method of comparison entitled FEER (Fundamental Equilibrium Exchange Rates), but it proved unsatisfactory. The writer concludes:

> What message should investors draw from all this? Mainly that economists never agree ... Indeed given the inadequacy of economics when it comes to understanding exchange rates, terms such as 'currency misalignment' or 'over-valuation' should be used sparingly.[47]

The markets thus remain a mystery and work as a muddle. Trusting them for wisdom and beneficial guidance is a piece of escapist superstition (or deeply cynical and evasive exploitation on the part of those with the power to play the markets). It is both difficult and hazardous for a non-expert to attempt to evaluate the operations of the financial markets and the claims made about them. Nonetheless if the rest of us are not to hand over our destinies to the money-comptrollers and self-styled experts the attempt has to be made. When the attempt *is* made the system does not look all that promising. Further, the experts and the expert commentators on the experts, do not agree. There is even evidence that the commentators themselves frequently take a suspicious and even cynical view of the markets. Consider a small (but, I suggest representative) sample of some comments collected from my survey of financial journalism.

I start with one of Barry Riley's regular Saturday articles in *The Financial Times*. It is headlined 'There Is No Safety in Numbers', with the sub-heading, 'Statistics can prove a real minefield for the unwary'. He refers to 'Top central bankers poring over the economic statistics this week'. After quoting one or two statistics he continues:

> Since it seems improbable that such a vast economy [of the USA] has wobbled in this way, it is more likely to have been a purely statistical effect. Not that it would really matter, except that a vast financial industry is devoted to analysing and predicting these reported short-term fluctuations and to second-guessing the reaction of the authorities.

He discusses monetary figures and comments:

> Money supply figures were the original inspiration of Goodhart's Law – the observation by a former Bank of England chief economist that as soon as an economic statistic becomes the focus of official targets, it would become meaningless. Suddenly, it will be worth someone's while to fiddle the figures or for people to change their behaviour.[48]

Riley goes on to give instances of other awkward problems connected with statistics, the difficulties of definition, of measurement and the uncertainties of interpretation and application. He includes the following two comments:

(1) In these insecure circumstances, most economists play safe by
     projecting the past. The developed world economy is forecast to
     grow at a little over two percent, not least because many of the
     forecasters have their salaries and bonuses paid by the global
     market and that is the kind of growth rate which bond investors
     believe will be non-inflationary.

(2) But then, the job of many financial market economists is not to
     project the real world but to guess the preliminary 'flash'
     figures, and forecast how the authorities will react.

Here is a sketch of 'the vast financial industry' which somewhat
depressingly confirms the picture presented in the blasphemy of Soros.

A similar picture is presented in a wry and forceful piece published in
the financial section of *The Times* towards the end of 1996. Under the
heading 'Exploring the High Demand for Nonsense',[49] Anthony Harris
quotes a favourite slogan of his first stockbroker – 'The market is always
right'. Of this he remarks, 'to an arrogant young economist, this seemed
obvious nonsense'. However he soon learnt that, 'The market may know
next to nothing about real life; but it does know (except at rare turning
points) where it itself is going.' After reflecting on the disparity between
real life and market behaviour, he continues:

> None of this matters in the least to market professionals: they make
> their money not by guessing what will happen in the real world, but
> by guessing in advance what less professional investors would be
> worrying about next. Tracking the real world through market prices
> is about as useful as observing a glacier with a high speed camera.

He proceeds to discuss the sort of nonsense which arises out of mistaken
attempts to correlate market behaviour and real world events.

> We have been warned endlessly, for example, that 'the market
> expects' British inflation or interest rates to rise. Since both fell
> consistently for years, this would argue amazing obstinacy; but in
> fact the yields are telling us no such thing. They told us simply that
> the professional speculators who were borrowing such astronomic
> sums in Japanese Yen preferred the Mark or the Swiss Franc for the
> long side of their 'play'.

Again, as Soros has suggested, the markets conduct their own games in
their own terms.

Harris then goes on to make a point which seems to me to be of considerable significance with regard to the power of the Market to effect events by its own expectations: 'Now we see something even odder: attempts to read the *political* future from the price charts.' I have my own example of such an attempt drawn from the 'JP Morgan Calculator' 14 July 1997, published in *The Financial Times*.[50] The Calculator, entitled 'EMU: Who's Going to Make It?', consisted of a table listing the eleven possible candidates for the European Monetary Union proposed for 1999. Each entry was given three percentage figures representing an estimation of the chances of that country entering the union. The percentages were calculated for (1) yesterday, (2) one week ago, and (3) four weeks ago. Germany, France and Belgium were assigned 100 per cent in all three categories. After that countries received varied percentages both up and down over the four weeks. The UK, listed at the bottom, saw its chances of joining in 1999 drop from 38 per cent 'four weeks ago' to 23 per cent 'yesterday'.

What is significant is the accompanying explanation:

> The EMU calculator reveals, real time, the probability of individual countries joining Germany in a monetary union in 1999 implied by financial market prices. Market probabilities are derived from the interest rate swops market in which investors swop floating rate interest payments for fixed rate ones.
>
> The implied probability of Italy participating in EMU in 1999 can be calculated by looking at where the spread between post-1999 lira and D.Mark swop rate lies between the zero level implied by EMU and the level we would expect if Italy is not in EMU. Italy's non-EMU spread is estimated by currency strategists at JP Morgan using the pre-1992 correlation of the lira – D-Mark swop spread with similar spreads outside Europe.

Surely this assumes that financial market rates predict 'history'.

Harris does not comment so widely but sticks to his theme of the nonsense involved in this attempt to connect market behaviour and predictions with political future and the real world. Picking up the theme of predictions about who will join EMU, he observes:

> Talk to a London trader who reveres the market, and you will hear that EMU – and even Italian first-stage membership is inevitable – 'a done deal'. Why? Because European Bond yields have converged.

Nonsense. What the yield curve tells us is that the professionals have been making what they call a 'convergence play'.

. . . They have made their money by now and are moving on to other 'plays'. George Soros, for example, is now reported to be going massively short of the Swiss Franc. This will interest you if you believe that anyone actually knows what Soros is doing; or if you suspect that Soros (or some other hedge speculator) has completed such a move, and is now trying to encourage others to buy his position. All absorbingly interesting to poker players; but not, surely, to economists.

So, is it the 'poker players' who allocate capital and decide our fate? There is a view that some form of monetary union will eventually go ahead because calling it off would cause monetary chaos, because speculators will find ways to profit from the ensuing volatility in the currency markets. Our politics are assumed to be at the mercy – not of a benign and wise Market – but of profit-making speculators. As my quotations from Goodhart indicate, the effects of their operations over time are quite contrary to their role in orthodox economics (i.e. to provide the wisdom and discipline which allows allocative efficiency).

The story of how financial markets actually operate in detail, and who makes what money out of what sort of transactions can be read daily in the financial pages of the broadsheets. Four years of such reading have convinced me that if one can believe that the financial markets are the presiding operators of the Invisible Hand which assures that the market operations deliver benefits for more and more, while promising increasing freedom for all, then one can believe anything.

The crucial question, however, remains. Can anything be done? Production has become our relentless god. Unless our profit-making continues to grow, our system – as we at present believe we are obliged to run it – collapses. We seem to be trapped on the treadmill of the Market as fate. But need this be so? Liberal proponents of the Market mantra are concerned about freedom. Are we sufficiently free to invent more healthy ways of wealth creation?

Notes

1 See quotations and discussion in Chapter 11 above, pp. 141–4
2 See Chapters 2–9.
3 See discussion on Mexico, Chapter 11, pp. 144 supra.
4 See Chapter 3.
5 Sometime business editor of the *New York Times* and then editor of the *Harvard*

Business Review, cited by David Korten, *When Corporations Rule the World* (London: Earthscan, 1995), p. 189.

6 *The Economist*, 23 September 1995.
7 Korten, *Corporations*, p. 189.
8 Philip Stephens, *Politics and the Pound: The Conservatives' Struggle with Sterling* (Macmillan, 1996), p. 43.
9 *The Economist*, 26 August 1995.
10 John Grieve Smith, *Full Employment: A Pledge Betrayed* (Macmillan, 1997), p. 216.
11 Anatole Kaletsky, *The Times*, 17 August 1995, 'Economic View: The Midas Touch game becomes more exciting'.
12 *The Guardian*, 27 January 1997.
13 See p. 11 of *The Economist* survey referred to on p. 21.
14 *The Economist*, 14 December 1996.
15 Jonathan Michie and John Grieve Smith (eds), *Managing the Global Economy* (Oxford: Oxford University Press, 1995),
16 Michies and Grieve Smith, *Managing*, p. 220.
17 J.K. Galbraith, *A Short History of Financial Euphoria* (1990; Penguin edition, 1994), p 19
18 Referred to in *The Times* of 19 December 1995.
19 As Kelly points out on page 215 of the chapter referred to above, the 'notional value [is] the underlying principal value used to calculate the cashflows resulting from derivative contracts'. So it is the higher figure which represents the denominated value of the primary assets on which the secondary derivative bets are being traded and which form the basis for calculating the cash made from such trading. Ruth Kelly, 'Derivatives – A Growing Threat to "The International System"' in *Managing the Global Economy*, Jonathan Michie and John Grieve Smith (eds) (Oxford: Oxford University Press, 1995).
20 Kelly, 'Derivatives', p. 215.
21 Kelly, 'Derivatives', p. 213.
22 David Korten, *When Corporations Rule the World* (London: Earthscan, 1995), p. 196.
23 Philip Stephens, *Politics and the Pound: The Conservatives' Struggle with Sterling* (Macmillan, 1996), p. 8.
24 Galbraith, *A Short History*, cited page 163 above.
25 Kelly, 'Derivatives', p. 221.
26 *The Financial Times*, 15 July 1997.
27 J.K. Galbraith, *The World Economy Since the Wars* (London: Sinclair Stevenson, 1994), p. 248.
28 Adam Smith, *Wealth of Nations*, book I, chapter II, conclusion.
29 *The Economist*, 12 August 1995.
30 Korten, *Corporations*, p. 197. Korten cites a survey, 'Frontiers of Finance' in *The Economist* of 9 October 1993 as his source.
31 Korten, *Corporations*, p. 193.
32 Both cited by David Korten, *When Corporations Rule the World* (London: Earthscan, 1995), p. 199.
33 George Soros, 'Capital Crimes', *Atlantic Monthly*, January 1997, reproduced in *The Guardian*, 13 January 1997.
34 To argue this through would take at least another chapter in a book which already threatens to be too long. Anyone who wants to follow up the questionable nature of the current arguments about Free Trade could find initial grounds for doubt marshalled, for example, in the chapter entitled 'The Size Thing' in *The Ecology of Commerce* by Paul Hawken (1993), especially pages 96 ff. More immediately current material is marshalled in Chapter 4 of *The Politics of the Real World*, edited by

Michael Jacobs (The Real World Coalition, 1996). An example of the available evidence of what commercial lobbying means in terms of power and influence is the book entitled *Who Will Tell the People: The Betrayal of American Democracy* by William Greider (New York and London: Simon & Schuster, 1992).

35   Paul Krugman, *Peddling Prosperity* (New York and London: W.W. Norton & Co., 1994), p. 223.

36   Krugman, *Peddling Prosperity*, p. 244.

37   Robert Skidelsky, *John Maynard Keynes: The Economist as Saviour 1920–1937*, (Macmillan, 1992), p. 596.

38   C.A.E. Goodhart, *Money, Information and Uncertainty* (Macmillan, 1975; second edition, 1989), p. 23.

39   Jonathan Michie and John Grieve Smith (eds) *Managing the Global Economy* (Oxford: Oxford University Press, 1995), p. 220. See page 62ff above.

40   The following quotations are from Chapter XVIII of the 1989 edition of Goodhart's *Money, Information and Uncertainty*.

41   Goodhart, *Money, Information and Uncertainty*, p. 440.

42   [LOOP] is the 'Law Of One Price' whereby, expressed in a common currency, a tradable good should sell at the same single price worldwide, i.e. another version of PPP.

43   Goodhart, *Money, Information and Uncertainty*, p. 441.

44   Goodhart, *Money, Information and Uncertainty*, p. 441.

45   Goodhart, *Money, Information and Uncertainty*, p. 444.

46   Goodhart, *Money, Information and Uncertainty*, p. 445.

47   *The Economist*, 26 August 1995.

48   *The Financial Times*, 9 February 1997. The more references to 'Goodhart's Law' I find, the more it becomes plain to me that its proper definition is: 'The money-operators in the Financial Markets can get round anything that puts checks on their money-making.' The Market which is in control is uncontrollable – so it is alleged or assumed. Hence the critical importance of facing the question of whether there is any truly reliable evidence, or any sufficiently justifiable theory, which demonstrates that the Market is a perpetually beneficent force.

49   Anthony Harris in *The Times*, 20 November 1996.

50   *The Financial Times*, 15 July 1997.

13 Facing the God of Our Production – The Market as Fate?

Interest on Capital and Effects on Society

According to the Market mantra the interest of capitalism is the interest of all of us across the 'the global market', into the indefinite future. The plausibility of this faith rests on the simple and obvious historical fact that capitalism is the first wealth-creating system the world has ever seen. For the first time in history poverty, starvation, disease and misery need no longer be inevitable for the vast majority of people. In the developed countries at least people have largely broken free from their historical fate of poverty, starvation and disease. So why be concerned? The Market is benign 'fate', or rather, promising opportunity.

This faith, surely, can no longer be taken for granted. A wealth-creating system as powerful and global as that which has developed into current capitalism is plainly a dynamic and interacting network of vast complexity. It is constantly adapting itself by internal feedback and changing its environment (the earth, human communities, their life-styles and possibilities). So what could hitherto be taken for granted can be taken for granted no longer. The system certainly cannot be guaranteed to expand indefinitely as the essentially motivating force of economic provision and improvement for the future.

My brief tour of current economic discussion has shown that economics has only recently allowed 'the future' into its theoretical considerations. In practical matters the practitioners of the Market and of ever expanding free trade, refuse to build into their trading practices factors which reckon with what is actually happening to people and localities. This is the issue of the 'two sets of data' I formulated in my initial scientific protest. There may be more and more money being made but how does that in practice relate to the 'well-faring', the 'well-being' and the 'well-doing' of the majority of people in the world as it is today and as it has prospects for the future? A sober investigation of the facts and the theories put forward to preserve the credibility of the Market mantra suggests that rather than promoting the interests of all of us, the interest of current capitalism is – simply – interest.

Capitalism finances enterprises in return for the first claim on the profits of the production it finances. This is the return by way of interest on the money loaned. This essential motivating role of interest is legitimated by Adam Smith in one of his typically pithy sentences: 'As something can everywhere be made by the use of money, something ought everywhere to be paid for the use of it.'[1] The critical question is: How much should be paid for this use? In Adam Smith's view the rate ought not to rise much above 5 per cent. He assumed that the law would regulate to this effect, believing that high interest rates were bad. They would, he wrote, result in:

> The greater part of the money which was to be lent [being] lent to prodigals and projectors, who alone would be willing to give this high interest. Sober people, who will give for the use of money no more than a part of what they are likely to make by the use of it, would not venture into the competition. A great part of the capital of the country would thus be kept out of the hands which were most likely to make a profitable and advantageous use of it, and thrown into those which were most likely to waste and destroy it.

Adam Smith, I suspect, would be at least as worried as George Soros about the dangerous effects of speculative interest rates in today's financial markets. The high rates of return and the requirements for rapid profits under which the financial markets now operate, are bringing about a state of economic affairs in which capitalism cannot afford to offer decent employment to growing numbers of people, while the earth, in turn, may not be able to afford to sustain capitalism much longer. Capitalism – that is – as currently practised and pursued.

Consider the evidence, starting with the issue of what capitalism can and cannot afford in relation to people. Current capitalism cannot afford to find jobs for anything like the number of people who need them if they are to play an effective part in the communities they live in. Further, an increasing number of the jobs which are available are (at least comparatively) poorly paid and involve conditions of casual and part-time labour which remove from these jobs the sort of security and promise which most jobs in developed countries had for the 'golden period' after the war (say 1950–73 or so). Aspirations and expectations about employment are sinking. Under the present conditions of capitalism economies do well, but more and more people do worse than they were doing.

A symptomatic example of the way in which economic commentators, while strong proponents of the faith of the Free Market mantra, are both aware of these facts and yet appear totally oblivious to the challenge they constitute to the orthodox faith in the Free Market, can be found in a concluding comment in 'Europe Would Do Well to Ape American Economic Policy', an article by Anatole Kaletsky.[2] After singing the praises of Mr Greenspan (chairman of the Federal Reserve Board, the USA's Central Bank) and of the US economic performance sustained by his guidance, Kaletsky concludes:

> America is far from perfect. I would certainly not want to bring up my children there. It lacks decent public services. It is marred by violence, extremism and grinding poverty. Altogether, there are many things wrong with America. It just happens that economic policy is not one of them.

What a breathtaking combination of simple faith in the Market and somewhat frightening logic! Is economic policy in no way related to whether or not a country is the sort of place in which one would wish to bring up one's children? Kaletsky's dismissal would seem to suggest that economic policy is simply about the making of money, regardless of how it is made and who gains what type of benefit from it. This, in fact, is broadly what my survey suggests the financial markets are up to. I imagined, however, that orthodox Free Market exponents held the view that, despite their limitations, financial markets actually facilitated real market operations which could be to the benefit of society at large. That is to say that the point of money-making is not to have more money but to facilitate the spread of beneficial effects to the improvement of the societies in which we all live.

Persons of Kaletsky's way of thinking would doubtless reply: 'Of course, but that is the subject of many other articles. First, and as a basis to everything else, we must keep the economy going with balanced (non-inflation producing) growth.' Future hopes for those people who find no hope in the present depend upon jobs; and jobs depend upon the capital markets being attracted by sufficiently profitable returns on their investments in interest made available through profits, for there to be that steady expansion of enterprise which promises eventual money and participation to all.

This basic faith is expressed with splendid brevity, and assurance, in the letter columns of *The Times* in October 1997. A group of letters commented on Mr Blair's speech as Prime Minister to the first Labour Party Conference after the Party's stunning electoral victory. In one Ian Morrow writes:

> The only way a democratic government can create full employment is to start a war. If the government gets the major items in the economic equation right (i.e. currency, taxation, inflation and trade unions) then private enterprise will be able to create an increase in jobs.[3]

But jobs for how many, at what wages, with what qualifications, for how long, under what conditions and to what ends? Kaletsky has frequently expressed the belief that the UK could be well on the way to 'full employment', while the USA, he believes, has as good as got there. If so, this is rather worrying in relation to any hopes of solving problems of poverty and social injustice through providing jobs. In the USA evidence suggests that the lot of the lower half of the population is not improving – and for many it is worsening. Thus, in a letter in *The Financial Times* contributing to a discussion about 'productivity as a measure of performance', Professor Layard of the LSE writes: 'So the US does lag in growth. European visitors do not normally see this because they meet the rich who are getting richer. They do not see the bottom half of Americans who are actually getting poorer.'[4]

This is not an isolated observation. In an article elsewhere in the same issue of *The Financial Times* – on its 'Markets' page – Tony Jackson, writing from New York, discussed the relationship between rates of growth and the value of stocks.

> the lack of correlation with growth, in particular, is easily explained. What matters for the stock market is not the level of growth but the proportion of growth which is retained by corporations in the form of profit. The present ratio of profits to GDP, at about 10 percent, is the highest for over fifteen years. This has largely come at the expense of the workforce. New technology and restructuring, with their associated lay-offs, have favoured the providers of capital more than the providers of labour.

A similar picture is supported in some comments provided to me by a correspondent who had been researching income statistics for the USA. In his assessment:

Average incomes have not risen significantly despite massive improvements in productivity – the median family income in 1994 was one percent below that of 1991. More strikingly the average weekly earnings of most rank and file workers adjusted for inflation fell by eighteen percent between 1973 and 1995. This is set against the real annual pay of corporate chief executives which saw a sixty-six percent increase after taxes ... Between 1990 and 1995 the productivity of all non-farm private sector employees increased by 10.3 percent. This had no effect on their income. A quote from Felix Rohatyn, senior partner of Lazard Freres, speaks about 'an advanced capitalism whose harsh and cruel climate [imposes] stringent discipline on its participants.' What is occurring is a huge transfer of wealth from lower skilled, middle-class American work-ers to the owners of capital assets and to a new technological aristocracy with a large element of compensation tied to stock values.

Broader grounds for questioning the claim that the USA economy is delivering increasingly worthwhile conditions of living for more citizens, were touched on at the World Economic Forum held in Davos at the beginning of February 1997. Mr Summers, the US Deputy Treasury Secretary, reported on the way in which the current US economy has 'lately been extremely successful'. At the same time he drew attention to negative lessons from America's experience.

A child born in New York today is less likely to live to five than a child born in Shanghai. A young American black man is more likely to go to jail than to college. We have seen a collapse of respect and trust for every American institution and community value. To summarise, as a model for making the economic pie as large possible, American capitalism is second to none. But as a means of creating a stable society and addressing the concerns of our citizens, the American model's superiority is far from clear.[5]

This uncertainty over the balance of values and prospects is under-lined by several social developments in the USA of which I mention two. The two are interconnected and would seem to be diagnostic of what is being brought about in a society where it just happens that economic policy is not one of the many things wrong with America, and where the economy has 'lately been extremely successful'.

A review article in *The Financial Times*, entitled 'The birth of Enclave Man',[6] reported the existence of 80,000 developments, housing some 8 million people, built as fortresses which have 'a twelve foot iron fence, security floodlights and bullet-proof guard boxes ringing their homes'. The author reports that the buyers of these protected houses:

> in most aspects mirror the people who lead the so-called 'white flight' to the suburbs in the 1970s and the 1980s. Most proceeded to fight for, and win, municipal incorporation for their bedroom communities, thus escaping the obligations and taxes of the fast-rotting cities they left behind. To some observers, the rise of the gated communities marks a critical further stage in the process of white flight.

In effect, these developments are more or less privatized local government enclosures.

> Most gated developments pay for their own private police patrols and security guards. Traditionally communal services such as schools, parks, entertainment facilities and even street cleaning and maintenance are often privatised within the enclaves. The inhabitants are ever more reluctant to pay higher taxes to main government and city services outside their walls.

Thus the middle-class are mirroring the retreat of the rich to their privatized and guarded ghettos.

Social commentators fear that this marks the abandonment of a sense of common citizenship and the traditional aspirations to social mobility and equality among Americans. The writer concludes:

> One result is that the economic and social segregation characteristic of societies worldwide is, in the US, taking on a physical form. 'Social barriers have always been there, but Americans climb over them', says Mr Blakely.[7] 'That is what America has always been about.' But walls, gates and armed guards – the essential elements of prison – present more substantial impediments; both to those trying to get in and those who want to get out.

As to involuntary imprisonment the present prospects are equally grim. In an article entitled 'Enemy Behind Bars',[8] Andrew Rutherford (Professor of Law at Southampton University), discussed *The Real War on Crime*, a 1996 report of the Independent National Criminal Justice Commission in the USA. The report documents, 'the unprecedented quantum leap in the number of people in prison', and goes on to state that:

> after seventy-five years of relative stability in the proportion of the population behind prison bars, in the early nineteen eighties the United States embarked upon an experiment in mass incarceration. The bare statistics tell the story: in 1980 the combined local, state and federal prison population was 493,000; in 1985 it was 759,000; in 1990 it was 1,179,000 and in 1995 it was 1,544,000. Whereas in 1980 the prison population translated into a rate of 210 per hundred thousand inhabitants, the rate today is 555 ... Furthermore the racial dimension to the American prison scene cannot be avoided: the incarceration rate is 306 per hundred thousand for whites, compared with 1,947 for blacks. In many American cities one third of black males aged 18 to 34 are either in prison or under parole or probation supervision.

Professor Rutherford adds that a spate of recent federal and state criminal justice statutes are bringing it about that the combined impact of the recent legislation, 'may well add a further 6 million to the total number in prison'.

The phenomenon of the voluntary imprisonment of the gated communities paralleled by the rise in involuntary imprisonment, presents a parable of devastating irony. The Free Market in which we invest our hopes, not only of prosperity but also for the promotion of freedom and democracy, is presiding over the multiplication of voluntary or enforced imprisonment among rich, middle-class and poor.

Moving to Britain, Professor Rutherford comments on the policies of the then Home Secretary,

> It is estimated by the Penal Affairs Consortium, that Mr Howard's plans ... will add 28,000 to the present record prison population in England and Wales. Should this come about, and if present levels of growth were to continue, the Millennium would be marked by a prison population rate which, in effect was no longer in the European league but taking its place alongside Singapore.

This link between imprisonment as socially diagnostic of conditions in the USA and penal policy in the UK was also made by John Gray in an article in *The Guardian* entitled 'Culture of Containment' (20.11.95).

> In seeking to emulate the American experiment in mass incarceration the Conservatives are guided by a sure instinct. When social cohesion has been undermined by policies which promote free markets regardless of their impacts on communities and families, the informal sanctions of public opinion cease to be effective restraints on criminal and anti-social behaviour, and only legal sanctions are left ... Since 1992 Britain's prison population has risen by nearly 30 percent (with results for overcrowding and discipline about which prison officers have repeatedly complained). This expansion of Britain's prison population has occurred as a matter of policy, not as a result of an unexpected explosion in crime. When communities are derelict and families fractured what remains that can hope to deter lawlessness aside from the threat of imprisonment? Here, as in the US, the regime of unfettered market is engendering a culture of incarceration as its primary defence against the disastrous consequences of its core social institutions.

Gray illustrates what he means by this:

> In 1979 fewer than one in twelve British families had no working members whereas today [1995] an astonishing one in five families is workless. Many of those in work earn too little to be able to found a family. Even when it does not create a workless underclass, revolutionary capitalism 'down-sizes' families 'by subjecting them to the pressures of declining income and incessant job mobility'. This has happened in towns such as Swindon, where an American-style culture of mobility has emerged, combining low levels of employment with very high levels of family breakdown.

It may be tempting to write this example of social commentary off as a typical piece of anti-market propaganda attributing the *causes* of social conditions to the Market in an improper and unscientific way. Let us consider next, however, the way in which economic commentators (such as Kaletsky and others) describe the logic of the Market system as it deals with the crucial issue of wages and unemployment.

Productive Requirements and Conflicts of Interest

Adam Smith has left us his understanding of the 'Accumulation of Capital':

> The annual produce of the land and labour of any nation can be increased in its value by no other means but by increasing either the number of productive labourers, or the productive power of those labourers who had before been employed. The number of its productive labourers, it is evident, can never be much increased, but in consequence of an increase of capital, or of the funds destined for maintaining them. The productive powers of the same number of labourers cannot be increased, but in consequence either of some addition and improvement to those machines and instruments which facilitate and abridge labour; or of a more proper division and distribution of employment. In either case an additional capital is almost always required.[9]

Both an increase in the number of jobs and an increase in the productivity of jobs, depends on the investment of capital. However there is about as much conflict as mutuality of interest between the capitalists and those who have nothing but their hireable labour to depend upon. The conflictual aspect of the equation is crystallized in an article, to which I have already referred, commenting on discussions at the 1997 World Economic Forum in Davos. Writing on 'Keeping up the UK Allure', Janet Bush comments:[10]

> Of course, there is often a divergence of interest between national economies and international companies. As UBS[11] says, the aim of national competitiveness is to raise living standards – primarily by creating jobs – while that of corporate competitiveness relies on raising profits, often by cutting jobs. This conundrum shot through much of the hand-wringing discussion of different economic models at the World Economic Forum in Davos, but nobody came up with a vision that side-stepped the preferences of international business.
> ... The world business community is far more worried about its inflexible and expensive labour markets for the reason that they make investing prohibitively expensive.

The cost of labour is too high to enable enterprises to make sufficient profit to pay a worthwhile return on capital invested so this investment is 'prohibitively expensive'.

The mechanisms involved here can be traced from observations made *en passant* by Anatole Kaletsky in his series of articles in *The Times*. In September 1996, writing about 'Wall Street Cheap at the Price', he refers to a 'brilliant' paper on 'Stocks and Bonds' by Brian Reading and published by Lombard Street Research. This shows that 'Market cycles can be divided into two very different types of movement' – short-term cycles and 'far longer and more powerful trends'. Kaletsky comments: 'These seem to be governed by technological and social phenomena, above *all the battle over income distribution that causes inflation* [my emphasis].'[12] There is a conflict of interest concealed within the alleged overall mutuality of interest in the capitalist system. Discussing one of the Bank of England's periodic rises in interest rates, Kaletsky wrote:

> Looking at the main structural causes of inflation – Government deficits, commodity prices and social struggle over the distribution of income and wealth – there are no serious worries. Public sector borrowing is firmly under control and commodity prices are falling in terms of sterling. The labour market where the root causes of inflation are usually to be found is remarkably quiescent . . . Workers are more nervous about their jobs and fearful of making extravagant wage demands.[13]

Descriptive diagnoses of 'the battle over income distribution' are reinforced in 'Look to an Old Theory to Explain Our Golden Age'.[14] In the course of a more general argument we find:

> Once full employment is reached, as it arguably now has been in America (although not clearly not in Britain or Europe) it is back to business as usual: long-run growth of about 2 percent annually in real incomes, profits and investment – and no particular reason to assume accelerating productivity or a continuing stock-market boom . . . There is little reason to believe that the new era of full employment will also be a period of ever-rising profits and accelerating productivity growth.

Kaletsky thus seems to be moderating the enthusiasm of many of the proponents of the Market mantra who look to continuous acceleration of productivity growth to ensure that the contest between wages and the distribution of profits does not become open conflict. The belief is that although the conflict *is* endemic, nonetheless all *will* prosper 'sufficiently' in the long run. Those who are hemmed in at the bottom of any earnings and insecurity league, so that the cost of their employment does not make 'investment impossibly expensive', will still flourish sufficiently to make the gross inequalities of distribution tolerable. Kaletsky's caution may thus simply imply that he expects improvement in the number of jobs and the rewards of those jobs at the bottom of the labour market to occur rather more slowly than enthusiasts are hoping for. In any case, he is fully aware of the conflict between the overt interests of the workers and the basic interests of the capitalists.

> Instead of seeking the magic elixir that might explain the miracle of non-inflationary expansion – be it technology, globalisation or even price stability itself – it would be more useful to focus on the pathologies that made full employment unattainable in the previous two decades. For Britain the most important of these pathologies was the neanderthal resistance of trade union leaders to modern working practices and adequate levels of profit. In other countries there were other problems ... What all these pathologies had in common was that they grew out of the prosperity of the 1950s and 1960s. They were by-products of the collapse of social discipline that followed the longest period of full employment and prosperity in history. When wealth creation seemed to be an automatic process, people naturally grew less interested in how further wealth could be created than how it might be shared out. A long era of full employment is bound to encourage such a breakdown of discipline in any democratic market economy ... What lies ahead is neither boom nor recession but a long spell of moderate non-inflationary growth when *the struggle of the income distribution between wages and profits will gradually resume* [my emphasis].[15]

This picture of endemic conflict between the workers and their employers being part of the nature of capitalism, is repeated in, 'Why I am a Prophet of Boom'. Kaletsky reiterates his belief that:

> in terms of economic growth, the 1960s were an unrepeatable period ... there is indeed no need to assume that globalisation or electronic technology will accelerate the long-term trend in productivity growth ...
>
> As every economist knows (but few say in public) the level of employment does not depend on productivity growth, technology or

globalisation. It rests on how many thousands or millions of people must be deliberately kept on the dole by dint of restrictive monetary or fiscal policies, to prevent wages from rising too rapidly and inflation spiralling out of control. The main reason for economic optimism today, at least in Britain, is that inflationary behaviour appears to have subsided dramatically, largely no doubt because of the insecurity about employment prospects engendered by the unstable conditions of the past twenty-five years. Sooner or later the over confidence of the late 1960s will perhaps return. Shop keepers will revert to price-gouging, industrialists will revert to business on the golf course, and workers will revert to striking for wages their employers cannot pay.[16]

Thus, although employers may contribute to future slumps by taking off for the golf course, it is really the workers who cause trouble when they cease to be frightened enough to stop them 'striking for wages their employers cannot pay'. Further evidence that this is part of the way the capitalist system has evolved, may be gathered from arguments deployed by Anthony Harris in his article entitled 'Sterling at One Hundred: Play it Again Tony'. He writes:

Exchange-rate volatility may offend the sense of order which is a management principal of Toyota; but, in the large view, there is an important trade off. Bigger financial swings mean smaller swings in the real economy. Within one country asset prices increases which result from falling interest rates make capital cheap and so help to end the recession that made rates fall in the first place. Exchange-rate swings have something of the same function internationally. Strong economies produce strong exchange-rates; weak ones devalue. As a result growth in one or two countries stimulates exports from the weaker economies. The more open the economies the more powerful are these forces of international stabilisation ... In due course this will produce a profit squeeze in the current strong economies *with a new round of cost-cutting and labour shedding*. Trade balances will swing into the red, which will provoke, no doubt, the usual hand wringing. But, in due course, the current strong currencies will follow their economies down, and *the whole cycle will start again* [my emphases].[17]

'The whole cycle will start again'. As one country, with its own sub-cycle, interacts with all the sub-cycles of other economies within the global economy, employment and wages will either creep up or fall more steeply down, and this yo-yo will go on rising and falling. Not much in this for the workers. Quite a bit in it for the successful capitalists.

Consider the enthusiastic article of an unashamed and out-and-out supporter of the Free Market in 'No Such Thing as the "Right Exchange-Rate"' by Bernard Connolly, Managing Director, International Economics at AIG International.

> Once capital could flow freely, the expected rate of return on capital was restored to its rightful place as the keystone of the economy – the variable that runs everything else. [cf. my statement that the interest of Capitalism is Interest.] If a truly capitalist economy is to survive and prosper, its government must put in place structural policies (not least low taxes) that generate bullish private sector expectations of the rate of return ...
>
> In other words, loosing 'competitiveness' in the upswing [of an economic cycle] is absolutely essential in a capitalist economy such as Britain's. Some manufacturers will have their rents reduced in the process; that is capitalism's 'gale of creative destruction'. The genius of a system that in two hundred years transformed hugely for the better, the every day life of ordinary people.[18]

What are our prospects if we continue to live under the dominance of 'capitalism's gale of creative destruction'? There certainly will be no steady improvement in the number of jobs at prospering wages for the ordinary waged labourer. Two *obiter dicta* in one edition of *The Financial Times* happen to underline this point.[19] In his regular Saturday article, Barry Riley, is evaluating the chances of the then current Stock Market boom turning into a bust. He writes that, 'much [about mortgages and wind-falls] is comforting, but the state of the labour market is considerably less so. Earning inflation has ticked up to 4.5 percent and will rise much higher as labour shortages develop.' This is 'less comforting' to the anxious observer when one notes, among a spate of articles on top salaries and fat cats a report entitled 'Fat Cats Get Fatter on Pay Packages of Forty Times the Average Salary'.[20] The rate of rise of these salaries is, of course, much less discomforting with regard to inflation than 4.5 per cent on wages because there are few fat cats and too many would-be labourers. This phenomenon of comparatively restrained wages growth interacting with incomparable magnification of salaries and perks is all of a piece with another symptom of the way the capitalist system actually works.

In spring 1996 *The Economist* carried a piece entitled 'Why More Looks Less'– dateline New York. It poses the question: 'Is America the land of opportunity or the domain of down-sizing?' The writer embarks on a case for maintaining that opportunity still prevails, but concludes:

> The nature of down-sizing itself also makes many Americans nervous ... The firms involved are mostly profitable – and the argument that they must cut costs in order to remain so can sound unconvincing. Especially, as a new study by the Institute for Policy Studies notes, if the bosses of down-sizing firms are richly rewarded. This study found that the chief executives of 1995's twenty-two biggest down-sizers saw the combined value of their share options upsize by $36.6 million on the day their lay-offs were announced. Small wonder that American workers, who in 1995 saw the smallest rises in pay and benefits for fourteen years, are unhappy.[21]

I draw my second *obiter dictum* from a first leader in *The Financial Times*, entitled 'An Answer to Dr Pangloss'. The piece considers whether we delude ourselves if we accept the view of many economic commentators that we are, for the time being, pretty near to inhabiting the best of all possible worlds. The leader asks, 'Can it last?' The writer's view is that it may for the time being:

> But unemployment figures, particularly in Europe, serve as a warning to anyone who thinks this is the best of all possible worlds. A large pool of excess labour might be a buffer against accelerating inflation – but only if countries cut their thickets of restriction which make workers too expensive to hire.[22]

The implication is that we could be quite close to the best of all possible economic worlds, providing workers take less wages or there are less jobs to go round.

Again, this may be necessary for our current capitalist system and there may be no alternative. But to suggest that the system's need for high interest returns is in the longer term interests of all is hardly plausible. People may be spared starvation (many still are not) but the conflict over the distribution of wealth is won hands down by the capitalists – and will be increasingly so if the accumulating data about the widening gap between the rich and the increasingly insecure middle-class on the one hand, and that between the middle-class and the poor on the other (in developed countries), is taken into account.

In early 1997 an article by Victor Keegan, from which I have already quoted briefly, illustrated the actual state of affairs:

> The value of all the shares quoted on the London Stock Exchange rose above £1 trillion for the first time last week. That is quite a lot of money: enough to buy Britain's entire economic wealth (the UK's gross domestic product is about £650 billion) with enough left over to buy Russia and a few other economies as well ... Those whose wealth was tied to shares enrich themselves by a cool 500 billion – about as much wealth accumulation as Britain has recorded in most of her previous history ... Economists and ministers start to worry if average earnings threaten to rise by more than 4 percent a year. Yet in recent years the average annual rise in wealth for share owners (dividends plus capital gains) has been between sixteen and seventeen percent. The politics of all this must seem as baffling as the ethics. People have felt bad during a period when most of them have never had it so good[23] partly because their comparative wealth improvement has coincided with an unprecedented worsening of the wealth of those at the bottom of the scale.
>
> ... There is a connection. Part of the reason pension funds are doing so well is that the companies they have shares in have been laying workers off, paying as little as they can get away with at the bottom end of the scale (unlike the salaries of directors) and generating a general sense of insecurity which makes not only their own employees feel bad but generally practically everyone else as well because, in the end, we all live in a community.
>
> ... Wealth and income distribution have not been off the agenda for the past seventeen years, it is just that the entire emphasis has been on redistributing wealth from poorer to richer people. The economic justification was that by making the rich richer, more wealth would be created which would trickle down to the poor who, after their initial forced sacrifice, would end up less poor. In fact the very poor are worse off than they were at the start of the experiment in absolute terms while economic wealth (as opposed to the bonanza on the stock markets) has been expanding less fast than it did in the 1960s and 1970s.[24]

This account of whose interests the system primarily serves is reinforced by the data assembled in *Inequality Within the UK*.[25] One of the authors, Paul Johnson, writes:

The growth in the gap between the rich and the poor is unprecedented in recent times. In the mid-nineteen nineties the poorest 10
percent of the population have incomes no higher than they did
virtually two decades ago. Over the same period, the income of the
richest ten percent has grown by a half. The richest ten percent now
control the same amount of income as the whole of the poorer half of
the population – each has just over a quarter of total income. During
the 1960s and 1970s the poorer half had about a third of total
income, the richest ten percent about a fifth. The shift in the
distribution of income, and therefore in the balance of economic
power, has been enormous ... In every region, in every age group,
among pensioners just as among workers, inequality has risen. The
gap between the rich and the middle-income earners has grown, as
has that between the middle and bottom of the income distribution.
   ... The central fact that inequality has spiralled upwards is not in
dispute. And the main reasons for it lie in earnings and the labour
markets, and in the failure of social security benefits, including
pensions, to keep up with earnings.[26]

We can no more afford welfare under the present system than we can
afford increasing jobs and increasing wages. The effect of all this,
Johnson adds, is that:

increasingly it looks as if public services are only going to be
provided at a very basic level as the Government continues to box
itself into desperately tight spending plans. As the rich start to opt
out, then we already have some evidence that they become less
supportive of public spending and higher taxes. So we end up in a
vicious circle ... The gap between the rich and the poor in their
private incomes then leads to an increasing divergence in the quality
of all the things that they consume.

Thus the visions and hopes of 1945–70 of decent welfare and decent
employment for nearly all have evaporated.
   This is not confined to the US and the UK. Anyone who pays
attention to reports about European Monetary Union and the follow up
to the Maastricht Treaty, will know that the trade unions in Germany
and France are deeply worried about rising unemployment and the
depression of wages and welfare conditions. The orthodox comment is
that they have refused, unlike the unions in the UK, to accept
the inescapable need for flexibility.[27] The condescension with which

workers are routinely berated about their expensiveness is a little hard to bear when so much data shows that as the worker's lot deteriorates the capitalists' profits go up. A recent report from the Club of Rome entitled *Factor Four: Doubling Wealth, Halving Resource Use* gives a graph which shows that

> until round about 1980, income from both labour and capital went more or less in parallel with the German GDP growth. Dramatic changes have occurred since that time. Workers' income has stagnated while income from capital has exploded.[28]

The authors also refer to the fact that, 'capital can easily evade higher taxes by emigrating, labour cannot'. An important fact to which further reference will be made below. This is all part of the evidence that, as the title of section (13.1) to which I am referring says, 'Free trade strengthens capital and weakens labour and the environment'.

The trouble which broke out in 1997 and continued into 1998 among the hitherto successful 'Tiger economies' of South East Asia surely underlines the case for doubt about this Market optimism. In the first stage of currently capitalist motivated growth conditions do improve for many people – and many millionaires emerge. But, quite apart from serious hiccups such as the Mexican crisis of 1994 referred to earlier and the financial turbulence which Thailand, Malaysia and the region round experienced towards the end of 1997 – why should it be assumed that the up and coming Asian countries will do better *in the long run* than the first developed capitalist countries? 'We' in the UK, USA, and Western Europe have already discovered that, under the conditions of current capitalism's interest in Interest, promises of better working conditions for most (with jobs for more and more) are prevented by the markets' requirement of flexible labour.

There are signs that this capitalist development is speeding up. Booms, as experienced in Thailand and South Korea, expire rapidly as the promised increases in employment and wages arrive, bringing with them conditions which cut them off. It is doubtful if all the troubles of these economies can be put down to corrupt governments and over-greedy bankers – especially as financial intermediaries taking vastly inflated profits are endemic to the whole global system.

In 1995 an interesting sequence of arguments appeared in *The Times*, articulated by Lord Rees-Mogg and supported by views and material from elsewhere. The theme is set out in a piece entitled 'Society's Dicey Prospects' with the subtitle, 'The information age will offer fewer chances to the middling mass of people'.[29] Rees-Mogg draws on work examining the distribution of intelligence among human beings and the correlation of this with earning power. Various studies, he claims, have discovered that

> The more intelligent people are the more likely they are to rise in society, the larger their incomes are likely to be, the more useful they are likely to be to society ... Measurable intelligence correlates closely with social position, and that gap between the 'very bright' and the rest is widening:
> 1) The cognitive elite is getting richer, in an era when everybody else is having to struggle to stay even.
> 2) The cognitive elite is increasingly segregated physically from everyone else, in both the workplace and the neighbourhood.
> 3) The cognitive elite is increasingly likely to intermarry.

He then spells out the predictive point of all this in relation to the generalized expectations promised by the Market mantra.

> The information age has created an enormous demand, greater than ever before, for certain relatively high skills, but is replacing electronically the skills of many of those in the middle of the intelligence distribution. The factory age rewarded those in the middle of this distribution exceptionally well; the information age will reward people of exceptional intelligence. This presents difficult social problems, of which the latest Rowntree Report on inequality gives warning. Societies that try to redress the balance by taxing their most productive people will lose them – the information age has produced an extraordinary geographical mobility. Thus to tax the rich will be the road to ruin in this new age.

I will take up the implications of the 'disappearing tax payer' below. First, consider Rees-Mogg's vision of the social prospect:

> There is bound to be popular resentment of the cognitive elite. There is only too likely to be an expansion of a matching but dysfunctional underclass. As the top of the intelligence and employment distribution glitters in the sun, the danger is that the middle may become bitter from disappointed expectations while the bottom rots. In absolute terms, most of the problems may be soluble. British

out-put per head will probably reach $50,000 a year by about 2040. The rich will be spectacularly rich, but the poor will not in absolute terms be particularly poor. There will be enough real wealth to take care of everyone.

We are indeed bound to the God of perpetual production. Rees-Mogg expresses the same diagnosis and hope in more detail in another article, 'The End of Nations'.

What sort of forecast could now be made for the year 2025? ... Three themes stand out: the second stage of the revolution in electronic communications, the rise of Asia, and the weakening of the nation-state relative to the citizen.
... The global population is now about 5.5 billion. In purchasing power parity terms, world product is around $20 trillion. That gives a world product per head of rather less than $4,000, about a fifth of the North American or European level. During the next thirty years world product is likely to grow at about 3.5 percent a year, which, compounded, means that it will be three times as great in 2025 as it is now. That would give a world product of $60 trillion in 2025, and if the trend were to continue, $180 trillion in 2055. Allowing for population growth, product per head would be about $8,000 in 2025 and perhaps $20,000 in 2055. In thirty years time, world average income per head may approximate that of South Korea now; in sixty years time it will approximate that of the EU.[30]

Is such perpetually compounded growth sustainable? And, if so, should we look forward with pleasure to its alleged affects?

The Necessity of Growth – Threat not Promise

Let us examine further Lord Rees-Mogg's vision of our future in his discussion of 'The End of Nations'. 'The communications of 2025 will have long since taken many, and perhaps most ... taxable transactions into cyberspace. That is a country with no taxes, the greatest tax haven, Bermuda in the sky with diamonds.' He later develops this:

Yet the most successful country of all will have no geographical location. The bright people, the so-called cognitive elite, will deal with each other on the networks of cyberspace outside the existing jurisdictions. By 2025 cyber-country will have at least 250 million citizens, some of them will be as rich as Bill Gates, worth over $10 billion each; the cyber-poor may be those with an income of less than $200,000 a year, but there will be no cyber-welfare, no cyber-taxes and no cyber-government. Cyber-country, rather even than China could well be the greatest economic phenomenon of the next thirty years.[31]

As far as Rees-Mogg is concerned, our particular opinion of such a future is probably neither here nor there. For a later article which echoes some of the same themes, entitled 'Decline of the Past', shows the author to be an economic determinist. He writes:

> Karl Marx saw a pattern in history in which changes in the methods of production lead to the rise of new dominant classes ... It is inevitable that the new methods of economic production and the class that controls them will prevail. Marx's mistake was to suppose that nineteenth century factory production was the final chapter of economic change which would inevitably lead to the dictatorship of the factory workers. Fortunately, it was not, as we now know ... All around the world a new class is springing into existence which can operate the systems of the electronic age to its own advantage. This class has some of the characteristics of the old Marxist bourgeoisie; it is certainly very far from the culture of the nineteenth century European proletariat. It places high value on consumer goods, on education, on fitness, on travel. It yearns for an uncertain spiri-tuality. It also places high value on personal excitement; if it is liable to be enslaved by anything it is by the craving for stimulation, by the New Age cults, by drugs, by sex and by Hollywood. This class is coming to dominate modern civilization.[32]

There is no romantic nonsense about democracy or equality of participation here. Those who command computers and money control all. The same prospect is sketched by Larry Elliott in a report from the 1997 World Economic Forum at Davos.

> Kofi Anan, the new Secretary General of the United Nations, summed it up well when he said that while developing nations acknowledge that they had to work with the private sector, there was no future in a world order only habitable for a small minority. But this is exactly what looks to be happening. Some US economists see

the America of the future as having 20 percent of well educated professionals earning $75,000 (£46,000) to $500,000 a year to carry out orders from the super-rich, while the remaining 80 percent that now have a median family income of $30,000 a year will do all the dirty work and see their living standards eroded year by year. In other words, a modern form of feudalism.[33]

The assessment of future distribution of income and power which leads to this reference to feudalism is sufficiently widely shared to be causing concern about prospects for taxation revenue. This taxation issue is raised more fully by a further Rees-Mogg article, 'When Tax Revenues Slip through the Net', subtitled 'the man with the laptop cannot be traced and taxed, so governments will have to cut spending'.[34] He quotes from a lecture of a taxation expert on 'cybertax': 'The Internet and other technological developments will tend to undermine the administrability of a tax system based on [current] concepts' and refers to:

> the disintermediation which is already one of the Internet's most striking characteristics. Instead of people dealing with each other through an intermediary, they are able to deal direct; they no longer need the distributors, brokers, bankers, and so on, who put them in touch with each other in terrestrial business, because the Internet lets them do that for themselves. But these intermediaries are the people who report taxable transactions to the authorities, and they are essential to the tax system. No intermediary, no reporting. Substantial taxable revenues will therefore just disappear, either because the activity is taxable only in another jurisdiction, or because the source of activity is not traceable, or because the activity will be no longer reported to the tax authorities ... In short, cyberspace is an impregnable tax-haven, and unfortunately a haven for money laundering as well.

A leader in *The Economist* entitled 'The Disappearing Tax-payer' and an accompanying article, 'Disappearing Taxes' widen the perspective.[35] The leader begins with the question: 'Can governments continue to levy taxes in a world in which companies, assets and people are mobile?':

> Not all firms, workers and products are equally mobile. Entrepreneurs, scientists, tennis players and film stars may be able to up-root

themselves in search of lower taxes, but the average worker is still unlikely to become a tax refugee. Although this may reassure governments, it implies that governments will eventually have to cut taxes on the most mobile factors of productions, notably skilled workers, while taxes on less mobile unskilled workers will have to rise. Over the past decade or so taxes on capital have already fallen sharply while those on labour have risen. In future it will be harder to tax firms or high-earners at high rates because they are the most mobile. The implication is *that unskilled labour will have to bear a greater burden* [my emphasis].

Comments from the main article include:

Modern tax systems were developed after the Second World War when cross-border movements in goods, capital and labour were relatively small. Now firms and people are more mobile – and can exploit tax differences between countries. This is the heart of the problem that governments face. Globalisation is a tax problem for three reasons. First, firms have more freedom over where to locate. Activities which require only a screen, a telephone and a modem can be located anywhere. This will make it harder for a country to tax businesses much more heavily than its competitors.

It is clear that capital is becoming more mobile, and some economists fear that as countries offer lower taxes to lure foreign firms, there will be 'a race to the bottom'. Taxes on company profits might even disappear.

Globalisation makes it hard to decide where a company should pay tax, regardless of where it is based. Multi-national firms design their product in one country, manufacturer it in another and sell in a third. This gives them plenty of scope to reduce tax bills by shifting operations around or by crafty transfer-pricing ... Foreign subsidiaries of American companies report higher profit margins in low-tax countries than in high-tax ones. What a coincidence.

The third reason why globalisation is a problem is that, as Swedish firms discovered, it nibbles away at the edges of taxes on individuals. It is harder to tax personal incomes because skilled professional workers are more mobile than they were two decades ago. Even if they do not become tax exiles, many earn a growing slice of their income from overseas, for consultancy work, for instance. Such income is relatively easy to hide from the tax man.

Taxing personal savings also becomes harder when these can be zapped from one side of the globe to the other; cross-border sales of equities and bonds have surged from 3 percent of America's GDP in 1970 to 136 percent in 1995.

The conclusion of this and much more is:

> A disturbing consequence therefore is that in a world of mobile capital, labour is likely to bear a growing share of the tax burden – especially unskilled workers who are least mobile. This will tend to exacerbate unemployment and blue-collar resentment. Add in the fact that the Internet will affect sales of basic necessities less than sales of luxury goods. And the result will be a more regressive tax system.

This is a particularly bland way of reporting how non-mobile workers (surely the vast majority of us) are to be reduced to poorly paid wage slaves (heavily taxed at that) to the new feudal elite of those who possess the required skills and control the necessary money.

The response of the Market faithful to all such evidence is simple. There is no alternative. As *The Economist* comments in discussing Chancellor Gordon Brown's decision to grant the Bank of England operational independence in monetary policy

> Although the Chancellor and Eddie George, the Bank's Governor, might deny it, the Bank will be engaged in the highly political task of choosing how many jobs to sacrifice in order to hit the inflation target quickly rather than slowly. The true case for independence is not that there is no such democratic loss, but that the loss is *more than matched by the economic gain* [my emphasis].[36]

Whose gain? On what specific timescale? To the benefit of what specific people? And who says so? As to the last question, one might borrow the answer put forward by Larry Elliott when he discusses issues closely related to the ones I am pursuing.

> The answer is, of course, the new class of feudal barons – the rich and the powerful who live in their walled fortresses protected by retainers, who avoid paying taxes whenever they can, and demand that the government keep the peasants in check with an increasingly draconian criminal justice system.[37]

To my mind that answer is more resonant with the actual conflicts being generated by our current market system than the bland tone of comments I have quoted above.

However, an intellectual investigation should avoid moral indignation. In the spirit of open-minded enquiry let me stick to my role of an anxious idiot seeking to find out what is really going on. I move on, therefore, to the questions about the sustainability of indefinitely compounded growth which Rees-Mogg cites as an assured future prospect, and on which market apologists rely for the eventual resolution of our concerns about unemployment, poverty and welfare.

In our current system of capitalism growth has ceased to be simply a means to meeting people's needs and aspirations in ways appropriate to our localities. Growth has become the demanding dynamic that keeps the system going for its own sake. Social conditions in developed countries are degenerating while in countries struggling to develop under World Bank and IMF enforced conditions, the poor are driven off the land to fester in cities. The world investment community insists on interest and debt repayments exceeding what such developing countries can afford, draining resources available for education, health and welfare, and even consuming sums made available as aid. All this goes along with the multiplication of pollution, resource exhaustion, waste production and ecological devastation. The details are open to controversy, the subject of as yet unsettled scientific investigation and are liable to differences of evaluation. Yet the *accumulating* effects of it all are increasingly undeniable. Who can ignore ominous signs such as the forest-burning smog afflicting Indonesia, Malaysia and Singapore in 1997/8?

The Market's demand for growth, however, seems to outweigh the urgent human need to consider *together* what this allegedly necessary production is doing to people, places and prospects for the future.

Perpetual growth with its compounding effects is an exponential progression which, being conceived of as necessarily perpetual, must, in application to the lives of human beings and the life of the earth, be experienced as steeply increasing growth *without limits*. So the Market is a system of production committed to (and, see below, *requiring*) increasing production in an exponentially aggregating way indefinitely. This system of compounding production inevitably depends on the natural systems of the earth which are essentially not indefinitely expanding in one direction but are *cyclical*. Given time and space the earth is renewable. But time and space is what the Market is violating. For the Market is run by a capitalist system whose interest is, as I have already said, Interest. And interest can only be earned at high enough rates to keep the system going if productive growth is profitable enough to produce enough Interest to satisfy the money markets whose sole concern is to make more money (i.e. produce higher rates of interest and return on the capital invested).

So the Market requires growth to keep going and make money not in order to respond to what people need; nor in order to provide ways of investment in communities and environments which would help them thrive, survive and be shareable; nor with a view to developing methods, rates and processes of production which could produce interactive rhythms between rates of industrial and commercial production (with their effects) and rates of cyclical renewal of the natural earth (with its own necessary rhythms of growth, death and renewal). The Market only requires to make money.

And the Market must always be making more money – for being an ever more highly leveraged system (that is having the nominal sums of money at use and at risk less and less directly related to any real assets) there must be more and more nominal money created to pay the various interest charges and discharge the various transactions involved in order to keep the 'credit' of the system going. I have illustrated the systemic risk in all this – as recognized by many of the authorities and operators in the system.[38] This apparently limitless process of making the connection between nominal money values and real assets on which people's survival ultimately rests ever more 'elastic' makes the demand for growth ever more necessary.

The entire system has only got to have a sufficient number of knock-on effects from defaults for it to collapse. For each set of real assets in the world is dangerously overloaded with credit secured on credit secured on credit. (Multiplying 'derivatives' and 'securitization' is the name of the money game.) Bill Gates may be the richest man in the world but his 'wealth' is not directly cashable into realities which would feed people, build up communities or check environmental damage. From this perspective the whole system is one vast pyramid scheme, dependent on continually increasing its number of investors, and reliant on no more than a small proportion of those investors ever attempting to cash in their investments at any one time.[39]

As commentators on the Market are clear, it is people at the bottom of the pyramid, and those people who lack the resources to take part in pyramid operations while they depend wholly on the productive operations of the pyramid for jobs and wages, who are expected to bear the costs of taxation and the liabilities arising if parts of the pyramid collapse. Like everyone else, they too (we too) depend on growth being maintained. This dependency on growth looks more and more like slavery to fate rather than a promise of freedom.

In order to keep profitably productive growth going the Market must concentrate on increasing the *wants* of people who have long ceased to be in any sort of real *need*. For it is they who have access to money and credit. Further, in order that such comparatively wealthy people may be freely supplied with the money they need to purchase these not *vitally* necessary goods and services – leaving them with sufficient surplus to invest in stocks, bonds and pensions – their taxation must be kept to a minimum.

Yet again the Market works against any provision through the system for the large number of people in the world who continue to suffer from *basic needs*. There is, after all, little profit to be made out of housing the poor or of setting up the sort of small-scale co-operative agriculture, industrial and commercial activities which could provide a reasonable standard of living for the millions of poor in Asia, Africa and parts of Latin America.

Similar pressures apply – *mutatis mutandis* – in developed countries. Here there is an 'underclass' who cannot be *profitably* employed because we have not been able to afford sufficient social investment out of tax revenue to establish decent housing, or continue a comprehensive free health service and thus send reasonably healthy and well-fed children to competent schools where they might learn to contribute to the responsibilities of being citizens in a society which had cared enough to give them this opportunity. Because of the Market we can no longer afford decent investment in the widespread education and employment of citizens. Instead we are forced to meet the rising costs of prisons and basic welfare payments, which by their paucity and rigor re-enforce the exclusion of those who receive them.

The faith that capitalism *is* perpetual growth and that perpetual growth is perpetual promise, is a fantasy which flies in the face both of the internal dynamics of the system and of the system's effect *now* on people, societies and the earth. We have reached the limits of the usefulness and promise of the amazing growth of the nineteenth century and of the Golden Spasm between 1947 and 1974. It is surely obvious that we need a new version of this wealth-creating system which tackles the problems of spreading participation in freedom and prosperity, and of establishing sustainability, given the limits of the renewability of the natural earth. The first problem of participation and distribution is the endemic political problem of democracy. The second problem of sustainability is the basic problem of survival. For to abandon the world to a Free Market whose dynamic is focused on pursuing the interest of Interest can only destroy the prospects of us all.

As George and Sabelli write, on the last page of their book examining *The World Bank's Secular Empire*,

> The Bank's nominal mission is to promote development. In the Bank's vocabulary the biological meaning [of development] is replaced by a concept of never-ending growth. The Bank's priest-hood specifically denies limits to growth and promises an *ersatz* eternity in the here and now. If such endless growth is supposed to lead to an American or European middle-class standard of living for over five billion people today, and who knows how many tomorrow, we already know this to be an ecological and biospheric impossi-bility, even assuming tremendous and rapid changes in technology. The Bank refuses to confront this last of all last things ... Incantations like 'sustainable development' stave off the moment when the finite must be at last faced.[40]

It turns out, therefore, that the Free Market mantra:

> The Market works, OK
> The Market rules OK
> And, even more OK, the way the Market works and rules is the only way to freedom and prosperity

is kept alive only by the persistence of what may be called the Three Con Trick.

The first con is that the Market promises prosperity to all. It does not. As I have shown,[41] even according to its supporters the Market cannot afford decent wages to those it employs, and offers expansive opportu-nities only to a cognitive elite.

The second con is that the Market offers freedom to all. In fact for many the Market offers slavery to the demands of growth and dependence on the lottery of picking up a job – and even that remains well beyond the possibilities of too many people in our present world.

The third con is that perpetual growth will, endlessly, enable even those at the bottom of the pyramid to have a 'comfortable' income. This is pie in the sky. Such perpetual growth is quite impossible. In the fairly short term the earth will not be able to sustain it. However much the proponents of the totally unrestrained Free Market may conceal the truth from us all, including, I suspect, from themselves 'the finite must at last be faced'.

A symptom of this is the decline in belief in the usefulness of calculating growth by GDP (gross domestic product). GDP includes all sorts of negative things, such as money spent on crime prevention or in dealing with pollution, and takes no account of such things as improvements in social amenities, health and welfare. (Not to mention the vast amount of unpaid work of carers in the home which sustains life in every community.) There are increasingly widespread attempts to come up with agreed formulas for establishing, for example, an index of sustainable economic welfare (ISEW). Attempts so far (although they are in their infancy) indicate that since about the middle of the 1970s whereas GDP has continued to rise in developed countries, any index of sustainable economic welfare has dropped steadily. This reinforces personal impressions of, for example, increased road congestion, or that life in cities is becoming more hectic, crime ridden and polluted. In so many ways 'more' does not mean better. And what 'more' there is does not improve the lot of something like the bottom fifth to the bottom third of our fellow-citizens in developed countries, let alone the lot of millions in developing countries.

Yet we are stuck on this treadmill of material production simply because if we do not continue, the system will collapse and we shall be even worse off. The Market has ceased to be promise for all; for more and more of us it is simply fate. If one is lucky enough to be born into the right family, go to the right school, get the right number of A Levels, defeat your equally qualified peers, and get into the right course in the right university, then (if you can avoid sinking under the weight of the loans) you may be able to get a well-paid job. Then, if you put up with all the stresses and strains and do not care too much about spending time with any family you may have acquired, you may ultimately clear your mortgage, pay your pension costs and enjoy anxious security for a sufficient time. Fate rules and beneficence is a sheer matter of chance for all but the elite.

This was not the vision of eighteenth-century enlightenment, nor of nineteenth century struggles for democracy. Are we to lapse into hopeless indifference now, disillusioned by the evident failure of the Invisible Hand to deliver what the Market mantra promised. We have supposed that this Invisible Hand (translated by philosophical argument into the evolved information system of the Market working by prices) magically ironed out all the negative effects, observable throughout history, of greed, of self-interest, and of deliberate power seeking. There is supposed to be power in the Market to overcome conflicts of interest. Despite the fact that every competitive episode must have a loser as well as a winner, the aggregate process will ensure that all will win and all shall have prizes. Surely the Free Market mantra out-Alices *Alice in Wonderland*.[42]

Do we abandon ourselves to fate and give up all hopes of greater justice, more freedom and shareable prosperity? Is there any possibility of recapturing the Market and regulating it for our requirements, both as citizens of local communities and as neighbours in one world?

These are political and value questions, not economic ones. Unless, of course, we are all economic determinists now, enslaved to the god of production. Surely we can be more free than that. Why should we succumb to the claim that there is no alternative to the god that we have ourselves produced?

Notes

1   Adam Smith, *Wealth of Nations*, Book II, section 4.
2   *The Times*, 'Economic View', 13 December 1996.
3   *The Times*, 2 October 1997.
4   *The Financial Times*, 13 November 1995.
5   Reported by Anatole Kaletsky, *The Times*, 7 February 1997.
6   *The Financial Times*, 20/21 September 1997.
7   The co-author of *Fortress America: Gated Communities in the US*.
8   *The Guardian*, 13 March 1996.
9   Adam Smith, *The Wealth of Nations*, Book II, section 3.
10   *The Times*, 11 February 1997.
11   In a paper emanating from UBS Global Research.
12   *The Times*, 17 September 1996.
13   Anatole Kaletsky, *The Times*, 8 August 1997.
14   Kaletsky, *The Times*, 12 September 1997.
15   Kaletsky, *The Times*, 12 September 1997.
16   Kaletsky, *The Times*, 23 September 1997.
17   Anthony Harris, *The Times*, 22 April 1997.
18   *The Times*, 27 May 1997.
19   *The Financial Times*, 20 September 1997.
20   *The Times*, 11 September 1997.
21   *The Economist*, 27 April 1996.
22   *The Financial Times*, 20 September 1997.
23   Is it most people? Surely not more than about 30 per cent of people at the most own shares and not many more have invested pensions.
24   *The Guardian*, 20 January 1997 (see also p. 130 above).
25   Alison Goodman, Paul Johnson and Steven Webb, *Inequality in the UK* (Oxford: Oxford University Press, 1997).
26   *The Guardian*, 28 July 1997.
27   Compare above from the FT leader on 'but only if countries cut back thickets of restrictions which make workers too expensive to hire'.

28   Ernst von Weizsacker, Amory B. Lovins and L. Hunter Lovins, *Factor Four: Doubling Wealth, Halving Resource Use* (London: Earthscan, 1997), p. 279.
29   *The Times*, 10 February 1995.
30   *The Times*, 31 August 1995.
31   *The Times*, 31 August 1995.
32   *The Times*, 30 January 1997.
33   *The Guardian*, 3 February 1997.
34   *The Times*, 2 December 1996.
35   *The Economist*, 31 May 1997.
36   *The Economist*, first leader, 10 May 1997.
37   *The Guardian*, 24 January 1996.
38   See Chapter 12.
39   Compare the recent worries over what would happen to the economy in this country if too many of the recipients of Building Society 'windfalls' attempted to realize their windfalls at once.
40   Susan George and Fabrizio Sabelli, *Faith and Credit: The World Bank's Secular Empire* (Penguin, 1994), p. 251.
41   See especially Chapters 11 and 12.
42   See the Dodo on the result of the Caucus race, chapter 3 of Lewis Carroll's *Alice's Adventures in Wonderland*.

14 Light from the Far East – The Market is not Fate but Finance and Fixing

My investigations have convinced me that there are no reasonable guarantees that the Market will work well. I have, however, been worried throughout my investigations that it might appear to remain the case that although we cannot rely on the Market for hopefully generalized prosperity, we cannot escape from it. It remains true that 'the Market rules', which means, in practice, that it is luck, chance or fate which rules.

I have been quite clear throughout my reflections that, as a matter of choice, determination and faith, I cannot accept as decisive any such conclusion about the Market as fate. I have not been clear, however, what arguments, other than exhortatory ones about human decency, compassion, solidarity and democracy (the powers of which I would not underestimate) could be marshalled against the threat of TINA. As I struggled with this, however, events took a hand in the form of the crises in the financial markets of several East Asian Tiger economies and Japan which emerged in November 1997. These crises, as they developed, provided illuminating evidence about the actual power and status of market operations.

What they revealed is that in a crisis the prime operators and proponents of the Free Market neither act nor argue coherently. Indeed, in notable ways they act and argue contrary to their claimed theories. To put it fairly crudely, when things start to go seriously wrong, the powers-that-be know that 'the Market' cannot be trusted and it has to be fixed.

The major operators in the Market know that power in this Market arises ultimately from the *operators in* the Market and not from the *operations of* the Market. There is no independent, innate power, which might be designated TINA, available to control the Market. People with the power to do so manipulate it. This means, therefore, that we need not surrender to the inevitability of market forces. For people with power can be counteracted by people who organize countervailing power. The real battle for our future is not economic, subject to mysterious innate rules known only to the initiates, it is political – as questions and issues of power always have been.

The practical example of the reactions of financial experts to the events of the developing financial crises in South East Asia and Japan in 1997/8 reinforces the perhaps more theoretical analyses of the main chapters of this book and prepares the way for suggestions about finding a more helpful way ahead.

My attention was caught by a first leader in *The Financial Times* in November 1997. It crystallized my suspicions of the sinister implications of an earlier leader in the same paper. The remark in this earlier leader, 'Global Risk', which I found particularly unsettling was that, 'Since many global players are likely to be deemed too big to fail if threatened with insolvency, tax payers of the world are heavily at risk.'[1] In other words, *The Financial Times* suspected that the financial markets would not be able to handle the risks that they themselves created.

On this issue the November 1997 leader, 'A Threat to the World', was absolutely explicit:

> Now is not the time for orthodox deflationary policies. Governments must credibly announce that they stand behind the soundness of their financial systems, if not individual institutions. Where foreign currency liabilities are an important source of a country's problems, international rescue operations must be large enough to convince lenders their debtors will remain liquid.[2]

The financial system, which through its innate wisdom is to be the saviour of our world's prosperity, cannot save itself from its own follies. Governments (and their available tax-payers) are exhorted to carry out this saving work, despite our being repeatedly told that markets are far wiser than governments, and that government intervention always makes matters worse. Money must be provided by sovereign states, either by increasing their national debt (by guaranteeing a share of the loans disbursed by themselves or through the IMF) or by printing more paper money – presumably with potential inflationary effect.

What of 'moral hazard' now? Up to this point we have heard only of moral hazard which makes it essential that Third World countries must not be allowed to default on their debts – nor can they be 'forgiven' them, so that they might have the chance to build up their own economies. Domestically we are warned of the equivalent of moral hazard in offering the unemployed welfare support which treats them as citizens rather than forcing them to look for employment – which may or may not be available. The poor therefore must not be subsidized but the banks which invest the money of the owners of capital must be bailed out for fear of the effects on investors and lenders. *The Times* was quite unashamed about this evaporation of 'moral hazard'.

> The most immediate need, as the Bank of Japan has recognised in the case of Yamaichi, is for large injections of public funds to protect depositors in collapsing banks, life insurance and other financial institutions; this is no time to worry about 'the moral hazard' of insulating the culprits from their mistakes.[3]

We note that 'moral hazard' has now retreated into inverted commas. What is morally forceful, just and inevitable for poor nations or poor people fades into a mere manner of speaking when the financial interests of the rich and powerful are at risk. Yet high returns are supposed to be justified by high risk. In practice capitalism is a system which must have its money protected at all costs. The welfare of the poor cannot be afforded unless and until the money system is kept in good working order and producing a high enough return for the international investment community. The interest of capitalism is indeed interest. Public money collected from tax-payers must foot the bill when things go wrong, while the rich grow increasingly skilled at avoiding taxation. The system is given a veneer of respectability and promise by those who profit from it by their persistently being 'hopeful about the Market at other people's expense'. We are not dealing with the inevitability of an evolved system to which 'there is no alternative' (TINA rules), but rather with one more example of the perennial human struggle for a chance for everyone to share in the prosperity generally cornered by the powers-that-be.

The pontifications of the high priests of finance and their faithful acolytes reveal the essential incoherence, rottenness and practical inadequacy of their faith which they promote with an accompanying bromide of promises. Our current politics are hopeless because they are based on a lie – the lie of the guaranteeing beneficence of the Free Market. Belief in 'the Free Market' is simply the latest human conceit about how the world is bound to be. Free men and women can still conceive of, and struggle for, something better.

The South Asian financial crisis of 1997/8 has made it crystal clear that the allegedly wise, disciplined and saving operations of the Market throw up situations with which it cannot cope unaided. The USA, backed up by the other members of the Group of Seven, forced the intervention of the International Monetary Fund with a package of loans (the major foreign banks, under pressure, agreeing to roll over certain short-term credits) to enable local financial systems to avoid bankruptcy. The aid enforced was tied to a series of conditions. These measures, laid down by the IMF, were all aimed at re-establishing financial stability and restoring credit-worthiness in the world's financial markets – the overall effect, however, was to ensure that the Western banks and other creditors involved did not lose their money.

At the centre of the wider crisis, South Korea suffered a particularly acute collapse. Its case is of particular interest since it has been a leading member of those 'Asian Tigers' who were once held up as wonders of the Free Market. South Korea's economic success was so impressive that it had recently been admitted to the Organisation of Economic Co-operation and Development (the OECD – comprising the industrial countries of the world) and was listed as the eleventh largest economy in the world. Neither the form of, nor the reasons for, this particular approach to financial breakdown are directly relevant to the point that I am pursuing. What I am interested in is what the commentators in the financial press have said about the activities of the IMF and the USA in responding to the crisis.

First, it is generally admitted as obvious that the IMF-focused set of interactions secured or repaid the investments of *private* investors from the banks and other financial institutions of the West and of Japan (that is of the G-Seven). Brian Reading (of Lombard Street Research) articulates this in 'Why the IMF Has Got it Wrong'.

> Who, precisely is being bailed out? It is not Korean borrowers. The IMF has stipulated that bad banks and over-committed *chaebol* must be allowed to fail ... It is not the Korean people ... Korea's problems of over-capacity and liquidity-crunch are to be made worse. The IMF has got it all wrong. Foreign lenders are the beneficiaries of this bail-out. US, European and Japanese banks are being rescued from the losses they would face if Korea defaulted.[4]

This view was frequently repeated. A *Financial Times* leader, 'Profiting from the Korean Crisis', put it pungently, with an additional turn of the screw, 'The upshot of such plans is also distressingly clear: the creditors that made some of the riskiest loans are going to be saved ... To add insult to injury, some of them will make a fortune.'[5] It was also agreed that these same western creditors bore a great part of the blame for the debacle. As Reading comments:

> The blame also lies with them. They lent willy-nilly to Korean banks and companies when they could – and should – have known they were cooking their books and were being manipulated by politicians. It lies with western greed, which conspired with Korean corruption to inflate the Korean bubble economy. And it lies with the western regulatory authorities which turned a blind eye to the risky investment policies of their banks.

This judgement is powerfully supported by a reference in an article by Martin Wolf:

> A study from the Washington-based Institution of International Finance released last week shows just how over-optimistic lenders to emerging markets became between the second quarter of 1995 and the third quarter of this year. The risk is that they may return to their old ways too soon.[6]

This links up with the whole issue of moral hazard and the way in which in 'saving the Market' the IMF acts contrary to the alleged principals of the Markets. As Wolf puts it in the same article, '[The IMF programme] has also helped bail-out foolish investors.' In another piece, 'Korea's Big Chance', Wolf takes this criticism further. Referring to arguments against 'the shielding of the population from economic risks', he writes,

> Many westerners concur: attempts to protect the Korean economy from Market forces must cease ... How passionately, it seems, do inscrutable westerners favour the Free Market – except when they start to lose money ... The IMF's legitimate function ... is not to bail-out foreign creditors which scream for the Market and reject the application of its disciplines to themselves.[7]

This reluctance to let market rules work is further documented in 'South Korea Rescue Raises Uncomfortable Questions'.[8] The writer draws attention to the radical change of policy in the approach of the IMF and the US to dealing with the crisis. Originally there was to be a limited IMF-centred programme with tough conditions attached to its loans. In face of the accelerating crisis, what emerged was a rapid extension of loans from public money and the involvement of western commercial banks. The effect was to establish 'a precedent that has underwritten debts of a troubled banking system – which the US said it would not do'. That is to say that the operation was a collusion in saving rash foreign investors and incompetent (if not also corrupt) local banks from the alleged cleansing and corrective forces of the Market.

The article reported that,

> In their defence, the IMF and US claim the alternative to what they did would have been far worse than what happened. It may have required some intellectual gymnastics but the emergency change of plan worked. 'If Korea had defaulted, or if commercial banks had failed to agree to rescheduling, we would have been blamed – and rightly – for causing an international virtual collapse', said one monetary official.

It is obvious to the experts in world finance that the Market cannot save itself. If we want to go on struggling for democracy, decency and shareable prosperity we shall have to do something for ourselves. Leaving it to the Market is hopeless.

This is underlined by a revealing comment in an earlier leader in *The Financial Times*, 'The IMF and its Critics':

> First, argues [the IMF's] critics, the IMF is increasingly dedicated to bailing out private foreign creditors from the consequences of their folly, thereby exacerbating the instability of the financial system it is supposed to strengthen. But this error, if error it is, is not one for which the IMF is responsible, *that is precisely what the great powers want it to do* [my emphasis].[9]

In other words, there is considerable, if not complete, incoherence about the applications of market principles in the financial markets of the world. It is briefly to be noted that incoherence is shown not only in practical approaches to market principles but also in the practical approach to the role of governments. The confusions between the theory of market proponents, and the political requirements of market operators is well illustrated in two leaders in *The Financial Times*. A leader entitled 'Bonuses and Safety-Nets' comments, 'Nor is it as if the biggest commercial banks run the risk of bankruptcy. They are regarded by central bankers as too big to fail.'[10] That is to say, once you are financially big enough, any risk of moral hazard has to be subordinated to the risk of systemic failure. Market forces cannot be allowed to operate and some mix of governmental and 'private' action has to take over. So much, therefore, for the claim that financial markets can be relied upon for a species of wisdom that operates in a self-corrective manner and can be relied upon for the long-term beneficence of all. 'The mystery is why governments continue to allow banks to punt on their own account in global markets knowing that if it all goes wrong the liability falls on the tax payer.'[11] This incoherence and confusion in the area of the relationship between markets and governments is spelt out explicitly in 'Profiting from Korea's Crisis'. (The 'profiting' is entirely western-orientated – although, once again, the mythical market mantra is appealed to in order to claim that sooner or later *all* should have prizes.)

> Is banking part of the private sector? As the crisis in East Asia unfolds, the answer turns out, *once again* [my emphasis], to be both yes and no: profits go to private owners, but losses, if big enough, to tax-payers. As a result, supposedly safe institutions assume vast risks, the result being endemic financial instability.[12]

At this point we need to remind ourselves that neither market activities nor government activities are ends in themselves. According to democratic theory, the private sector and the public sector exist for citizens at large, together with the ordering and preserving of the earth at large. In practice, of course, people seem to want to get into government to exercise power and the business of business is to make money for people in business. Whether we can resume a struggle to make better sense and hope than this is precisely the subject of this book. At least I hope it will establish that to leave the hope of human betterment to the workings of the Free Market on its own is simply not good enough.

In any case, a theoretical approach to economic and political affairs which lays it down that private economic activity is spontaneous and, generally, to be relied upon for good, while government activity is secondary, usually power-seeking and generally to be suspected of making matters worse, is an ideological fable, formed under the powerful but baleful influence of Karl Marx's dialectical reading of the processes of human activities in history. Market activities and government activities are much more intertwined than that and the location of wisdom and promising beneficence in human affairs much more problematic.

The discussions surrounding the South Asian crisis also reveal a good deal of confusion about what is 'government' and what is not. One simple example of this confusion occurs in 'Uncle Sam Sees off Asia's Paper Tigers' by Richard Lambert. Although Lambert warns against hubris, the general theme is that 'today it seems that Wall Street has won the battle' (over Asian styles of capitalism). He concludes, 'So let's hear it for America's regulators. They are an obscure and generally unloved group of people. But it turns out the free markets will not work well without them.'[13] It would be interesting to have had some clearer indication as to which 'regulators' Lambert had precisely in mind. He refers to their work earlier in his article, 'by contrast the American financial system is transparent and open and the banks are kept under close scrutiny'. This seems unduly complacent, or possibly, simply US domestic-centred. For others complain (such as Brian Reading, cited above) about 'western regulatory authorities which turned a blind eye to the risky investment policies of their banks'. George Soros is more sweeping, stating baldly that, 'the private sector is ill-suited to allocate international credit'.[14] Further, 'the regulators' would seem to be bodies authorized under law who, if not part of 'government' are certainly part of 'governance'. But whose interests are they to be trusted to pursue?

Another complicating issue in this area of confusion between private sector and government activities is revealed in the part played during the crisis by particular persons who apparently moved around as 'financial experts' in a closed circle of financial institutions, some of which were directly governmental, some international – set up and supported by governments – and some in private sector banking. Thus 'Observer' in *The Financial Times* carried the following paragraph of cosy financial gossip under the heading 'Rhodes's Collar'.

> The sight of bankers scurrying between hastily convened meetings in New York yesterday to prevent the financial crisis in South Korea from getting out of hand, brought back memories of fifteen years ago when Latin America was at the centre of the storm. Some things don't change. Other banks involved in the talks say Bill Rhodes, the City Corp Vice-Chairman who led the banks through the discussions over rescheduling the Latin debt, has been in the driving seat again in recent days, pushing for an agreement giving Korean borrowers more time to repay loans.

Rhodes hasn't been the host of this particular show; New York Fed president Bill McDonough brought the banks together, then tried to retreat into the background to preserve the impression that this is a private sector effort. Also in evidence has been Ernie Stern, the former World Bank president and now JP Morgan managing director.[15]

If we check through this list of names – the reference to 'the former World Bank president' reminds us that Lawrence Summers, the US Deputy Treasurer, who was equally active in the South Asian rescues, was chief economist of the World Bank. The US Treasury Secretary, Mr Rubin, used to run Goldman Sachs and the mention of J. P. Morgan reminds us that things change very little. In his review of a book on *Manias, Panics and Crashes: A History of Financial Crises*, Richard Lambert refers to the author recalling that,

The great J.P. Morgan more or less single-handedly stopped the crash of 1907 by the force of his personality and his ability to raise capital. Ninety years later the Morgan bank is actively involved in the South Korean rescue – but do not expect it to stick its neck out too far. No single individual or bank can possibly stop the rot – even the International Monetary Fund does not have the resources to draw a line in the sand.[16]

So, what is new? Bankers run the world.

But what is new is that whereas, as Lambert writes, 'in the past, an old-fashioned panic generally led to old-fashioned failures', nowadays things are different. The Market cannot be left to deal with its own malfunctioning. (By means of those 'gales of creative destruction' whereby bankrupting mistakes bankrupt and the Market promotes the survival of the fittest.) Now too many interests are involved; the scope of interlocking market operations is worldwide and the huge sums of money 'sloshing about' are too volatile and subject to self-feeding panic. Crises, therefore, threaten to spiral out of control, and all possible forces must be rallied to suspend the supposed wise and prosperity promoting, guiding rules of the Free Market. Maybe, this time around (and several more times around) the financial powers-that-be will stop the whole system slowing down into serious economic decline on a world-shaking scale. I am not concerned with predicting the likelihood of the next capitalist slump or how big a bust is likely to follow the current (western) boom. I am pointing out that the claim of the Market mantra that Free Markets tend on the whole to be economically wise and to promise general beneficence is explicitly disproved by the current financial goings-on.

The simple and adversative distinction made between the activities of government and the activities of private enterprise in relation to the operations of the markets is obviously false. Governmental, inter-governmental and private financial institutions are all mixed up together in working out responses to events and none of the money experts, in whichever sector, is ready to leave it to the markets. So why should 'we', who are the vast majority of the people in the whole world, and the majority of people still, even in the developed world, who are compara-tively without money power – why should we trust the money experts when they assure us that if we leave things to the Free Market it will all work out for our eventual good?

The international interventions in the Asian crises of 1997/8 are depressingly revealing of more than incoherence of practice in relation both to market economic theory and to the understanding of interactions between the governmental and private spheres in the Market. It is at this point that the issue of rottenness emerges. This rottenness is exposed in the quite explicit way in which the conditions of the bail-outs conducted by the IMF (clearly guided by the US, backed up by the G7 powers) in effect rescued western and Japanese creditors at the expense of pushing ordinary South Asian savers and workers into unemployment and poverty. And in addition ensuring that financial agencies and organized investors in the West (and especially in the US) were given the opportunity to buy-up significant parts of the eastern economies at bankruptcy knock-down prices. What the IMF was actually promoting was not the stability of present market systems for the eventually increasing prosperity of all, but the scope of the western financial powers-that-be to increase their opportunities for financial control and profit-making.

This is spelt out in the financial pages of *The Times* and *The Financial Times*:

> There is plenty of scope for things to get worse. Far more than the realistic terms the IMF asked of Britain in 1976 or its school masterly approach to the poor and the wayward, the IMF's loan terms to Korea have the punitive tone of a treaty imposed on a defeated foe after war. Nor need Koreans speculate on conspiracy theories. Americans openly seek to use this opportunity to shackle Korea and promote Western trade interests.[17]

In *The Times* of Christmas Eve 1997, in an article entitled 'How the West Cages Asian Tigers in IMF Trap', Janet Bush writes:

> The fire sale of Asia has begun. Goldman Sachs is today reported to be prepared to spend $4 billion on buying up bundles of asset-backed loans from stricken Japanese banks ... Other American investment banks who learnt the art of buying and repackaging bad loans during the Latin American debt crisis of the 1980s will surely follow. These forays are the very early signs of an American take-over of Asia's financial and banking sectors aided and abetted by the International Monetary Fund ...
>
> It is hard to avoid the conclusion that its 'bail-out' of Asia amounts to a deliberate policy of laying the region open to take-over by foreign interests ... At the same time as the IMF is ensuring a brutal shake-out of Asian financial institutions, it is demanding that Asian governments open their financial markets to foreign investment at their point of maximum vulnerability and when assets are cheapest.

She then makes the important observation,

> Lest anyone dismiss this as a silly conspiracy theory, just remember the speech that Mickey Kantor, former US Commerce Secretary, made to the Confederation of British Industry this month. He told his audience that the troubles of the 'tiger economies' should be seized as a golden opportunity for the West to reassert it commercial interests. When countries seek help from the IMF, he said, America and Europe should use the IMF as a battering ram to gain advantage.[18]

This comprehensive indictment is supported by considerable evidence elsewhere. John Burton, for example, writing in *The Financial Times*:

> Korea Inc. is up for sale ... The survival [of South Korea's conglomerates] depends on rapidly shedding excess businesses by selling them to foreign investors ... The International Monetary Fund's ... rescue has forced the country to drop restrictions on foreign take-overs ... Moreover, Korean companies are likely to be sold at bargain prices.[19]

His article also contains the interesting comment,

> Share prices are so low that the total market capitalization of the

Seoul Bourse last week amounted to Won 66,350 billion (£26.6
billion), about the size of the Dutch Banking Group ING, the
world's seventieth largest company.[19]

That is to say that the world's seventieth largest company can command
more capital than the stock market of the eleventh largest economy in the
world. Of course bankers and businessmen run the world. They
command the nominal money supplies (they are the capitalists of
capital). It is the tax-payers of the various 'sovereign states', supporting
their 'sovereign currencies', therefore, who ultimately bear the costs of
risk while the bankers and businessmen juggle with the profits. Is there
no political way of effectively raising once again the issue of 'no taxation
without representation'? Or has the Free Market thrown off both the
pretence of the evanescent Invisible Hand of Adam Smith and the
nonsense of democracy – despite muttering mantras about prosperity
and freedom.

Footnotes on the theme of the West seizing its opportunities continue
to appear. Thus, *The Times* business commentary remarks on a visit of
George Soros to Seoul:

> Mr Soros's presence in Seoul captures some of this ambiguity. His
> hint that he might make a 'quite substantial' investment in Korea
> could be seen as the ominous arrival of a big buyer at the car boot
> sale now under-way in Asia. By forcing Asian economies to open up
> their markets to foreign ownership just when assets are cheapest and
> their need for cash most pressing the IMF has ensured rich pickings
> for foreign investors.[20]

A couple of days later, the same commentator observes,

> This week's chosen victim for global humiliation is Indonesia.
> During decades of profitable expansion there, the West found it
> convenient to ignore the sheer unpleasantness of Indonesia's
> Government. Suddenly Washington, long defender of the politically
> indefensible, has become a nit-picking financial prosecutor.[21]

And so it goes on. It is all quite clearly a power game, as Janet Bush
pointed out in an earlier article, 'US and Europe Play Power-Games'.

> The focus of the battle of influence now raging between America
> and Europe is the proposal, first mooted in Hong Kong of a Japan-

led Asian bail-out fund. Both America and Europe have fiercely opposed the idea, arguing strongly that the IMF ought to lead any financial rescue. The reason for this is obvious. America and the large European economies are the dominant shareholders in the IMF and can, therefore, exert influence indirectly ... It looks like Japan will capitulate to intense pressure and that the Asian fund will be quietly dropped or down-graded. The IMF and its powerful shareholders will determine the nature of Asia's recuperation. Asia is not, however, the only object of interest. The tussle between America and Europe goes far deeper than this; it goes to the very heart of which will dominate the world financial system in the future.[22]

Such a context seems to validate my choice of the word 'rottenness'. As Janet Bush writes:

The IMF may genuinely believe that West is best and that Japan and South Korea will end up with a sound financial system much more quickly if their banks are run by Goldman Sachs or Citycorp. But there is still something faintly obscene in the way that western commercial interests always appear to profit from others' misfortunes (and avoid paying for their own mistakes in the case of US banks who lent so wildly in Latin America).[23]

A similar point is put more strongly by Mark Atkinson in 'No Bargains for Korea in this Sale'.

There is something morally distasteful about the IMF lending money for Korea to pay off its short-term foreign debts and in return demanding draconian reforms which will ultimately benefit the West and meanwhile requiring Korean shareholders, depositors and employees to suffer.[24]

Atkinson ends his article with a suggestion about what would have possibly been a better market solution.

Armed with a competitive currency following the devaluation of the Won, Korea might have been better off left alone to export its way out of trouble and restructure using internal financing drawn from a high level of domestic savings. The difficulty is that this would not have gone down well in the West, which would have seen its share of export markets eroded without any off-setting benefits. As it is, following the IMF bail-out Korea as a production base will still enjoy a significant cost advantage over the West. But the profits of Korea-based enterprises will flow to US, European and Japanese owners, not the Koreans.

Despite the protestations of such as Lawrence Summers, the Market is not left alone to work according to 'eternal verities of finance'. Where market processes threaten the money-making powers of the West, they are forcibly manipulated to preserve – or even to enhance – those powers. Not only is this acknowledged by western financial commentators, but both the commentators and government spokesmen refer thankfully to how market failures in South East Asia – at least for the time being – help to maintain Market prosperity in the West. A typical example of this is to be found in a report 'Living Under an East Asian Cloud'. At the end of his paragraph on 'will US inflation come back?', Gerard Baker writes: 'The Asian crisis could knock half a point or so off US growth next year, quenching inflationary fires and providing the economy with another near-perfect soft landing.'[25] It is remarkable how chance in the Market serves the West. It will be recalled that back in February 1995 Anatole Kaletsky commented on the Mexican Market crisis to the effect that the slow down this was about to produce,

> in other developing countries ... will come at a handy time for the rich industrial countries of Europe and North America ... Flagging demand in the Third World should counteract inflation, weaken commodity prices, and reduce the pressure for higher interest rates in Europe and the US.[26]

So the prosperous western world is blessed once again in 1998 – at other people's expense. There would seem to be a rottenness here which ought to be deeply troubling humanely because it is both globally threatening and humanely deceitful. The responses provoked by the late 1997 crisis in South East Asia reveal that, in practice, even its self-styled practitioners do not believe in the Free Market faith.

The Market faith is false and to persist in maintaining it and in peddling the promises which go with it without serious qualification is to persist in deceit. But it would be worse than useless to construe this as indicating that we must now return to seeing the world in terms of a basic conflict between the exploited have-nots and the greedy and unconcerned haves. There are two initial reasons for avoiding such a return to nineteenth-century dialectics.

The first is that if it were not for the amazing productivity of investment and markets in the nineteenth century and onwards there would be no widespread fruits of such prosperity for the have-nots to feel excluded from enjoying. The second reason is that there is a great deal of evidence that the majority of enthusiasts and operators of the Free Market faith are themselves self-deceived about the prospects of it. It is necessary therefore to develop some understanding of the likely sources of this shared delusion about the Free Market if we are to dispel it and develop more hopeful ways forward into a future which has more realistic promise in it of increasingly shared prosperity. We need to build political and social coalitions for developing mutual freedom and sustaining the viability and enjoyability of the earth. We have, in fact, to develop a fresh sense of shared responsibility and shared morality in developing our entrepreneurial, productive and trading activities into the millennium.

Notes

1　*The Financial Times*, 15 July 1997; already cited above, p. 166.
2　*The Financial Times*, 20 November 1997.
3　*The Times*, 25 November 1997.
4　*The Financial Times*, 20 December 1997.
5　*The Financial Times*, 5 January 1998.
6　'Why the IMF Has Got it Wrong', *The Financial Times*, 20 December 1997.
7　*The Financial Times*, 15 December 1997.
8　*The Financial Times*, 2 January 1998.
9　*The Financial Times*, 17 December 1997.
10　*The Financial Times* 22 December 1997.
11　*The Financial Times*, 22 December 1997.
12　*The Financial Times*, 5 January 1998.
13　*The Financial Times*, 23 December 1997.
14　'Personal View' *The Financial Times*, 31 December 1997.
15　'Observer', *The Financial Times*, 30 December 1997.
16　Review by Richard Lambert in *The Financial Times*, 10 January 1998.
17　Business Commentary, *The Times*, 12 December 1997.
18　*The Times*, 24 December 1997.
19　*The Financial Times*, 29 December 1997.
20　*The Times*, 6 January 1998.
21　*The Times*, 9 January 1998.
22　*The Times*, 19 November 1997.
23　*The Times*, 24 December 1997.
24　*The Guardian*, 5 January 1998.
25　*The Financial Times*, 27/28 December 1997.
26　*The Times*, 2 February 1995 (already cited above, p. 145).

15   Rediscovering Democracy and Redirecting the Market

Emergence of the Moral Challenge

It is my contention that faith in the Market, and the activities that enforce its practices on others, is not just a matter of mistaken judgement but also involves elements of deceit. This case against the proponents and practitioners of the Market faith is underlined by the fact that, in a crisis, their actions and comments reveal that they do not trust the precepts they themselves claimed to be following.

Pursuing this challenge further becomes an uncomfortable matter because it involves challenging the morality and sense of responsibility of a great number of people who, perhaps without much analytical reflection but in reasonably good faith, are involved with various degrees of enthusiasm or indifference, in a vast range of market operations. But if there is serious truth in the analysis which I have developed, then the proponents and practitioners of this market faith which I have been describing and analysing throughout this book are, *in effect* liars; and they *ought* to recognize the case for the making of this accusation against them.

Introducing a charge of immorality and irresponsibility into a discussion of economic activities, and the theories supporting them, may seem offensive and sound like condescending moralism. The issue however is critical to the possibility of finding new ways ahead for political and social collaboration in rescuing the Market from its current distortions. New efforts are needed to secure the benefits of our productivity and trading for people at large in the world at large. The energy required for this task will not be generated without a shared sense of our moral responsibilities as free human beings who are neighbours and citizens in one limited world.

As we approach the twenty-first century we are facing a severely practical challenge. The Market cannot be relied upon to promote human prosperity and freedom on its own. Its operations have to be guided and checked by human morality, collaboratively exercised, through political means. This issue of shared immorality and irresponsibility involved in accepting where the Free Market is at present taking us therefore has to be addressed. I hope to be able to pursue this necessarily uncomfortable theme of the personal immorality and irresponsibility which is *in effect* involved in an uncritical espousal of the Free Market without appearing to pass a moral judgement on any particular person or class of persons. I do not consider myself to be in any position to make direct accusations of irresponsibility and immorality against particular persons. A particular person must be responsible to his or her own conscience. I am seeking to point out that conscientious questions do arise.

It is at least clear that proponents of the Free Market appear to ignore the realities of the power structures involved in the Market. In the face of all counter-evidence the alibi of the true believer in the Free Market remains the claim that actions promoted within financial markets to secure the protection of the money-making capacities of the Market, as currently operating and dominated, will ensure that the innately resilient Free Market will resume its beneficent functioning to the eventual prosperity of all. For example, the 'bone carving pain' of the ordinary people of South Korea referred to as their immediate prospect by their President-elect in early 1998 will eventually bring blessings to us all, including these people of South Korea. But my investigations have surely shown this alibi to be threadbare.

It is true that all proponents of faith in the Free Market admit to the imperfections and malfunctioning of this market. But the types and degrees of malfunctioning are not counted as sufficient evidence to undermine seriously the basic and hopeful faith. In the words of Professor Krugman,

> By the way, saying that market economies are imperfect does not imply a longing for some other system. Winston Churchill once said of democracy that it is the worst system of government known to man, except for all the others. Similarly, a real as opposed to an idealised market economy is a highly imperfect system which works better than anything else we have come up with. The point of

emphasising market imperfections is not to condemn the market system, but simply to explain how things can sometimes go wrong.[1]

Samuel Brittan, too, appeals to Churchill:

> The case for accepting markets as a system for allocating resources does not depend on the belief that they can infallibly tell us either what will happen or what ought to be done about it by policy makers. The case is rather the one that Churchill argued about democracy: that it was the least bad system he knew.[2]

It has never seemed to me that the Churchillian dictum licensed the conclusion that nothing should be done to improve the way that democracy works. Indeed, political attempts to reform the practice of any democracy are surely inherent in any consistent commitment to democracy. The use of the dictum to justify the dismissal of market malfunctions as being of only secondary significance with regard to what we can expect of the Market seems one more indication that the combined claim about both the necessity of the Free Market and its beneficence is based more on faith than on argument. 'Democracy' on its own neither has a fixed form of operation nor, on its own, guarantees freedom and efficient government. Why should 'the Free Market' on its own have a fixed form of operation and guarantee freedom and prosperity? This type of dismissive belittling of obvious market malfunctioning and inconsistencies is typical of the way in which believers in the Market struggle to maintain the *appearances* of coherence and beneficence in the Market in face of the *realities* of actual market operations.

The production of 'more', whatever it is, does not imply 'better' for whoever we are, wherever we are. It was always blind and bland stupidity to suppose that multiplying indiscriminate productivity promises a solution to human woes and produces no new problems for people and the world. But now it is quite obvious.

The conflict between owners of capital and the people dependent only on their labour-power is quite as evident as Marx ever said it was, however destructive his political proposals for dealing with this may have turned out to be. Under the current pressures of capitalism the promise of improvement to the poor in developing countries or to the workers in developed ones is always jam tomorrow and either further restrictions today, as in the European countries struggling to meet Maastricht criteria, or being precipitated back to poverty from which they had hoped to emerge as in South East Asia or Latin America. In

Latin America the standard of living of the increasing number of the poor is worse now than at the beginning of the decade, however successful the 1994/5 rescue of Mexico from its financial crisis was for western bankers and world financial stability. As to the USA, admittedly the most successful economy in the world, a recent study from the Centre on Budget and Policy Priorities shows that

> despite the boom, America's richest and poorest are growing farther apart. Whereas in real terms the income of the richest fifth of families with children has grown by sixteen percent since the mid-1980s, that of the poorest fifth has fallen by three percent. Take the comparison, in a new study from the Centre on Budget and Policy Priorities, back to the late 1970s and the gap is wider still: the income of the richest has grown by thirty percent and that of the poorest has fallen by 21%.[3]

According to a chart accompanying this report, it is only the two top quintiles of families that have seen an increase in real income between the late 1970s and the mid-1990s. That is to say that during this period of America's great economic success 60 per cent of American families have become at least comparatively worse off – and the poorest fifth grossly and absolutely so, given the vast improvements in the lot of the top fifth.

If this is what economic 'success' in 'wealth' production does, what hope for the unsuccessful? Wealth in nominal money terms is increasingly made, but overall evidence suggests that things are getting worse (if 'better' is supposed to mean that more people become more free because of their participation in real wealth). The promises made to the unsuccessful are false. In all probability this falsity is inherent in the system. The cost of capital is too great for the development of enterprises which could 'profitably' employ sufficient numbers of the average and the poor at any level of decent living. But, in any case, the promises are *practically* false for their fulfilment (even if the current system could eventually develop to allow this) is evidently long, if not indefinitely, delayed. The general hope in capitalism is, in foreseeable practice, at other (or most) people's expense.

The hopes and promises of the Free Market as currently operated, look more and more like an illusion, yet there seems to be a widespread determination not to face up to the evidence. Instead the illusory hope has been transformed, by some sociological chemistry, into a shared delusion that the hope really exists and that the Free Market, through some mechanical or organic self-correcting dynamic, will bring the fulfilment of hope ever nearer, all the time incorporating more people in its cornucopia of blessings on its way. Any attempt therefore to build up seriously organized opposition to this deluded surrender is undermined before it can gain a proper public hearing.

I do not see how anyone who has attended to the lines of argument and the types of data which I have touched on in the chapters of this book can reasonably maintain the soundness of the claims made for the Free Market. Yet these claims are used to justify the politics of all the countries in the world – led by the prosperous West and Japan. Politicians and financiers are constantly telling us and themselves that these claims are valid, promising and irrefutable. The claims are declared rationally sound because they are alleged to rest in reasonably secure economic theory. The claims are practically sound because they rest on the deliverance of amazing production so far. The claims, further, are morally sound, for morality is either irrelevant to market transactions in themselves or is satisfied by the promising results of market operations.

Since 'being moral' is now widely held to be an individual matter, moral issues arise only about what individuals choose to do with their money after they have made it. The making of money in the Market is therefore, strictly speaking, an amoral matter. But fortunately, as by an Invisible Hand, or by blind evolutionary chance, the overall effect of the Free Market is moral. The rational theory of the Market economically and the practical deliverance of the Market combine to promise that everybody will eventually obtain access to enough money to have their own power to exercise their own morality. They will be able to expend the money which in one way or another they receive through the Market in ways which they choose. Thus everyone will be free and sufficiently prosperous and it is the Market and the Market alone which promises us all a sufficiently material, secular and moral salvation – one day.

It is plainly absurd to leave to the Market the responsibility for enabling us to be moral. Morality, freedom and shared prosperity can only be *our* responsibility. The maintenance of TINA (There Is No Alternative – and nothing better can be found because nothing better has so far been found) depends on power, on inertia and on collusion in a delusion. It does not express or reflect any innate necessity in the nature of things. The Market is neither a prudential dispensation nor a deterministic natural emergence. It is produced by human beings, worked by human beings, maintained by human beings and defended or manipulated by human beings. The ways of the Market can therefore be changed if there is sufficient awareness and will, focused in sufficient organization and backed up by sufficient political power.

This is a very big 'if' but it is not a theoretical or economic 'if', it is a practical and political 'if'. The world of human intercourse and activity is not ruled by any theory. It is at the mercy of us, including our theories of how it works. If one theory temporarily establishes itself as the latest fatal conceit then we are dominated by a deceitful illusion. In any case we have to cope with the effects and opportunities of our behaviour and choices, including our theories – assisted by any resources of human insight, morality and endurance, including any spiritual and transcendent resources that may seem to be available to us. To claim that there is no alternative to the Market as we now understand it and expound it (TINA) is to turn one, rather crude and simplistic, version of a set of doubtfully coherent and certainly intensely debatable economic theories, into a crude political ideology.

This point about ideology is stressed because it is a universal weakness of apologists for the Market that they ignore the persistence and ubiquity of ideology and especially the connection between ideology and power. There is a total unwillingness to acknowledge the possibility that the reliance on TINA to justify submission to the Market and excuse its malfunctions is not a reliance on indisputable reasoning and on undeniably observable data, but a claim to power. The powers claimed include access to an economic expertise which gives the experts the right to establish the theory that supports the reasoning for the Market and the right to select the data which define the successes of the Market. These two powers converge in the maintenance of, and justification for, the economic powers-that-be maintaining themselves in power. There is nothing new in such claims.

Turning temporary successes into ideologies and idolatries of power and exploitation is a pattern frequently repeated in human behaviour. However, a central feature of recent human history has been the attempts to penetrate, modify or overthrow the ideologies of the powers-that-be in order to expand the range of human freedom and participation in both prosperity and freedom. The liberty to pursue, protect and expand this human search has been a constant aim and vision of human aspirations and politics for at least as long as has the extraordinary outbursts of human energy and productivity which have formed and driven the Market.

We seem to have forgotten the once famous warning given a classical shape late in the eighteenth century (apparently by one John Philpot Curran in a speech on the Right of Election to the Lord Mayor of

Dublin in July 1790) 'eternal vigilance is the price of liberty'.[4] Whenever people succeed in dominating the current structures of power (whether, for example, land and the military in feudal times, or money and the Market in modern times) they do not lightly desist from cornering the benefits from it. As the currently growing gap between the rich and the rest show, the riches and wealth over which the powerful gain control are out of all decent proportion in relation to the wealth, or even the possible livelihood and subsistence, of all the rest of human beings on the earth. The powerful and their acolytes have always invented an ideological justification for such an imbalance, claiming that the way things are are the ways either God or evolution have determined that things shall be. Some form of the TINA argument is as old as the time when slaves first gained the nerve to question the right of their overlords to the powers they exercised. Who said that the gods or fate or necessity decreed that things should always work this way?

By the end of the twentieth century the market-makers have become the market-takers and are organized to remain so. All that is new is that our modern overlords now bend scientific, technological and economic arguments to their interest as these are the types of argument that are now assumed to have obvious and so *neutral* authority.

The way power is exercised is a human responsibility which must not be hidden behind alleged necessity, whether of the Market or any other sphere of practice and power. If progress towards generally spreading prosperity and freedom is to be maintained, eternal vigilance is required *all round* – including vigilance about the workings of the Market and the powerful groups that fix the Market in their own interest. To claim that the Market is bound to work in such and such a way and, further, that the way is bound in the longer run to work to the interests of all of us is a blatant example of what Lord Dahrendorff called 'the fatal conceit that we can impose one comprehensive view on a recalcitrant world'.[5]

To accept the type of fatality about the Market involved in the current alibis for the Market is a betrayal of the dedicated human pursuit of democracy, freedom and a just and participatory society for all, which has been such an important part of our history in the same last two hundred years. It seems that we have completely lost our nerve. The great moral tradition of democratic concern for human freedom and mutual responsibility has simply been abandoned to a materialistic myth labelled 'the Free Market'. The Market has been reified, and even, deified. It has been turned into a powerful 'thing' in its own right, as if it were a built machine or an evolved organism with its own clearly distinctive existence and its own self-supplied and self-regulated driving mechanism or dynamism. No such mere 'thing' could deliver any truly human freedom or prosperity. To believe so is to abandon ourselves to an utterly inhuman determinism.

Mercifully and hopefully no such distinctive 'thing', machine or organism exists. The 'Market' is a metaphor labelling a set of goings on operated by people who produce and trade; 'goings on' which are increasingly dominated by people who trade in money, by credit creation and other financial transactions. If we are to look for growth in general human prosperity, shared human freedom and our ability to preserve the sustainability of the earth, we have to face up to the power, the manipulation and the distortion of those who make the Market work to their own prosperity and dominance. We need to see through the propaganda to reality. 'The Market' does not 'work', it is people who work. 'The Market' is a metaphor and the 'Free Market' an illusion. What is real are the human beings who through a variety of institutions (public and private), in which they are ordered, grouped and inter-locked, have partly evolved and partly manoeuvred themselves into a position, where they control the money transactions and therefore dominate the trade transactions of the globe. Adam Smith's beneficent Market, guided 'by an Invisible Hand' has become the corporate playground of international financiers who manipulate money for further money-making and clearly have the upper hand.

We need to sort out the confusion of both our ideas and our language. It would help to avoid false generalizations, for instance, if the activities of the immense variety of institutions, locations and activities engaged in human productivity, trading and exchange were simply referred to as 'markets' with a small 'm'. The phrase 'the Free Market' is then clearly marked out as an ideological one labelling a certain construction put upon selected aspects of activities in the markets of the world.

The phrase 'financial markets', however, is of a different verbal status. Financial markets clearly have a concrete existence and exercise func-tions of a particularized kind. The ideological construction of 'the Free Market' is used to co-opt these financial markets into the myth of the guaranteed beneficent effect of market forces for human prosperity and freedom. This co-option is not convincing if one examines the actual workings of the financial markets, the effects they produce, and the excuses and explanations made for them.[6] What one actually encounters in the financial markets is the upper hand of those who can manipulate money and credit. There is nothing mysterious about this, although there is much that is complicated and a good deal that is concealed. But, at least, an examination of the financial markets makes it clear that we are up against nothing more mysterious than old-fashioned power, greed and fear. Thus, we are not ultimately constrained within a vast and unalterable system with its own innate rules of inevitability. We need to recover our human nerve and organize ourselves to challenge the upper hand of the economic powers-that-be.

Seeing Things Differently and Doing Things Democratically

The first wealth-creating system human beings have ever known is now running amok and askew. The central political, economic and human task now, therefore, is to develop a second wealth-creating system which will recapture trading and productivity as a humane activity for all human beings and as a sustaining activity for the future of the world.

It must be possible to work out such a politics and economics. For if 'we' (some of us) can fix things in and through the Market, then 'we' (all or most of us) can organize to change things, Market and all. The basic, determining and vital problem for the twenty-first century lies in the will we can muster to dispel the collusive delusion of the current Free Market faith. Sufficient people have to find the shared courage to set out on a renewed set of political activities, informed by political realism, driven by moral and responsible human concern and designed to make things better for as many as possible. For all its imperfections politics has to be reasserted over economics.

The greatest heresy of the Market as it is at present sold to us is that some mysterious force in it neutralizes power and greed and guarantees beneficence and sharing. This is quite as much an impossible utopian illusion as the most dedicated Marxism ever was. Both of these very powerful utopian illusions produce, in their respective spheres of influence and dominance, collusive delusions. The fatal flaw or conceit which gives sustaining dynamism to both the delusions is a simple-minded and limitless faith in production. Marx thought that this meant working with the material dialectic. We think that this means working with the Free Market itself as the immanent and unfolding expression of the genius and beneficent force of productivity. The crisis and opportunity we now face is that the Free Market as the force and form of the god of our production is now clearly revealed as discredited and discreditable.

None the less, faith in the Free Market is still upheld as common sense and it remains so despite the fact that it is becoming less and less plausible to claim that this is a promising way forward. Therefore, if we care for truth and if we dare to believe that we human beings have a capacity to strive for a better future for both ourselves and our earth then the impracticality of the Free Market faith has to be challenged head on. This brings me back to the challenge I formulated earlier that proponents and practitioners of this market faith are, *in effect* liars and they *ought* to recognize the case for the making of this accusation against them.

This accusation of being liars put forward against persons of acknowledged status and expertise who are publicly in good standing, and may be generally assumed to be in good faith may seem extreme and impertinent. The pertinence, however, is this. Arguments about the Free Market are not just arguments about economics. They are arguments about what the world is really like, how human beings should really be treated and about what 'we' as human beings together can reasonably and rightly hope and strive for. To promote the Free Market as the promising way forward for us all is to make practical and powerful statements about the truth and reality of the world of human beings. Free marketeers are telling a story about us and the world which is put forward as so true and realistic that all of us *have to fit in with it*. This claim to truth is exposed as an ideological claim to power. The unsatisfactory nature of the grounds for this claim and the threatening effects now being produced by it have to be recognized and refuted so that both productive and political power may be redirected.

This redirection requires political activities supported by sufficient public interest and concerned public opinion to have effect on the way power is exercised in both political and economic matters. Destroying the collusive delusion of the Free Market faith and working out the political, public and consensual activities necessary for redirecting the productive possibilities of our trading activities as human beings require personal rethinking and activity organized into collective and political action. All persons actively engaged in the Free Market and its activities have therefore to be challenged with the shared political and individual responsibilities of each and every one of us with regard to the Market.

This is why it is, in my view, realistic, and, above all, potentially hopeful to say, the proponents and practitioners of this market faith are, *in effect*, liars. This is to confront the advocates of the Free Market in as pointed and as personal way as possible to face the fact that there is something shocking, undesirable and deeply disturbing about the way the Market operates at present and the way we all collude in ignoring this. As the Free Market story gets it increasingly wrong about the world and about people, we are colluding in producing a good deal of misery. It is of the utmost practical urgency, therefore, that all who promote the Free Market or acquiesce in it take some personal responsibility for it.

There is a serious personal moral issue involved here for each and every one of us as individuals, citizens and neighbours. Taking an enthusiastic part in market operations, making active contributions to maintaining the collusion in the delusion of the Free Market faith, or simply acquiescing in it are all ways of living a set of lies and promoting them as a set of promises. This is not a decent way of being oneself or of treating one's fellow human beings. This corrupting falsity and indecency are endemic in the Free Market system as it is worked at present by the financial and business powers-that-be. This falsity and indecency therefore remain even if I firmly believe, or simply suppose, that my involvement in profit-making is a direct and unambiguous contribution, however small, to the well-being of everyone in the world. The world, I may have been led to believe, is so organized that my making what money I can contributes to everyone having the chance to make what money they can and so we shall all prosper together someday fairly soon. Even if I do not think much of this or occasionally have grave doubts, what is the good of thinking further about it? After all there is no alternative on offer and, even if there were, I certainly am in no position to divert the established momenta of the Free Market. What a relief therefore to accept assurances that issues of morality about market goings on can be left to individuals as they, individually, see them arising, while issues about the effects of market goings on can be left to the longer term operating of the Market itself.

It is precisely this acceptance of the Free Market delusion, with an accompanying admission of fatalism (There Is No Alternative) and claim to legitimate irresponsibility (I can do nothing about it) that has to be challenged in the name of realism, humanity and hope.

The practical difficulty in mounting an effective challenge, however, is that we have no practical alternative pattern of production and trading sketched out with which to confront the free marketeers. The urgently required challenge to the present operations of our Free Market system, therefore, cannot be mounted under the banner of an alternative system. We appear to be brought up short then, by the validity of Professor Krugman's alibi for the Free Market:

> saying that market economies are imperfect does not imply a longing for some other system ... a real as opposed to an idealised Market

economy is a highly imperfect system which works better than anything else we have come up with.[7]

I have argued before that this alibi for the Market is an evasion, and I continue to do so. The reason it is an evasion despite there being no alternative system to the Free Market in sight lies in what is involved in the understanding of the Free Market as a 'system', combined with the implications of the idea that this system 'works better than'. For the very ideas of the Free Market and its guiding dynamic of productive capitalism are not just drawn from a straightforward description of something like a set of natural phenomena. The claim that this system 'works better' than anything else we have come up with has built into it an assumption about 'the more production the better', which also forms part of an ideological perception of the workings of the world and the interactions of human beings. The collusive delusion about the viability and inevitability of the Free Market system casts its cloud of unreality and confusion over the way arguments are supposed to carry weight and the way data are to be selected and interpreted. The battle to break through this Free Market delusion is a battle for liberation from the domination of a false description of our human situation and false promises about how this situation can be enabled to 'work better'. The heart of this delusion lies in the wholly mistaken belief that reality is 'dialectical'. That is to say that it is literally true of reality that it has a power working within it which, if one system of life, work and economics fails, then the system of life, work and economics which takes over will on its own internal dynamic be guaranteed to succeed, or, at least, will do the best that can be done for us and that we can hope for.

An illustration of the way in which a dialectical way of interpreting market ideology continues to dominate our common way of looking at the economic and political affairs of the world, is provided by what Kofi Annan, the UN Secretary General, is reported to have told a gathering of businessmen at Davos early in 1998. He, 'pointed out that Market capitalism has no major ideological rival. Its biggest threat is from within. "If it cannot promote both prosperity and justice, it will not have succeeded", he said.'[8] As there is no major ideological rival there is no readily available alternative game-plan for developing and handling human productivity and trading. This may be true but the disappearance of any alternative and opposing 'major ideology' to market capitalism does not mean that the ideology of market capitalism has therefore won a dialectical victory and therefore established itself as the one, true, inevitable and promising ideology for the world and all human beings in it. Market capitalism is not rightly to be thought of an established system with an innate dynamic which is correctly described by an ultimate and saving ideology. To maintain this ideological line about the Market is to continue playing the game as it was mapped out by both Marxists and capitalists in the nineteenth century. Marx dared to dream that once the proletarian revolution had gone far enough in controlling and deploying the means of production, the state would wither away and every man would be free to follow his inclinations after making his necessary productive contribution to the prosperity of all. With the problem of shared prosperity solved by endless production properly organized freedom would be general and idyllic. It is perhaps a measure of how much less idealistic we have become that, for example, the Rees-Mogg vision looks forward to a rich entrepreneurial class, assisted by a well-paid mobile cognitive elite and all looked after for the ordinary routine things of life by a large service class who would, none the less, have a sufficient income to be content with their lot. The vision appears to presume that the lower orders would not be troubled by aspirations to a more participatory role in running their affairs. Both human self-interest and human self-respect for the majority of people would, on this scenario, be satisfied enough by a modest sufficiency of ready cash. Any disturbing tendencies among the lower orders to attempt to better their material lot by organizing crime or strengthening their political influence by organizing revolution – or any lesser social or political disturbances – will be avoided.

This late twentieth-century vision is scarcely idyllic nor does it seem very feasible. However, Free Market theory seems to work on a limited, trivializing and degrading model of human beings, as consumers, customers and competitors driven by self-interest. It may not be surprising, therefore, that a leading proponent of the Free Market faith should expect the majority of human beings to be reasonably satisfied if they have regular provision for the consumptive use of cash. The Market working model for human freedom is, after all, an individual exercising free choice in a market. With such a trivializing and degrading view of what is at the heart of being human it is no wonder that market enthusiasts have such a degrading view of the human future for the majority of us.

There has to be something more open to us. The amazing possibilities of our human productive and trading activities of the past two hundred years or more cannot just go to waste. Hence my attempt to focus the concerns and discoveries of an anxious idiot which have been built up through the previous chapters of this book in the couple of sentences of personal moral challenge and criticism which I have been repeating through this sector of my investigation, *viz*. 'The proponents and practitioners of the Market faith are, *in effect* liars. You are relying on what is untrue and you are promoting, or at least condoning, what is immoral.' It may look as if I am merely repeating a personal moral incantation to exorcise the Market mantra which I have attributed to the proponents of the Free Market, but the issue is far more fundamental. It is about freedom and our human capacity for choice – just as the most enthusiastic and morally concerned proponents of the Free Market faith say it is.

In promoting, or acquiescing in, or just going along with, the current Free Market faith, one is choosing a way of life and a way of looking at the world. Thus, either by positive choice or by default one is at least contributing to the choosing of one's humanity. By deciding to give in to the Market as it is presented to us in the propaganda of the Free Market faith we are making, or acquiescing in, several decisions. We have accepted the decision, for example, that human beings are for practical purposes rightly defined as primarily consumers of goods and services. We have chosen to be aligned with the assumption that our central aim is to increase this consumption indefinitely in both diversification and amount. We are identified with the decision that as human beings we are primarily driven by individual self-interest and, further and most crucially, that our primary relationships with other human beings is driven by this self-same self-interest.

This means among other things that when we talk about 'we' we are either being entirely vague and rhetorical or else, in reality, 'we' are referring to what as individuals we regard as our own self-interest group. It is hardly surprising, then, that acquiescence in the Free Market faith erodes ideas of common good, is suspicious of the notion of public goods, and promotes the idea that governments are necessary evils to be as limited as is practical in their resources and sphere of action. (Taxes, for example, are generally to be regarded as infringements on individual liberty and property.)

This picture implies a very bleak and ungracious view of human beings. It is clearly a very partial view of the much more exciting range of possibilities which human beings actually display. However, proponents of the Free Market faith claim that this view of us and our world is true because it is supported by sound economic theory and the practical evidence of the deliverance of amazing productivity combined with the moral results of the working of the Market's amoral but invisible hand or evolved price system.

But there is ever-increasing evidence that this is a false faith and a vain hope, even if it were a hope worthy of human beings. Refusing to face the probability that the faith is false and the hope deceitful therefore becomes a moral issue which raises the question of the responsibility of each and every one of us. The object therefore of my repeated accusation and challenge is to draw attention to the inescapable element of moral and personal responsibility which is inherent in any involvement in market activities.

My working assumption is that the majority of persons concerned in market activities share with the majority of all of us some concern and aspirations related to human decency, the moral exercise of our freedom and choices, and a proper responsibility to our neighbours. We urgently need to renegotiate our understanding of the Market in relationship to our personal responsibilities and our moral stance about human decency and our neighbours. As the Market guarantees nothing, responsibility has to revert to us in whatever coalitions we can organize for the purpose. It is both ironic and pathetically defeatist that modern and sceptically informed men and women should be so ready to hand their moral responsibilities for one another and the earth over, to such an ideological construction as 'the Free Market', promoted as the means and the mystery of our secular salvation.

The discovery that the Free Market faith compounds lies about processes with deceits about false promises is, if properly received, a liberation rather than a condemnation. Appearances no longer have to be kept up to prop up the Market faith. Realism can therefore return about the actual positive and negative effects of particular market activities with regard to real people, actual localities and future prospects. This ought to make a contribution to deepening the humanity of our dealings through the markets with one another.

One of the most anger-inspiring and indecent aspects of the talk of faithful proponents of the Market faith is the apparently indifferent way in which they comment on what happens to people, their homes and their prospects under market momenta. Market operations are saved at no matter what cost to, say, Mexican peasants, Indonesian or Thai employees, or the poor families in various African states in their health care and education under the requirements of a World Bank or an IMF structural adjustment scheme. Maybe these happenings are inevitable under our current ways of the Market. If so must we not hasten to find another way? I suppose such a thought cannot trouble the minds (let alone the hearts) of the prosperous, for unless our prosperity is preserved, how will the whole system keep going and promise prosperity to all? It is precisely at this point that the prospects for more prosperity for all pose a direct moral challenge to all of us who promote, or simply acquiesce in, the activities of the Free Market faith.

Even prudence, or self-regarding fear, might suggest that an increase of moral awareness and sense of responsibility would be useful here. For how long is it supposed that the disappointed poor will put up with their delayed 'dividends' from the Market – especially when they have begun to enjoy some relief, as in South East Asia, or see conspicuous consumption among their own elites and on the television? This point was well put in a letter to *The Financial Times* from Mr Foster-Carter, a senior lecturer in sociology in the University of Leeds, picking up what he describes as a 'complacent Panglossian panegyric' in a particular article on globalization. After criticisms of detail, he wrote:

> Far more than history is at stake. We have seen how alarmingly easy it is, even in rich countries, to rouse a rabble against a 'Europe of bosses' or 'faceless Brussels bureaucrats'. *A fortiori*, how will nations where globalisation means years of pain for many and gain for a sleek few resist the siren song of national socialism?[9]

The complacent discussion of the ups and downs of the Market by financial commentators shows such indifference about actual human beings as to verge on the obscene. How long do they, or we, expect the poor of this earth to put up with what is going on – now that they have access to pictures and knowledge of the prosperity they are themselves denied?

Such pressures and possibilities, however, seem to have no place in either public discussion or practical decisions about the worldwide operations of the Market. This would seem to be a further reason for seeking to bring issues of morality and responsibility directly into both market discourse and market operations via the aroused awareness of market operators. As I said above, I am assuming that most market operators share with most of the rest of us concerns related to human decency and the moral exercise of a responsibility for the use of our freedom and towards the concerns of our neighbours. The issue, however, is not the moral status and intentions of particular individuals but whether what the proponents of the Free Market hold to be true and hopeful in varying degrees of good faith is now increasingly shown to be – in effect – bad and false faith. If the case for this is strong then, as I suggested at the beginning of this chapter, they *ought* to recognize the case for making the accusation of bad faith against them.

It is very important, however, at the same time to be clear that the issuing of this accusatory challenge is not equivalent to saying that all proponents of the Free Market are, personally and individually, liars and cheats. One of the implications of getting rid of the idea that our actions or our motivations are largely determined by whether we are on one side or other of a dialectic confrontation, is that we are all generally freed from any obligation to hold that individual persons are defined by the overall ideology of a system they are committed to. People may espouse an ideology or get caught up in it but they are not defined and determined by it, nor are they necessarily aware of the implications of their commitment or practice. There is more to being a human person than being classified by an ideology. For ideologies are not determinative patterns which fix a person's ideas of reality by tying then up in a dialectical determinism but only patterns of ideas which people develop and use uncritically. Therefore we are not entitled to stigmatize the moral standing of individual persons because of a commitment to a particular ideology. This is why I have been careful to formulate my repeated accusation about lying and cheating in the clumsy form that practitioners of the Free Market faith 'are, *in effect*, liars'.

The human, practical and political purpose I have in inserting this modifying phrase in my formulation is, however paradoxical it may seem, that I intend the accusation to be taken as an invitation – an urgent invitation to reconsider together the actual prospects for the future of ourselves, our societies and the earth. I have, therefore, to make it clear that there is a distinction between exposing the immorality and irresponsibility of a widely accepted pattern of thought and action and making indiscriminate accusations of lying and cheating against all or any individuals who subscribe to this pattern. This distinction between the immorality and irresponsibility of shared patterns of thought and action, and the moral standing of the persons committed to, or joining in, these patterns is of great practical importance. We need to initiate realistic discussions between people who have become deeply hostile to the operations of the Free Market faith and those who are committed to that faith and part of those operations. For what is at issue is how we all understand ourselves as human beings and how we believe we should work together for our future.

We shall get nowhere in this literally vital argument if we allow ourselves to get sucked back into the dialectical, either/or style of economic argument over the last one hundred and fifty or so years. Both the present and the future are much more complex, and more open and potentially hopeful, than such a deterministic form of dialectical argument allows. If we are to develop the required changes to our present economic ways, we need to resist the temptation of searching out some new economic system in dialectical confrontation with the system of the Free Market.

The assumption of this would be that the system of the Free Market which, for a while, triumphed over the system of socialist collectivism is now in its turn found dangerously unsatisfactory, so now we have to find out what will *replace it*. This would be desperately backward looking. Both the critically anxious and the optimistically enthusiastic have got to sustain one another in the great mental and imaginative effort required to realize that the whole idea of an economic system which can both embrace the world and be relied upon to promote the prosperity and freedom of more and more of the inhabitants of the world is a delusion. There is, can be and will be no such system. The notion of a self-contained, self-motivated and self-controlling system which, if we get it right and discern the right rules, will move us progressively towards greater happiness, prosperity and freedom is clearly a collusive delusion.

People and power are involved in every level of all the operations to do with productivity, trading and profit. Neither the definition of the terms used, nor descriptions of the rules to be followed, are plainly declared by simple inspection of 'the system'. This has been sufficiently demonstrated in the previous chapters of this book. The way things go economically are developed, discerned, declared, defined and worked by people. It is people, therefore, who have to monitor the results of the various operations, evaluate their effects and get together to modify trends, check miseries and enhance benefits. We have to recognize and accept our responsibility. There is no saving economic system. We need to develop institutions and organizations which will accept perpetual provisionality, monitoring and reordering, related to open experimentation and participation. We do not need a new 'system' but new perspectives for seeing our problems and possibilities. Within these perspectives we have to invent new ways of living with the problems and the possibilities. The adversarial mindset is too limiting. We need collaborative ways which can embrace varied and experimental options as we pick up our democratic responsibilities once more.

The problem in all this for practical, political and power purposes is: Who are 'we'? The Free Market faith claims that democratic freedom is enhanced by its operations because the Free Market is based on individuals making free choices in markets. As many writers and commentators have pointed out, this is not true in practice. It is only those with access to sufficiently large sums of money and credit who effectively count.

Is it possible to revive a democratic search with universal implications in face of the overweening power of the Market? Is it mere stubborn anachronistic idealism to entertain the idea that the basic answer to the question Who are 'we'? must be – every adult person who is a citizen in any state or community anywhere in the world? Common humanity promotes this answer because we are all affected by an economic network, and a communications network, which are 'globalized' in the simple descriptive sense that they operate throughout the world. Further, this is a limited world, so whatever its possibilities and constraints are they affect all of us. As the Free Market is supposed to be the only hope and sure promise of freedom and prosperity eventually for all of us, we are universally concerned if the Free Market project proves to be a cheat. Here, then, is the democratic challenge of the new millennium.

Recovering Our Political Imagination and Working Out Our Future

If we are freed from the dictates of either the material dialectic or the competitive Free Market, then we are free to develop a renewed and renewing political imagination. So how should we now work together to find ways forward to something more generally hopeful and sustainable, and less inflicting of pain and poverty on too many of the poorest of our neighbours? The challenge is given a potentially dangerous edge by the increasingly visible fact that a fortunate few do immensely, and even grossly, well for themselves. Are we going to see a revival of a twenty-first century version of class conflict?

To put any hope for positive change in such an outbreak would be to abandon ourselves to disruption rather than progress. The hope that the dialectics of history will produce a worthwhile result for all when an old order is overthrown through violent revolution has been shown to be a delusion and a disaster. We must surely have learnt by now that there is nothing inherent in either history or humanity which ensures that progressive good comes out of conflict as such. But, on the other hand, we are also discovering that there is nothing inherent in either history or humanity which ensures that progressive good comes out of competition as such. The dialectic does not work from either end because there is no dialectic. Consequently processes – of economics, of politics, of social negotiation and of living together – cannot be turned into contributions to human progress automatically by simple decision taking of the 'either/ or' type.

Such a dialectic still lingers. Take the Free Trade policies pursued through the World Trade Organisation, for example. Proposals for outlawing particular tariff barriers or local tax discrimination are supported by arguments of the form that *either* these practices hinder free trade as defined, *or* they do not. If the former they must be banned. The decisions do not take into account the immediate effects on particular groups of industries, people and communities nor the efforts of local governments to protect the environment. According to the Free Market faith freeing markets enables more production and therefore more resources will become available which can, in due course, be applied to jobs for the unemployed, resettlement for dislocated communities, measures to restore disrupted environments, and payments to protect threatened species. In other words, economic decision-taking is determined by the Free Market game-plan as understood, interpreted, and applied by the experts, gurus, and operators of the Free Market. It is their 'either/or's which determine the regulations to be enforced, leaving the world at large, and the livelihood of local producers at their mercy.

There is the further complication that the most powerful economic and trading nation in the world, the USA, does not pursue free trade matters according to the received game-plan of the Free Market but according to its understanding of its own interests. Just as, in fact, as I have already pointed out,[10] the experts and gurus do not play according to the received game-plan in a crisis. Why then do I go on probing further into the whole matter of market, politics and people? Why not simply denounce the whole thing as fraudulent power play for the benefit of the powerful and the exploitation of the poor? I see no positive use in such a blanket denunciation, and I persevere with my enquiries because such a denunciation would ignore the promising role of our human capacities for enterprise, production and trade.

Economic and political issues could well be more hopeful than they appear at present. But to propagate this hopefulness it is essential that we do not succumb to the seductive simplification of the 'either/or' with its accompanying submission of vital decisions to the self-styled experts. To do so is to accept that the rest of us, being ignorant of the mysteries and powers of the economic game-plan, can have no influence over decisions, but only play our allotted roles according to the game-plan rules as the experts apply them. Such an approach is a blatant betrayal of the possibilities of human freedom and creativity – even if the economic liberals who promote it believe that human freedom is the most important thing that the Free Market protects.

Economic activities, theories and expectations have been enclosed in this heretical strait-jacket which has been forced on to human history and freedom. But rejection of the ideological idea of the dialectical nature of conflict does not mean that there are no serious conflicts of interest, possibilities and power. There is clearly an unresolved conflict in the way we currently run our economies between the capitalist interest in Interest and indefinitely delayed promises of spreading prosperity and freedom for all among the majority of the world's population who remain poor. But this obvious and continuing conflict of interest in current economic operations has no hope of being hopefully and promisingly resolved, or positively directed, if it is looked upon as another 'either/or' conflict. This is where renewed and renewing political imagination is urgently required. There is no serious prospect of a beneficent victory by following the economic experts. They – as we can now see – are false-hopers. But what beneficence can be expected to come out of disturbances created by the disappointed and the disillusioned who have become no-hopers?

The currently developing scenario divides all human beings across the world into three main groupings dictated by economic fates. The first group consists of the international financiers, corporate businessmen and women and attendant economic experts in both governmental and private organizations. They keep up the good appearances of the current economic system while making their profits. The majority group are the so-far left-outs who are supposed to suffer whatever the economic system inflicts on them in the hope of eventual co-option into at least minimal prosperity. The third group is a 'middle' class, experiencing increasing insecurity about jobs, prosperity and welfare.

In such a scenario conflict, insecurity, disappointment and resentment are endemic. Peaceful progress to further prosperity and freedom for all is scarcely likely. For one thing any trickle-down of wealth that there is moves very slowly and erratically, and is often withdrawn. So there is very little encouragement to the no-hopers. Meanwhile the ostentatious wealth of the first group grows rapidly and obviously. When this inherently unstable social situation is matched by the evident volatility of over-leveraged capital and stock markets where vast nominal sums of money 'slosh around' the world in unregulated and predatory ways, the overall set of interacting processes looks volatile and threatening. Is it therefore the case that any hopeful and socially stabilizing politics have been paralysed by dominance of the Free Market economic myth over the worldviews and life-expectations of all of us?

The answer must be that this depends on us. And this returns us to the question – if the answer depends on us, who are 'we'? As I have already indicated, this 'we' has to be seen in the perspective of potential universality. This necessity does not derive, in the first place, from idealism but from practical realism. Through global markets and global communications we are all located in an interlocking set of systems and sub-systems which interact with one another and so make us literally 'members one of another' in a limited world on whose resources we all necessarily depend.

This interlinking aspect of practical reality is significantly matched by the idealistic perspective of democracy which has grown up alongside the immense expansion of enterprise and productivity since the late eighteenth century. A vision has been conceived that every human being, as such, should have the right to be sufficiently recognized as a person and a citizen to enjoy some sense of respect and identity. This recognition has been formulated in terms of an entitlement to opportunities for responsible participation in contributing to the maintenance and running of the society in which one is a citizen. This democratic agenda remains unfinished and deeply problematic in practice. It is certainly not applied all over the world, and uncertainty surrounds what the basic rights, privileges and responsibilities of every human being as such should and could be. But the very existence of the attempts at democracy is of fundamental importance with regard to our understanding of human worth.

To hand over this concern for the protection and enhancement of human worth to such an ideological construction as 'the Free Market' is a betrayal of other people's human worth and therefore a betrayal of one's own worth. In 'Market' terms millions of poverty-stricken human beings or, indeed, thousands of struggling middle-class human beings are mere accumulations of statistics in the book-keeping calculations of profit and loss which are the essential means of operation in current market transactions. Under the compulsion of the high rates of return demanded by the present financial markets of the world the fate of miners in Durham, England, of temporary employees in South East Asia, or peasants in Mexico may, therefore, be held – *under current circumstances* – to be inevitable. But it must never be supposed to be acceptable. Who has constructed this 'inevitability' as an alleged prevalent feature of markets and human enterprise, productivity and trading – and who maintains this 'inevitability' *now*? If it is unshakeably believed that the Market does indeed require the rejection 'it' inflicts on millions of men and women, then at the very least the unshakeable holders of this Free Market faith should be much less triumphalist in their claims about the promises of this Market. They should also, collectively, be much more ready to put efforts, commensurate to the efforts put into money-making, into finding ways of mitigating the lot of the victims of the Market. Schemes need devising, for example, for investing some proportion of the large amount of money made in current market trading into low-return enterprises which can provide immediate relief to the millions of small producers and communities which might, given the chance, be self-sufficient at lower standards of living than could offer the opportunity to make profits at the rates required normally by the current financial markets.

These assumptions, inflictions and indifference, inherent in the Market faith, insult humanity and they contradict democracy. This is why all of us with any sort of power, influence and activity in the actual operations of markets under the dominance of the Free Market myth have to be confronted with – even if we will not face up to – our personal and individual involvement in, and collusion with, immorality and irresponsibility.

But what about those who still believe in this Market faith? What those who operate at various levels in various market activities from finance to local manufacturing and trading consciously and conscientiously believe they are doing as human beings, both for other human beings and to other human beings, is by no means a simple matter to discern, categorize and stigmatize. If one is looking for collaboration to bring about change, simple condemnation of those being invited to change is hardly likely to be helpful. It is also unlikely to be morally justifiable. In making serious charges of immorality and irresponsibility against classes of persons it is necessary to take into account the actual ambivalence, complexity and confusion of the individual moral stances of all of us as individuals. This is particularly important when one is trying to get persons influential in market operations to acknowledge that accusations of immoral irresponsibility have sufficient realism and basis to require them and all of us to think again about free market operations as a whole. The accusations are intended to be perceived as justified invitations to take part with others in developing plans and proposals for altering the way things go on in the markets of the world.

To attempt to challenge the consciences of free market enthusiasts and free market hangers-on is to ask all of us who are involved with the Free Market to reconsider what we are making of our shared humanity, our shared world and our shared future. Such an accusation, invitation and appeal has to be addressed to the awareness and conscience of individuals. The moral and individual element in the challenge to see things differently and develop a new and effective political imagination cannot be avoided.

But, just as the events and effects of free market operations cannot be evaluated by a simple and dialectical 'either/or' so the moral responsibility and stance of individual human beings cannot be assessed or categorized by a similarly simple and dialectical 'either/or'. It does not do justice to the complexities of individual responsibility nor the perplexities of living in relation to the goings on of the markets to take a stance which implies that everyone in favour of the Market is immoral and irresponsible while the only moral and responsible human stance is to oppose the Market and all its works. This is to go back to the either/or dialectic which I have been trying to criticize.

In making an attempt to rally democratic forces for political action to change the current operations of the Free Market there are two principal reasons for not adopting an unyieldingly critical and combative stance against the proponents of the Free Market myth. The first is that, practically, we must not and cannot write off the achievements of markets, fed by capital, over the last two hundred years. The efforts of the 'haves' to produce and have more is complexly interwoven with both the longings and the exploitation of the 'have-nots'.

The second reason is that, morally, we cannot write off the intentions of individual free market proponents with regard to human prosperity and freedom. The evidence accumulates that uncritical supporters of the Free Market myth, are *in effect* liars and cheats in this respect, but this does not, of itself, show that all free market supporters are individually and personally to be characterized as liars and cheats. It is *the effects* of their beliefs and promises which are described falsely and presented deceitfully. The motivations, commitments and hopes of free market proponents as individuals are another matter. This is why I persist in pressing the accusation of effective – but not necessarily intended – immorality and irresponsibility as a challenge and an invitation. We must all together think again about what free market operations are actually doing to the hopes and prospects of all of us as human beings living together on a globally 'marketized' earth.

Our common freedom and prosperity – and, in all probability our worthwhile survival – depends on our breaking out of the domination of the Free Market myth. This widespread domination is the result of a confusion of factors which at least include elements of delivery, of delusion and distortion to which I have already referred. The delivery factor is the emergence of the first wealth-creating system the world has ever known and its remarkable achievements in enterprise, productivity and trading which the dynamics of capital investment have brought about. People who are committed to efficient and innovative enterprise, production and trading or marketing are committed to a basic human project of fundamental importance.

The delusion factor is that the prestige of the delivery factor has blinded people to its limitations and unaccounted for costs so that 'the Free Market' as the agent, machine or organism of productive growth has been mythicized and idolized as the reality which, in its own right and under its own momentum, guarantees worthwhile and shareable deliveries in ever extending ways. This is such an apparently promising and comforting delusion that there is widespread collusion in it – a collusion entered into with a widespread spectrum from total enthusiasm through modified and doubtful acquiescence, to apathetic acceptance or resentful surrender. Given the prestige of the delivery individuals cannot automatically be fairly blamed for collusion with, or co-option into, the delusion.

The third factor is that of distortion. This is the emergent operation of a self-interested ideology. History demonstrates that it is customary for powers that have emerged to fight for the right to remain the powers-that-be. This is principal reason for reminding ourselves of the need for democratically organized 'eternal vigilance', allied to imaginative political attempts to organize countervailing power to restrict the capacity of the prevailing powers-that-be to be socially destructive in their pursuit of self-interest.

This conflict is endemic in human history and living. It is not a dialectical conflict but a perennial one. So we cannot rely on the emergence of some non-providential but evolved 'system' like a Free Market to resolve it happily for us all. We have always to struggle for better ways forward which make better uses of our great but ambivalent powers of innovation, enterprise, productivity and trading. We have to move on and once again rally human commitment to the aims (never fully achieved but essential to be pursued) of wider democracy, greater freedom and increasing justice for all. To fail in developing this unending pursuit is to succumb to closures of misery and poverty, of tyranny and endemic conflict.

In renewing this struggle and pursuit we have to take into account that abuse by the current financial and market powers-that-be distorts market activities and market effects to a gravely threatening degree.

That, however, does not deny the vital importance of human productivity and trading for not only sustaining but improving human living and livelihood. Also, because of a mixture of the proper prestige of the delivery of the markets and the widespread confusion and collusion of the Free Market delusion it is neither prudent nor just to fall back into old habits of dialectical confrontation politics. A democratic challenge to renew and redirect our politics must be directed to all. Such a future cannot be built without market activities and expertise of all kinds, and it is not realistic to stigmatize individuals solely because they are rich any more than it is to invest saving hopes in individuals solely because they are poor.

Still, the critical challenge of immorality and irresponsibility as human beings who are neighbours and citizens in our currently globalized earth, must be addressed more particularly to the rich, the prosperous and those of us clinging on to a comparatively prosperous position despite the down-sizing, redeployment and the threats to our pension prospects. It is no longer good enough simply to take refuge in the cloud of our collusive delusion about economics and the Free Market. To refuse to think again about these matters is to reveal a personal and individual failure in morality and responsibility. Economic theory politically used is not a technical non-political and amoral matter. It involves a fundamentally human and moral question of how we look at the world, ourselves and our neighbours and what we choose to do about it. Both our responsibility and our freedom are involved. Hence the urgent need at every level of human understanding, from the practical through the prudential to the compassionate, to develop democratic countervailing powers that will assist to rescue our productive and trading activities for the prosperity of all. We have to dispel the illusion that if you make a profit under any circumstances then you automatically contribute to the promising and promised prosperity of all.

A practical democratic programme, therefore, has to be built up from three principal considerations. First of all, we require an appreciation of what capitalism has so far made possible by way of productivity and trading. Then we have to recognize the threats and dangers which current free market capitalism is now producing and multiplying. This recognition has to be matched by a determination to develop political measures by democratic means to search for new ways. The excessive and distorting powers of the controllers and creators of money and credit have to be confronted. We have to re-establish the powers of governments to play a balancing role in the global workings of markets and trade. We must recover powers and possibilities for people locally for this is how the vast majority of human beings in the world live. Therefore they must be enabled to contribute and develop their own economic activities, communities and environments.

What human powers have achieved by various forms of organization, coalitions and confrontations, can be corrected and redirected by appropriate new forms of organization, coalition and confrontation. Are we to sell our possibilities of sharing in prosperity and freedom on a sustainable earth for 30 trillion pieces of financial paper denominated in nominal sums of overleveraged credit? Who do we think we are, who do we propose to attempt to become, and what chances of success do we suppose we have? The markets have got to be recovered and redirected for us all. Ways have to be found of pursuing the concerns of democracy and of morality along with an interaction with the concerns of capital and of money-making. We cannot wait until enough money has been made to exercise morality, promote democracy and seek to enjoy liberty. The price of liberty, as of freedom to develop a future worth sharing, is organized and democratically responsible vigilance now, on all fronts and in all sectors, including, most urgently, the economic sector of our lives. Money must not be allowed to take unchecked precedence in the affairs of human beings. It allows too much power to get into the hands of too small a minority and its benefits are increasingly unbalanced by its threats. In any case, money and the ways of manipulating it, are human inventions and activities. Money is not a guaranteed and guaranteeing token of exchange which will certainly work for human prosperity and freedom. Possibilities for human progress and freedom lie in the nature of human beings, if they lie anywhere. We have got to rely on ourselves – for good or ill.

Notes

1   Paul Krugman, *Peddling Prosperity: Economic Sense and Nonsense in the Age of Diminished Expectations* (New York and London: W.W. Norton & Co., 1994), footnote p. 213.
2   Samuel Brittan, 'Markets Can Be Wrong', *The Financial Times*, 20 November 1997.
3   Reported in *The Economist*, 20 December 1997.
4   Or words to that effect – a fuller version cites, 'the condition upon which God hath given liberty to men is eternal vigilance'. This seems to me to be a very likely original as it reflects Adam Smith's eighteenth-century basis for faith in the Invisible Hand. (That God has so ordered the world that rational behaviour produces harmonies and beneficent results for human beings.) Given our modern context we have to leave 'God' out of the argument. I myself believe firmly that this is a fundamental miscalculation about the resources that are open to us. I also believe, however, that God does not order human and earthly affairs 'providen-

tially' as is too often maintained by those who express faith in Him. He suffers through with things and provides never-ending resources for openness and for fighting against all idolatries and all attempts at closure in human affairs. That is to say, in my understanding God is a resource against succumbing to any claims of the TINA type. But that is the subject of another book. The immediate practical point, however, is clear. Nothing works on its own – least of all the Market – to produce perpetually increasingly beneficent results with regard to human prosperity or freedom. We have to exercise eternal vigilance if we are to maintain progress in the direction of desirable and shareable objectives.

5   See discussion on page 8 of my Initial Scientific Protest.
6   See especially Chapters 11 and 12.
7   Paul Krugman, *Peddling Prosperity: Economic Sense and Nonsense in the Age of Diminished Expectations* (New York and London: W.W. Norton & Co., 1994), footnote p. 213.
8   Reported by Mark Tran in 'Notebook', *The Guardian*, 23 February 1998.
9   Letter published in *The Financial Times*, 19 May 1997.
10 See Chapters 13 and 14.

16 Outline of an Agenda and a Confession of Faith

As I wind up this journey of an anxious idiot, the Free Market project is smouldering at the edges. With the smoke still drifting from the devastating forest fires in Indonesia, 1998 has seen the Asian Tiger – and even the Japanese – economies crash one by one. The amazing productivity of capitalism has aroused great expectations of wealth, prosperity and freedom for all. But capitalism, in its present form, has passed the peak of its usefulness and promise. It has taken off on the impossible pursuit of perpetual growth, including growth in the rates of return on capital invested. In pursuit of competitive growth of profitable productivity of no matter what, for whatever use, under whatever circumstances, capitalism is increasingly promoting forms of economic growth which sideline the *needs* of the majority of the inhabitants of the world, and ignore the *limits* of the adaptability of both the natural earth and of stable, cohesive human communities.

The persons and organizations that control and create money, invest in the economic operations of the world, and so create and direct the dynamic effects of productivity, trading and markets, have developed habits which are now more threatening than promising for the future of all of us.

Capitalism (the shorthand for the activities of capitalists) always requires 'more' if it is to maintain its momentum. This requirement is still stubbornly interpreted as producing more and more goods and services which, simply by being 'more', are held to promise expanding prosperity in money terms, and freedom in human terms. But this simple faith in simple expansion is being shown to be simply false.

Once one has followed the questioning trail of an anxious idiot the uncertainties of the Free Market scenario are not at all surprising. In a cool and detached hour how could anyone possibly imagine that a global system whose basic dynamic was competitive self-interest could, of its own momentum, promote the prosperity and freedom of all? A theory or story about the world and human activity which treats the human disposition which sets people against one another, as the very means by which we shall all prosper and serve one another, would seem to be too clever by half. No doubt competitiveness has a powerful place in the nature of things, but we still have to get on with our neighbours and we cannot afford to destroy the resources of the earth on which we live. As human beings, we have a history of a much more positive vision of communities which are worth living in, human beings who are worth sharing with, and an earth which has glories and possibilities which go far beyond short-term provision to us of material for production, consumption and waste.

Consciousness has to be aroused about the real effects of the Free Market delusion. *Consciences* have to be challenged about the responsibilities of each and everyone of us with regard to this. *Coalitions* have to be formed between active politicians, members of the numerous campaigning and pressure groups which are multiplying, locally and internationally, with regard to common threats to environments and social cohesion. There are many potential recruits waiting among the millions of dissatisfied or angry citizens who are anxious about what is going on, but who feel powerless on their own to crack open the truth shrouded by the experts, or to make their voices heard against the chorus of complacency about the Free Market, with its undertone of 'and in any case there is no alternative'.

Freedom is not so easily to be denied and we are all entitled to demand that the whole spectrum of facts be faced. The basic prudence required for survival demands such realism. Market accounting is hopelessly partial, even when it is not obviously manipulated. Governments have to be pressurized to use their powers as constituent and contributory members of international bodies such as WTO, the IMF, the World Bank, and various agencies of the UN, to broaden their agendas so that financial matters and dogmatic theories about free trade are not the sole concern of these primarily financial bodies. Trade, aid and environment have to come together and influence one another.

Globalization has got to be co-ordinated for the sake of localities. For it is in localities that all but the smallest minority of human beings live. It is the equivalent of secular blasphemy to allow the fate of communities to be determined by an elite international class of 'expert' financiers, who have no local loyalties and are accountable to no sovereign community and state. Governments who set up and maintain organizations such as the IMF must find powers to bring them down to the earth where everyone else has to live. Similarly, ways have to be found to regulate and restrain the powers of the corporate business elite. For instance, measures should be taken to ensure that the officialdom of the various organizations are not dominated by personnel who switch between private banking, large corporations and employment by the relevant agencies. These appointments are ultimately made or approved by governments. It is necessary therefore to promote intensive-political activity to insist that governments take their democratic duties seriously and do not surrender them to the operations and operators of the Free Market.

At the moment it is widely held that such political movements cannot happen. But there is growing awareness in world financial circles themselves that international finance and capital need some form of restraint and regulation – just as there is some growing concern, although it is channelled through different organizations, about the environment. Governments, responsible to informed electorates, need to reassert control over international organizations in the interests of people and the earth, and give up the notion that surrendering priority to the interest of Interest will always save and bless us all.

The internal dynamic of the Free Market has passed the stage where it expresses any interest in meeting the *needs* of the millions of people whose basic needs remain grimly unmet in a globalized world where plenty runs to the grossest excesses for some. Under the current interest in ever-rising Interest we are told we cannot afford social investment. Our 'prosperous' economy will cease to prosper in today's fiercely competitive world if we divert money, via taxes, into improving our health and education services. We cannot afford sufficient welfare payments to ensure a decent standard of life for all citizens, which will enable the upbringing of a generation who might have the commitment, the health and the training to serve as citizens and contributors of the future. We cannot afford investment in viable society and instead we foot the rising bills for prisons, household protection and insurance. So under the current free market orthodoxy we cannot afford what, collectively and as a society hoping for a viable future, we cannot afford not to afford – and we pay out just the same – for utterly uncreative imprisonment, utterly wasteful insurance and increasing urban misery and congestion.

The growth in the more and more does not improve our prospects in society. The Free Market is far too slow in adjustments, via costs and prices, to deal in a positive way with the externalities of resource exhaustion and pollution. Natural occurrences such as the 1997/8 forest fires in Indonesia and the Amazon are amplified into environmental disasters by indiscriminate logging practices dictated solely by profit. Environmental attempts to control, say, noxious emissions, become a matter of bargaining between experts working for the fuel industries and government advisers who fear the reactions of car-owning voters. Open and genuine negotiations, taking account of all available facts, are simply not possible because the proponents of the Free Market buy the experts and threaten the politicians. Once again, the Free Market demand for the more and more has simply left the needs of the inhabitants of the majority of the world behind.

How do we expect our communities and societies to have the cohesion, trust and social discipline to survive in any civilized and hopeful way through the Market switchbacks? Who can be relied upon to show sufficient neighbourly solidarity and goodwill to protect us, together, against the increasing threats to law and order? (Consider for example the growth of ghettos for the rich in the USA – the most successful market economy in the world; or the spread of a mafia in Russia; or endless banditry and guerilla warfare in many parts of Latin America.)

The evidence is mounting that we have reached a stage of development in free market affairs in which, as human beings together and for the sake of our common shared and limited world, as well as for the healthy viability and cohesion of our societies, we can no longer afford the Free Market in its current form, rationale and operations. If, as a community, we cannot recognize that this is an indecent system, we ought at least to be capable of recognizing that it is a precarious one. The widespread impoverishment and threat of social unrest carried by acute recessions, combined with the evident failure of current free market trends either to promote the prosperity of the poor, or protect the viability of the earth, ought at least to stir up some *fear* in the prosperous, the nearly prosperous and the hopefully would-be prosperous. Perhaps we shall not progress with the urgently needed rethinking until some pretty frightening economic collapses and/or outbreaks of social disturbance occur.

How much better it would be if some shared *prudence* took root among us so that we could collaborate in looking again at where the mythical Free Market faith is taking us. And if we start to consult prudentially together, from our various disciplines, occupations and perspectives, perhaps we should discover among ourselves some shared commitments to *decency* which would make us uncomfortable, or even ashamed, of our current abuse of the earth and our neglect of the less prosperous and the radically poor. Such a sense of decency, and the promptings of some sense of shame, might remind us that human resources have often included longings of compassion, visions of sharing, and ideals of democracy. How can we relate our economic practices to the possibility of participation for all in the recognized rights of citizens, rooted in a general recognition of the needs of citizens, and therefore the encouragement to a general owning of the duties of citizens? Of course such visions are never finally realized (the price of liberty is eternal vigilance), but they do recall us to a direction for politics and economics, of citizenship and neighbourliness, which reflects some of the most worthwhile hopes and achievements of human beings.

The developments of human invention have put such powers and possibilities of productivity and prosperity into human hands, need we let them be squandered in a selfish pursuit of the more and more? Those who dominate the Free Market are so directing the allocation of money (the capital of 'capitalism') that the future is contracting for most of us in the world, while reducing the quality and viability of that world. Unrestrained competitive individualism has run out of control. This is clearly true in both practice and trends however much the faithful of the Free Market continue to whistle to keep their spirits up in the deepening gloom.

It is discomforting to find oneself coming to the simple conclusion that the public faith, which is held to be the only practicable and hopeful basis for our living together, is simply false. If everyone publicly agrees that they are right, how can an individual (even though he or she doubtless has many worries in common with a good many other individuals) convey the conviction that they are wrong?

My enquiries as an anxious idiot into the highways and by-ways of the currently maintained practices of the Free Market operators have put me into the role of the questioning child who observed that the emperor had no clothes. 'The Free Market' has no sufficiently valid arguments to clothe the claims made for it. Indeed, the underlying logic is even weaker than that. For the emperor does not exist – either in the ghostly form of an Invisible Hand, or in some other evolved formation, such as a global information system which determines prices, in ways which turn out to be beneficial for more and more people, through more and more production, or in a Darwinian dynamic of the ruthlessly competitive survival of the fittest, where the capitalist 'fittest' miraculously turn out to be producers of prosperity and freedom for all.

'The Free Market' is a metaphorical labelling of an ideological description of the ways in which the economic practices which have spread worldwide in the last two hundred years or so, are said to have worked up until now. These ways, it is claimed, are innate and must go on working as they have done into the indefinite future. This is a simple secular heresy made up of two elements. The first is that human affairs and, in particular, human economic activities, are determined by processes which can be definitively described and then relied upon as fixed, and so to repeat themselves as such. The processes, therefore, are held to determine the outcome of human economic activities. But this is a travesty. Human affairs are not determined by process; they are worked out by human beings. Human affairs are not the output of processes, but the outcome of human activities. These outcomes then have to be observed, responded to and corrected by further human observations, activities and chosen operations. The mistaken reliance on self-operating processes replacing the actual role of self-guided human beings, confronts us with the current demand that economics must direct politics, and that markets are properly more powerful than states.

The second element in the heresy is this. It is not only held that economics must guide and direct politics. It is further held that the 'Free Market' can safely and promisingly be left to do so. That is to say that economic processes promise human progress. Where does the promise come from, and who or what guides, informs or directs the processes so that they are, in aggregate and in the continuing long run, promising? The non-existent emperor of the Free Market not only has no adequately argumentative clothes, he has no powers. For he is either the ghost of a providential Invisible Hand, or a surprisingly super-stitious modern personification of materialistic and natural forces of an evolutionary type. In fact and for the future, the only sources of both activity and process known to us who can possibly multiply promising progress in and through the processes of the world, are ourselves. Human political activity is therefore essential for any promising, prosperous or survivable future. Human economic activity simply cannot be 'left to itself' for there is no 'self' to leave it to.

Economic operations cannot be trusted. Human economic operators have to be collaborative in caring for the earth, and in promoting viable communities with reasonable opportunities of participation and sharing. Otherwise capitalism's 'creative gales of destruction' will undermine the lives of ever more of us. Our capacities for enterprise, innovation and trade have to be redirected into a second wealth-creating system which corrects the excesses and nonsenses which the present one has now arrived at.

Practicable prosperity will require limitations on the current over-weaning demands of capitalism for ever-increasing interest. (This will, for example, have to be related, 'even', to the demands of Mutual Funds for ever higher and quicker returns. We pensioners, too, have to take account of the real cost of shareable, sustainable and mutually enjoyable, real wealth on a limited earth.) We have got to organize ourselves politically to find ways of affording what it is increasingly obvious we cannot afford not to afford. Possible mutual freedom, on the other hand, involves widespread rethinking of the overweening demands of ultra-individualism. The development and maintenance of individual freedom and fulfilment are not possible without social relationships and a social framework. All citizens who have the means of affording it, will have to accept sufficient taxation if we are to build up social cohesion. This will involve agreed restraints and duly voted sacrifices which, at the moment, seem to be off the political agenda. In fact, however, prudence requires this – for fear of society's collapse. Decency demands it – for in a globalized world we are all clearly neighbours of one another – and compassion invites it. We must throw off the notion that we are, collectively and individually, nothing but a set of short-sighted, greedy, insensitive and competitive animals.

The political task is, therefore, to develop countervailing powers to the powers-that-be in the current market and financial operations. This requires focusing political pressure from, and a giving of voice to, all those of us who share anxieties about the generally passive acquiescence in a free market faith. We have to multiply our efforts to stimulate people's consciousness as citizens, to challenge people's consciences as human beings, and organize coalitions of concern, collaboration and, where need be, confrontation, to restore the primacy of politics over economics.

Pressure groups for the awareness of particular problems, agencies and networks which are carrying out their own experiments in developing alternative economic ways forward, are multiplying. A glimpse into this growing field of activity can be obtained from the publications, for example, of such bodies as the New Economic Foundation, or the Real World Coalition, or from the catalogues of publishers like Earthscan, or documents produced by Oxfam, the World Development Movement, and literally hundreds of other sources. But the time has surely come when every effort has to be made to insist that the issue of whether or not to go on investing our trust in the present operations of the Free Market must be placed at the centre of our general political agenda. We must not allow this crucial issue to be obscured because of the multiplication of particular issues, pressure groups, and organizations.

As my discussion of a dialectical approach to politics and economics has, I hope, made clear, I am not looking to renew political protests after the fashion of nineteenth-century communism or nineteenth-century socialism. Nor am I raising a party political point. All the parties at present active in the current UK Parliament are committed to living by the Free Market faith – in one version or another. Rather, I am making a plea that, on all the evidence available to us, the twenty-first century needs a renewing political imagination and economic innovation. We have to arouse the awareness, and the consensus, to break out of the deterministic future into which we are being rail-roaded by the current Free Market juggernaut of the more and more.

Sustainable prosperity and freedom in the twenty-first century requires us to develop a new perspective on *risk*. Whatever may have been the case in the nineteenth century, when the risks of capitalism developed such an outburst of amazing productivity and growth, the risks we now have to take as human beings together in a limited earth have shifted sharply from competitive risks to the need for collaborative and political risks. One of the most unsupportable assumptions of the Free Market faith is that the Free Market has developed a system of risk-taking which has evolved so as to overcome the interactions of multiple economic risk-taking, to produce an aggregate result which promises that, in the longer run, all shall profit. This is Alice-in-Wonderland economics. In the real world there is no innate force to balance out risks, or ensure that they can be hedged against, or recovered from when they go wrong. Only we, as human beings, can decide which risks are most risky at any time, and only communities can build up the insurance of social cohesion and collaboration to enable any particular set of inhabitants, in a particular country, to weather the turbulence when risks go wrong.

I do not feel any obligation to offer a comprehensive list of what these risks might be. It is we, as citizens together, who have to wake up to what is going on, and we, as a community, who have to work out what our appropriate political and economic response will be. New political and economic imagination is something that has to be developed collectively – which is why I took such tedious pains earlier in this book to argue that 'capitalists' who were, collectively and as a class, 'in effect' liars and cheats, are not to be cast out, individually, as possible partners in developing the renewing imagination, and the new activities which are required for our future.

There are, however, already many suggestions for alternative risk-taking to purely market ones around. A few examples include:

- The risk of developing (via the World Bank, IMF, WTO, Bank of International Settlements and UN agencies) international agreements to regulate capital flows, tone down currency speculation, and limit the capacities of capital to move about scooping out its profits without any accountability, or paying any taxes to any sovereign state. (A starting point for readjusting the balance might be the necessity of 'sovereign money' as some sort of last resort in crises, and the regulations of states as a means of enforcing contracts.)
- The risk of building up a consensus that increased taxation is necessary to fund what we now say we cannot afford but know we should afford. The object would be to assist in social cohesion and the development of well-housed, well-fed, well-educated citizens who, being well-trained and well-treated, might develop a sense of their *duty* to contribute, because they had the *choice* of participation, and therefore a reasonable basis for their *rights* as citizens.
- The risk of exercising our current economic and financial sophistication to devise new forms of money creation and credit availability which would finance enterprises at low-levels of return on capital to enable the development of small local enterprises and co-operatives in heavily populated areas in underdeveloped countries, or in run-down areas in developed countries. If we can think the unthinkable about 'welfare' why are we not clever enough and informed enough to think the unthinkable about 'capital'?
- The risk of developing some scheme for basic or citizen's income – linked to a drastic simplification and integration of taxation and welfare payment systems, so that there is less means testing, less overlap and less administration as well as a much more simple distribution of the means to meet basic needs.
- I would judge that we have to take the risk of adopting some carefully worked out form of proportional representation, for all levels of representative government. Clearly there are risks of political parties fragmenting to too great an extent (especially in an age where the general approach to political expression is more often through pressure groups than a general concern for wider issues). The need to buy the support of too many small parties might threaten a government's ability to act rationally and decisively. But this might be guarded against by arrangements over thresholds and so on. In my view, the overriding concern is to put a end to the idea

that politics is chiefly conducted by one party, who is right, being opposed by another party, who is wrong. The current oppositional shape of our Houses of Parliament denies the complexities of current issues – and the plain fact that no one has any definitive solutions. We need forms of opposition, collaboration and controversy which assist governments in managing their areas of responsibility, contribute to the process of working things out, as well as holding those in power to account. Manifestos promising this and that are just political exercises in marketing. A new and more realistic form of election might encourage a more realistic form of constant negotiation in the light of developments, whether in respect of policies, particular pieces of legislation or spending.

- The risk of reconstituting local government – related to the particular national governments that are coming into existence and linked with regional organizations of some sort. The risks of bureaucracy and the multiplication of layers of government, here, are obvious. But somehow or other people have got to be brought back into local participation and influence to complement a more responsible approach to expenditure and taxation. The renewal of local life, responsibility and cohesion is essential to survival and mutual support when so much is 'globalized'.

- The risk of international agreements, possibly often for limited periods, to *protect* particular economies, localities or, even, industries. States must be able to protect and guide specific communities through transitions to change. There must also be space for state governments to protect their own reasonable environmental measures. To develop WTO regulations or multilateral investment agreements which allow purely commercial decisions about what is allowable in trade, and what is illegal protection, is to hand far too much over to the dogmaticians of the Free Market, who are doing quite a job at undermining environments and communities as it is.

We cannot trust the lords and gurus of the Free Market. They do not have our interests at heart. As the orthodox theory of the liberal market economy declares, they are far too self-interested for that. They may deceive themselves, as well as us, that nonetheless the mystery or myth at the heart of the Free Market dynamic will transmute naked self-interest into mutual prosperity and freedom. But this theoretical repudiation of morality and responsibility is as implausible and impractical as it is immoral and irresponsible.

There are, in fact, no lack of imaginative and carefully thought out proposals, experiments and hard-working groups around whose suggestions and experience could be built into opening up new ways of wealth creation, new disciplines for protecting the environment and our communities. What is needed is a consciousness of the problems, which stirs consciences about neighbours and the world and inspires a readiness to organize to confront the powers of established self-interest groups and institutions. There has to be a challenge to the attempt of these groups to legitimize their efforts through the claim that 'if you let us grow as rich as possible then one day you will be at least somewhat better off'.

If out-and-out supporters and promoters of the Free Market are genuine in their belief, and sincere in their wishes that all should profit, then they should have the courage of their sincere and genuine commitment to recognize that the Free Market, as at present operated and delivering, is no way to what they genuinely and sincerely wish to achieve. They should observe the facts, review the incoherence of the theoretical arguments for free market guarantees, and join in the search for fresh political and economic imagination which will seek the sustainable wealth-creating system which the world of the twenty-first century and beyond so urgently needs.

The central question which faces us all is: who do we think we are? And what resources do we believe are available to us for living hopefully with our neighbours, who, under the globalized market, are all our fellow inhabitants of the earth? I refuse to believe that all the materialistic prestige of economic productivity, and all the discoveries and complexities of science, technology, innovation, enterprise and communication, have generally reduced us human beings to competitive pursuers of ever-increasing consumption. Autobiographically, my own encounters with striving human beings, whether in India during army service, or in the North East of England during the local crisis of the miners strike of 1984/5, have given me no reason to believe this. Personal encounters lead me to suspect that the wealthy person's pursuit to become richer and richer is the acme (or nadir) of materialistic corruption and utter self-centredness. If one is rich enough, one can indulge the illusion that everyone depends on you and you depend on no one.

Whatever generalizations personal experiences may incline or encourage us to make, the basic motivating question is the perspective within which we look at the world, other people and ourselves. How far do I go in perceiving that I live with an awareness of some possibilities of compelling worth, and some hope of promises and possibilities that draw me in pursuit – however unsuccessfully – or however often I am in practice indifferent to these claims and that worth.

Why, then, should I 'refuse to believe' that we human beings are to be reduced to being treated, primarily, as consumers and competitors? Because of what I have found through experiences of compelling worth, and what I have glimpsed of promises and possibilities which draw me in pursuit. These experiences have built up a conviction, a faith, that I do not direct the finding of this worth and value but something in, or Someone in and beyond, the worth and value finds me. So I believe in God. I find my belief in God constantly fleshed out for me in what I learn of the things focused in Jesus. I am, therefore, by increasing conviction and in persistently unsatisfactory practice, a Christian. This pilgrimage of faith informs the perspective within which I struggle to apprehend and respond to the goings on of the world – and of my neighbours within it.

I have, therefore, a fundamental faith in the possibilities of human beings, and our capacities for relationships, creativity and freedom. This goes with an intuition that the earth is, in some real and serious sense, a promising gift to be shared, rather than an inert source of material to be exploited and consumed. All this I locate within a calling to worship and follow a God who is as involved and down-to-earth as Jesus, and as ubiquitous and immanent as the Holy Spirit.

I have been driven to write this book by an unfolding conviction that, whatever are the personal understandings, motivation, intentions and hopes of very many free market activists, nonetheless, the assumptions on which free market theory works, and the practices which free market operators follow, have reached a point where they disgrace the earth and diminish and demean us human beings. Quite possibly by sheer human overenthusiasm, inadvertence, and lack of careful attention, the Free Market has become a worldwide idol with dangerously threatening results – and, of course, utterly empty promise, for no idol can deliver.

Hence my detailed attempts to observe and understand matters economic. The results of my enquiries have given me hope. The way the Free Market at present works is not the product of evolutionary fate but of human fixing. What human beings have fixed other human beings can liberate for more sustainable and shareable purposes. This is where my perspective of faith on human beings and the earth comes in. My christian faith in God is by no means universally shared. (Not least because of the many instances of ungodly and unchristian behaviour

among us Christians in the world at large.) But it is evident that much of
the important resonances of christian faith, as I have come to understand
it, are widely shared. People from many faiths and many secular
perspectives have their own version of, and commitment to, 'human-
ism'. As human beings, both as individual persons and in communities,
we are of intrinsic worth and immense potential. Love, longing and
compassion are as much a real part of us as self-interested suspicion,
greed and ambition. Human experiences of pilgrimage, intense commitment and great sacrifice, are as evident as selfishness, indifference and
stupidity (besides being so much more exciting, challenging and shareable). There is a world-wide search for what we may perhaps call
spirituality – matters of depth, intensity, mysticism, exploration and
sharing at levels difficult to explain, and yet they remain there to be
explored. And there is a worldwide network of various forms of concern
and respect for the earth, which tap into a deep sense of reverence and
enjoyment. It is amazing and encouraging (and often very humbling) to
discover how many people, at some time, have a sense of an overriding
and inviting worth which is so great that it is worth taking the risk of
wholly investing in it – even if the risk does not seem likely to 'pay off'.
(For myself I suspect that this is what incarnation, crucifixion and
resurrection are about.)

It is therefore quite plainly practical nonsense and human betrayal to
collude with the notion, however widespread and powerful, that the
Free Market has the last word on human possibilities – economic,
political, social or personal. Of course we can change things, and of
course we have to find our ways forward to a much more generally
enabling future. There is a whole spectrum of human commitment,
collaboration and capacities for innovation, which is sustained from a
whole variety of human perspectives and motivations. They range,
perhaps, from perceptions of 'you shall love the Lord your God with
all your heart, with all your soul, with all your mind, and with all your
strength – and your neighbour as yourself' to various versions of 'don't
let the bastards get you down'. All can direct human freedom and all can
contribute to working out new ways forward.

Progress does not come from discerning a historical game-plan, nor
from imposing a correct ideological map from any source whatever. It
comes from human collaboration in carefully chosen purposes and
realistically shared visions. We must not collude with the Free Market.
We must collaborate with one another. Then we might all profit in a
sustainable way from our skills in marketing, productivity and innovation. One thing is clear – it is up to us.

Index